meXicana Encounters

AMERICAN CROSSROADS

*Edited by Earl Lewis, George Lipsitz, Peggy Pascoe, George Sánchez,
and Dana Takagi*

meXicana
Encounters

The Making of Social Identities
on the Borderlands

Rosa Linda Fregoso

UNIVERSITY OF CALIFORNIA PRESS

Berkeley / Los Angeles / London

Excerpt from the poem "Our Father Who Drowns the Birds," by Barbara Kingsolver, from *Another America* © 1992, 1998, appears by permission of the publisher, Seal Press.

Excerpt from the poem "and when I dream dreams," by Carmen Tafolla, from *"Sonnets to Human Beings" and Other Selected Works by Carmen Tafolla*, published in 1992 by Lalo Press, appears by permission of Carmen Tafolla.

Parts of chapter 3 were previously published in "Recycling Colonialist Fantasies on the Texas Borderlands," in the anthology *Home, Exile, Homeland: Film, Media, and the Politics of Place*, ed. Hamid Naficy (New York and London: Routledge, 1998).

An earlier version of chapter 5 was published as "Re-Imagining Chicana Urban Identities in the Public Sphere, cool chuca style" in *Between Women and Nation: Transnational Feminisms and the State*, ed. Caren Kaplan, Norma Alarcón, and Minoo Moallem (1999). Permission to reprint granted by Duke University Press.

University of California Press
Berkeley and Los Angeles, California

University of California Press, Ltd.
London, England

Library of Congress Cataloging-in-Publication Data
Fregoso, Rosa Linda.
  MeXicana encounters : the making of social identities on the borderlands / Rosa Linda Fregoso.
      p.   cm. — (American crossroads ; 12)
   Includes bibliographical references and index.
   ISBN 0-520-22997-5 (cloth : alk. paper) — ISBN 0-520-23890-7 (paper : alk. paper)
     1. Mexican American women — Mexican-American Border Region — Social conditions.   2. Women — Mexican-American Border Region — Social conditions.   3. Women in popular culture — Mexican-American Border Region.   4. Women in motion pictures.   5. Mexican American women — Ethnic identity.   6. Group identity — Mexican-American Border Region.   7. Popular culture — Mexican-American Border Region.   8. Mexican-American Border Region — Civilization.   9. Mexican-American Border Region — Social conditions.   10. Mexican-American Border Region — Ethnic relations.   I. Title. II. Series.
F790.M5 F75   2003
305.48'868720721 — dc21   2003000594

For global justice

There is a season when all wars end:
when the rains come. . . .

There is a season when every ancient anger
settles, conceding
to water the grass.

Barbara Kingsolver, "Our Father Who
Drowns the Birds," in *Another America*

Contents

Illustrations

Preface

In my home in Oakland, California, you will find an appropriate metaphor for the inverted temporal order of this book: a small image of the Sankofa bird of Akan philosophy. Carved into a piece of wood, this feathered creature is suspended in motion, its billowing body moving forward while its head contorts, facing backward. In the present tense of its carving, the majestic Sankofa bird looks back toward history as it moves into the future, as if to say, "We must go back and reclaim our past so we can move forward, so we can understand how we came to be who we are today."[1] The future is enabled through the recognition of the presence of the past.

This book is an exploration of the symbolic role of Mexicanas and Chicanas in culture. I begin at the end of a long journey through a century of representations of meXicanas (pronounced "me-chi-canas") in various institutional, social, and cultural sites. Inverting the chronology of history and memory, *meXicana Encounters* looks at the vital role of culture in the formation of social identities on the borderlands. Looking back from the perspective of the present, I dramatize the significance of cultural practices and symbolic forms in shaping, representing, and defining social identities in our contemporary world. By emphasizing the role of social identities in nation-building narratives, I aim to offer an account for the apparent contradiction between the visibility of meXicanas in cultural representation and their invisibility in the history of the nation.

For me, this exploration has been transformative, and the ordering of the chapters reflects the evolution in my thinking about the cultural representation of meXicanas. Oriented to the future while moving through the past, each chapter stages an encounter with the symbolic visibility of meXicanas from the perspective of the present, from a social location that is constantly being transformed and shaped by social interactions, events, narratives, and power relations in the life of, in Barbara Kingsolver's words, "Another America."

A comment on the term "meXicana": As the interface between Mexicana and Chicana, "meXicana" draws attention to the historical, material, and discursive effects of contact zones and exchanges among various communities on the Mexico-U.S. border, living in the shadows of more than 150 years of conflict, interactions, and tensions. "meXicana" references processes of transculturation, hybridity, and cultural exchanges — the social and economic interdependency and power relations structuring the lives of inhabitants on the borderlands.

Not recognizably Chicana or Mexicana, "yet geographically and historically localized" — echoing the lyrics of Chavela Vargas's song, "Ni de aquí ni de allá" (Neither from here nor from there) — meXicana is a metaphor for cultural and national mobility.[2] And even though the term is an amalgamation of "Mexicana" and "Chicana," it does not signal an erasure of difference, but rather calls attention to the intersections among the multiple narratives of race, gender, sexuality that inform nation building.

My concern with how the making of social identities is structured in dominance, within narratives of racism, sexism, and classism, guides the focus on practices of representation. In the first three chapters of the book I consider the role of violence in reproducing racial, class, gender, and sexual hierarchies, emphasizing the interconnections between experiential and symbolic forms of violence.

Current debates over nomenclature are based on legal distinctions between "Mexicanas" as immigrants to the United States and Chicanas as native. While such distinctions may serve policy interests or demographic aims, in the realm of cultural representation, the difference between "Mexicana" and "Chicana" is often obscured and erased. The term "meXicana" reflects the complicated imbrication of "Chicanas" and "Mexicanas" in the formation of subjects in the nation. My readings of mainstream cinema in the United States, especially in chapters three and seven, will take up this amalgamation of Mexicana and Chicana within cultural representation. My focus here is on the shared history of othering, on how dominant culture collapses differences and homogenizes Mexicanas and Chicanas into a single social category as "other." Chapters four, five, and six examine the politics of othering that excludes identities of women from conceptions of the Chicano and Mexican nations. In this case, the term "meXicana" charts an encounter with a shared history of exclusion and subordination within the cultural and political practices of various patriarchal nationalisms, those emanating from the nation-state (the United States) as well as from nationalist, antiracist movements (the Chicano nation). In this manner, *meXicana Encounters* probes the role of Mexicanas and Chicanas as figures of otherness within cultural discourses of the nation.

Clearly, however, my story of the making of social identities on the borderlands is far from a one-way process of othering within culture. At each stage, *meXicana Encounters* recuperates the counternarratives emanating from and giving voice to new social collectivities. From the politics of grassroots activists in Ciudad Juárez (chapter one) to feminist subversions of gender arrangements (chapters two, four, and five) to a star persona's disruption of gender roles (chapter six) to my grandmother's countermemories of Tejano film culture (chapter eight), *meXicana Encounters* affirms the production of new cultural citizens on the borderlands.

Even so, the utopic borderless world many of us imagined seems increasingly distant these days. "Borderlessness" seems more like a dystopic nightmare, a design reserved for the new global empire of the United States as it reasserts its imperial role as state above all states and as beyond the rule of international law. In a climate of fervent nationalism, the banner of counterterrorism is currently the pretext for emergent forms of state terrorism against immigrants, the poor. The state is intensifying border militarization as it develops new forms of policing and surveillance of immigrants and dissidents — the excluded citizens of the nation.

The normalcy of state terrorism in our own historical moment makes the movement for global social justice more urgent than ever before. My writings join the common and overlapping struggles on behalf of social justice among many people throughout the world. Like others, I am driven by a sense of urgency, by the recognition that what is at stake today goes beyond the survival of ethnic, national, or racial groups; it involves the very survival of our planet.

If the growth of state terrorism and the nativist obsession with territorial borders are new political realities in the twenty-first century, so too are the new social forms of transnational migration and group membership. Mexicana and Mexicano immigrants no longer reside solely in the Southwest, but are living in every state of the United States, from large metropolitan centers like New York City and Atlanta to the hinterlands of rural Pennsylvania and Kentucky. Nor are these immigrants and their native-born children bound territorially to a single nation-state.

New forms of cultural citizenship are in the making wherein Mexican communities forge binational and multistate networks and affiliations. Maintaining vital ties with their hometowns in Mexico, Mexicanas and Mexicanos contribute directly to the political and economic lives of their communities of origin but also culturally enrich and economically revitalize their resident communities. Today, you will find Mexican agricultural, poultry, and hotel and restaurant workers in states like Kansas and Rhode Island, and Mexican tienditas and tortillerías in Delaware and Georgia. These transnational immigrants represent the social and political crosscurrents, riding against the growing tide of state terror and racist nativism. They are the new cultural citizens claiming social space, rights, and recognition. These transnational immigrants are creating the conditions of possibility for the emergence of a new political consciousness, brewing in many of those hidden corridors throughout the new borderlands a consciousness that joins the ancient call for social justice everywhere.

Acknowledgments

Mil gracias to all who have supported me through the years I spent writing this book. I own enormous debt to the colleagues and friends who left their imprint on my work. My sisters, Angela Fregoso and Maria Teresa Araiza, resurrected family memories and offered editorial suggestions, *del mero corazón*. B. Ruby Rich, Isabel Velásquez, and Ian Haney López provided exceptional commentary on earlier drafts. I am especially grateful to Dana Takagi and George Lipsitz, series editors of "American Crossroads," and Lisa Lowe for their intellectual generosity and superb editorial suggestions. Monica McCormick, Jacqueline Volin, and the readers at the University of California Press contributed invaluable assistance. Special thanks to Sue Carter for being such a thoughtful and engaging copyeditor. I was fortunate to count on the skilled research assistance of Erin Maya Higgins, Graciela Berkovitch, Kim Owyoung, Jesikah Marie Ross, and Deb Vargas.

Portions of this manuscript were written during my tenure at the University of California-Davis. Numerous colleagues as well as students in Women and Gender Studies deepened my understanding of feminism and critical race studies. I would like to acknowledge the support and friendship of my UC-Davis colleagues, especially Sarah Projansky, Judith Newton, Gayatri Gopinath, Susan Kaiser, Shaunna Ludwig, Kent Ono, Beatríz Pesquera, Lorena Oropeza, Lynn Hershman, Wendy Ho, Dianne MacCleod, Michael Peter Smith, Luis Guarnizo, JoAnne Cannon, Sergio de la Mora, and my theoretical hermana del alma/co-conspirator, Angie Chabram-Dernersesian.

I feel fortunate to have gained new fellowship and solidarities with my move to the University of California-Santa Cruz. Ongoing dialogues and exchanges with my students have advanced my intellectual and political understanding of cultural politics. I am grateful to be in the company of such inspirational colleagues in Latin American/Latino Studies. I am especially grateful to Jonathan Fox for news clippings of current events in Mexico.

My deepest gratitude for their dedicated scholarship and teaching to Rosaura Sánchez, Susan Kirkpatrick, Iris and Carlos Blanco, and Herb Schiller, who unfortunately passed away while I was writing this book.

Throughout the years of working on this project many colleagues have advanced and enabled my thinking. I especially thank those of you whose writing inspired me along the way. I am also grateful to the colleagues who invited me to present my work at conferences and college campuses. I hope that I have honored the feedback I received in these various forums.

Special thanks to the filmmakers, musicians, and artists who continue to feed my soul. I would like to acknowledge the guidance of my guitar maestro, Richard Spross; Clairemarut Evasco and Robert Zeiger have also supported me along the way. I have been fortunate to work with a vibrant community of film and video makers through the Film Arts Foundation under the leadership of Gail Silva.

Over the years my creativity has been sustained by passionate conversations over good wine and food in the company of Lourdes Portillo, Ellen Gavin, Beth Hass, Chip Lord, Lata Mani, Ruth Frankenberg, Pam Ivy, Aida Hurtado, Craig Haney, David Wellman, Ruby Rich, Mary Peelen, Alvina Quintana, Ed Guerrero, Angela Davis, Gina Dent, Sara Garcia, Victor Fuentes, Reneé Tajima-Peña, Armando Peña, Brenda Cabral, Kevin Fitzpatrick, Ian Haney López, and Deb Cortez-Dickerson.

I received financial support from various sources. At the University of California-Davis, I thank the Faculty Career Development Office; the Office of the Dean of Humanities, Arts, and Cultural Studies; and the Chicana Latina Research Center. At the University of California-Santa Cruz, I thank the Division of Social Sciences. The Rockefeller Foundation provided a Bellagio Residency Fellowship. I also appreciate the kind generosity of Gianna Celli, Yolanda Garcia, Gina Dent, and Angela Davis.

I can never repay my compañero Herman Gray for his companionship, unwavering support, intellectual acumen, and devoted teaching. He deserves a medal for enduring my intractable writing and study habits. I am forever indebted to my two children, Xochitl Magaly and Sergio

Emilio, and my grandson, Jasim, for replenishing my heart throughout the years. I appreciate the support of my mother, Lucia Orea Chapa, my father, Francisco Fregoso Gómez, and my sisters and brothers. Finally, I would like to express my deep appreciation to social activists everywhere for reminding us that peace and global justice matter.

CHAPTER ONE

Toward a Planetary Civil Society

Cruelty has no unearthly punishment and often no earthly reason.[1]

Jean Franco

The campaign to end the killing of women in Ciudad Juárez took the name "Ni una más." Ni una más en Ciudad Juárez. Not one more murdered woman in Ciudad Juárez. Mothers and grandmothers, women's rights and human rights groups, and friends from both sides of the border joined in a movement of denunciation, demanding an end to the most sordid and barbarous series of gender killings in Mexico's history. By mid-2002, there were 282 victims of feminicide in this city across the border from El Paso, Texas, and more than four hundred disappeared women.[1] "Ni una más" stages women's visibility and invisibility in the nation as well as a confrontation with the historical and social trauma in the region.

The politics of gender extermination in this region took the form of the apparently random yet seemingly systematic appearance of brutally murdered women's bodies and the equally horrific disappearance of many more. What is now understood as various forms of "feminicide" started in 1993, a year after the signing of NAFTA, and continued on through the tenure of three Mexican heads of state: Carlos Salinas, Ernesto Zedillo, and Vicente Fox.[2] As the numbers grew, the state continued to turn a blind eye to the violence afflicting women.

In spring 2001 a number of nongovernmental organizations (NGOs) involved in human rights work, including Grupo 8 de Marzo, Comité

Independiente de Chihuahua de Derechos Humanos, and Taller de Género de la Universidad Autónoma de Juárez, delivered a report, "Cases of Murdered Women in Ciudad Juárez, Chihuahua," to the special rapporteur for human rights for the United Nations, Dato' Param Cumaraswamy. The authors of the report had compiled files for 189 women murdered between January 1993 and April 2001.[3]

By early 2002, according to a report prepared by La Red Ciudadana contra la Violencia, the number of murdered women had increased to 269, with an additional 450 disappeared.[4] Between 1985 and 1992, by contrast, thirty-seven women were murdered in Ciudad Juárez.

Records of the identities of the assassinated and disappeared women are kept by the nongovernmental organization Grupo 8 de Marzo of Ciudad Juárez.[5] They were poor women, most were dark, and many of them had been mutilated, tortured, and sexually violated.[6] Although there have been random appearances of dead bodies in public places throughout the city, most of the bodies were found near the outskirts of Juárez, in the desert, near poor *colonias* (shantytowns) like Anapra, Valle de Juárez, Lomas de Poleo, and Lote Bravo. Ranging in age from eleven to fifty, the murdered and disappeared women shared humble origins and, in many instances, their migratory experience to these borderlands.

Sensationalistic media accounts of these murders have exploited the stereotype of single or multiple serial killers violently and systematically exterminating young women. However, in a highly perceptive study, Julia Estela Monárrez suggests that the murder and disappearance of women in Juárez cannot be considered simply as the work of psychopaths. Rather than the aberration of a single individual or group, the murders of women are "politically motivated sexual violence" rooted in a system of patriarchy.[7] In fact the various feminicides in Mexico make evident the exercise of power across the social spectrum: the power of the state over civil society; the rich over the poor; the white elite over racialized people; the old over the young; men over women. It is a novel kind of "dirty war," one waged by multiple forces against disposable female bodies. The women targeted in these unprecedented border feminicides represent the "stigmatized bodies," those "marked for death in drug wars and urban violence."[8] Feminicide in Juárez makes evident the reality of overlapping power relations on gendered and racialized bodies as much as it clarifies the degree to which violence against women has been naturalized as a method of social control.

"Yet another massacre, another mass grave," writes Jean Franco. "In our time, only too often we are given the image of the mass of bodies —

the massacres of Rwanda or Kosovo — out of which it is difficult for those of us watching the television screen or looking at news photographs to construct a meaningful narrative."[9] In the course of my investigation for this book I found this difficulty often compounded by the competing discourses used to construct a narrative.

In September 1999 I attended the Burials on the Border conference, held at New Mexico State University, Las Cruces, where I witnessed a struggle over the meanings of these gender murders. There, before an audience of activists, researchers, and family members, representatives of the Mexican state publicly blamed the victims of feminicide in Juárez. The heated exchange I witnessed between representatives of the state and civil society derived in large measure from competing interpretive frameworks. For the purpose of my own study, this public struggle over the social identities of the victims and the meaning of their deaths raises broader issues of cultural representation and its role in our effort to construct a meaningful narrative. In this chapter I intend to unpack the competing and often overlapping narratives that have been used to interpret the murders of women and, in the process, expose the subject that is constructed within each account.

From Negation to Disaggregation

One would expect the modern state to intervene on behalf of its citizens and limit extreme expressions of gender violence such as those unfolding in Ciudad Juárez, but the Mexican government has failed dismally. It has justified its failure through a rhetorical strategy of deflection that has taken two narrative forms: negation and disaggregation. Early on, state officials repeatedly framed their interpretation of the killings within a discourse of negation, refusing to acknowledge the reality of systemic and calculated acts of violence against women.

The state's early response, negation, involved at first a denial that the killings were systematic. Then, when the state could no longer deny this reality, officials shifted the blame onto the victims, committing further sacrilege against already violated bodies.[10] In many instances the state emphasized women's nonnormative behaviors, accusing them of transgressing sexual norms, either of lesbianism or of leading a "doble vida" (double life) — that is, engaging in respectable work by day and sex work by night — as though nontraditional sexual behavior justified their killings.[11] Indeed, the Comisión Nacional de Derechos Humanos

(National Human Rights Commission) found that police authorities had violated the victims' rights by making declarations such as these to members of the commission: "Many of the murdered women worked in factories during the week and as prostitutes during the weekend in order to make more money."[12]

The discourse of negation thus tended to discredit the murdered women by emphasizing their alleged transgressive sexual behavior: "She visited a place where homosexuals and lesbians gathered"; "She liked dating different men and was an avid patron of dance halls."[13] Such expressions of nonnormative sexuality have been so relentless that the mother of murder victim Adriana Torres Márquez responded indignantly: "Don't they have anything else to invent? They have said the same in every case: that it's the way women dressed or their alleged double life."[14] Nonnormative sexuality is central to the causal chain that goes from transgression of patriarchal norms to murder.

To establish legitimacy for this narrative of negation, the state enlisted the testimony of scientific "experts" whose testimony linked transgressive sexual behavior to newfound independence. A Spanish criminologist echoed the by now standard "moral panic" about the dangers of modernization: "As a result of the influence of the United States, women are joining the workforce at an earlier age and therefore discovering independence. This means young women could become more promiscuous. Some of these independent women have maintained sexual relations with more than one person. This behavior leads to danger."[15]

Again, nonnormativity became the lens through which the killings were interpreted, although the criminologist's comments also laid bare the patriarchal nostalgia for an earlier era of male authority in which women remain wedded to the private sphere of domesticity and motherhood. Like those who champion the conservative "family values" campaign in the United States in the 1990s, Mexican state officials blamed women's growing independence and mothers entering the workforce for the "disintegration" of the family and, first and foremost, the loss of male authority in the domestic sphere.[16]

It bears emphasizing that the subject constructed within the state's discourse is an "immoral" one. The patriarchal state's initial preoccupation with women's morality and decency is a form of institutional violence that makes women primarily responsible for the violence directed against them. Thus, those women who do not conform to the mother/wife model of womanhood (lesbians, working women, women who express sexual desire, and so forth) are suitably punished. In effect women are transformed into subjects of surveillance; their decency and morality become the object of social control. What's more, shifting the blame toward the victims' moral character in effect naturalizes violence against women.

By the end of 2001, both the state's investigation of the murders and its dubious interpretive framework had been placed in question because of the convergence of a series of events that galvanized the public during that year: the assassination of human rights lawyer Digna Ochoa, the unearthing of the bodies of eight women in an empty lot adjacent to the headquarters of the Maquiladora Association, and the police assassination of a defense lawyer in Juárez. A broad-scale social force emerged within civil society. Hundreds of nongovernmental organizations — feminist, civil, and human rights groups from both sides of the border — joined the existing network of local grassroots activists and women's groups that had been denouncing the killings for several years. Media coverage of the killings zeroed in on state corruption and indifference.

Negating the reality of widespread violence against poor and dark women proved to be not just a transparent, but an obscene, interpretive strategy. To counter the growing national and international movement of outrage and denunciation, the state adopted a less ideological strategy, this time enlisting the techniques of science to transform its narrative of interpretation from outright denial to disaggregation.

In December 2001 the office of the governor of the State of Chihuahua released the document "Homicidio de mujer en Ciudad Juárez, enero 1993–noviembre 2001" (Homicide of woman in Ciudad Juárez, January 1993–November 2001).[17] Although a month earlier, special prosecutor for Juárez, Zulema Bolívar had acknowledged the murder of 259 poor women, this recent document in effect proceeded to disassociate the cases of the murdered women in Juárez as a phenomenon and reformulate most of the murders as discrete, unrelated cases.

The state authenticated its new narrative through technologies of statistics and forensic evidence, thus shifting the discussion away from broader social issues and isolating each "case" from the more general and systemic phenomenon of violence against women. In other words, the state now conceded the fact of the murders, but it refused to accept their interconnection, claiming that only 76 of the 261 murders exhibited traces of sexual violence or were related as "multiple homicides."[18] As the months passed, the discourse of disaggregation served the state in several ways. First, it provided the state with a veneer of "scientific" authority and professionalism to counter its image as a corrupt "Third World" police force, especially in meetings with representatives of international organizations and media. Second, disaggregation bolstered the "scientific" claims of the state, especially regarding the universal aspect of the crimes, as a "common" occurrence in any major city. Claiming the normality of the murders in Juárez, state officials cited the recent serial killing of fifty women in Canada. Finally, the state used disaggregation in a discursive war, a campaign to discredit women's rights and human rights activists meeting with representatives from the United Nations and the Organization of American States by accusing activists of "politicizing" the murders.[19] To some extent, the discourse of disaggregation has proven to be an effective strategy, providing the state certain legitimacy with U.S. state officials and international media, where the new narrative is reported uncritically.[20] Ironically, the state's disaggregation of "the rest" of the murders as "crimes of passion, drug traffic, theft, sexual, intrafamilial violence, vengeance, [and] imprudence" does not preclude linking violence against women to gender hierarchies within a patriarchal state.[21]

Globalism on the Borderlands

Whereas the state's narrative anchored the meanings of the murders of women at the microlevel of the individual, other accounts of feminicide constructed a narrative out of macro processes, as is evident in the discourse of globalism.[22] Unlike the state's narrative, this discourse grew out of a progressive impulse, one critical of the expansion of transnational capitalism and global neoliberalism under the coordination of the IMF, the World Trade Organization (WTO), and the World Bank. Established as a major interpretive framework during the mid-1990s, the discourse of globalism equated *exploitation* with the *extermination* of gendered bodies, tracing both conditions to a single process: economic globalization. And, on the Mexico-U.S. border, globalism was most visibly embodied in the maquiladora industry.[23]

The murders of women in Juárez came to be seen as part of the "more insidious — and far more widespread — violence of work on the global assembly line."[24] Given the geopolitics of the region, connecting feminicide to the maquiladora industry proved to be a compelling narrative, especially since the murders of poor and dark women began in 1993, a year after NAFTA (the North American Free Trade Agreement), the treaty that solidified the project of neoliberalism and economic globalization in this part of the world. One of the features of global capitalism today is the creation of export-processing zones throughout the Third World. During the 1990s, Ciudad Juárez was the largest export-processing zone on the border, host to roughly 350 manufacturing plants owned primarily by U.S. transnational corporations. These plants employed roughly 180,000 workers who were paid around $23 US per week in take-home pay, a little less than $4 per day, or fifty cents per hour.[25]

In many respects, the geopolitical and economic characteristics of the region lent legitimacy to arguments that the *exploitation* of bodies on the "global assembly line" and the *extermination* of bodies in the public sphere were part of a singular process. In studies of the worldwide grid of export-processing zones, researchers like Saskia Sassen have contributed important insights about the role of women as laboring bodies for global capitalism, documenting the "incorporation of Third World women into wage employment on a scale that can be seen as representing a new phase in the history of women."[26] It is precisely this body of work on the "feminization of the proletariat" that is used to construct a narrative about the murders of women in Juárez, to make claims about how their "lives and deaths centered around the global assembly line."[27] In other words, since both "exploited female bodies" and "exterminated female bodies" are expressions of the exercise of power and gender hierarchies, the cause of one condition (exploitation of gendered bodies) has served handily to explain the other (extermination of gendered bodies).

I do not mean to dismiss the value of critical theories of globalization, especially since they undoubtedly help to explain the structural transformations in export-processing zones like Ciudad Juárez. It is important to recognize how under current conditions of capitalist expansion, transnational corporations function as "the masters of a 'new imperial age' spreading an inhumane model of development . . . with islands of enormous privilege in a sea of misery and despair."[28] Antiglobalization perspectives provide valuable insight into how Juárez figures as the "local" embodiment of the wave of global neoliberalism (market-based development) under the coordination and direction of the G-8, the IMF, the WTO, and the World Bank; of the concentration of economic power in transnational corporations; of the internationalization of social divisions; and of the subordination of national economies to global forces. There is no doubt that global and transnational dynamics implode into the geography of Ciudad Juárez.

To be sure, the effects of this newly constituted global economic order impact the most vulnerable communities — the bodies of the poor and Third World women, who are its disposable targets of labor exploita-

tion.[29] And critical globalization theories have rightly noted the uneven-
ness of development in Ciudad Juárez, the further exploitation of the
poor, and the lack of infrastructural development — housing, sewage, elec-
tricity, health and other basic services — to accommodate the many poor
immigrants recruited from southern Mexico and Central America by the
maquiladora industry. And, although there is no doubt that the process
of economic globalization is "out of control,"[30] globalism is a monolithic,
top-down analysis that neither captures nor explains the complexity of
feminicide. Nor does conflating the *exploitation* of gendered bodies with
their *extermination* offer us the nuanced account of violence that feminicide demands.

Attributing the murders of women to processes of globalization has
created the enduring myth of "maquiladora killings," one in which the
killers are allegedly targeting maquiladora workers — a cliché that continues to this day.[31] For a Left drawn to critiques of global injustice, the
maquila murders are certainly alluring victims.[32] As convincing as this narrative may be, there is ample evidence disputing the myth of "maquiladora killings," especially in the research of independent journalists and aca-
demics in Mexico. A study conducted by Benítez et al. of murders
between 1993 and 1998 identifies only 15 maquiladora workers out of 137
victims.[33] Drawing from a larger sample — 162 murdered women between
1993 and 1999 — the research of Monárrez further corroborates the earlier
figure of 15 maquiladora workers killed, citing additional occupations for
the victims: students, housewives, sales clerks, sex workers, domestics,
and drug traffickers.[34] Since the publication of these two studies, there
have been several more maquiladora workers murdered, but they are still
in the minority. Rather than targeting "actual" maquiladora workers, it is
much more accurate to say that the misogynist and racist killers are targeting members of the urban reserve of wage labor of the maquiladora
industry, namely a pool of female workers migrating from southern
Mexico and Central America and living in the poor surrounding colonias
of Juárez.

The Subject of Globalism

In positioning the maquiladora industry as its unifying trope, the discourse of globalism elides the multiple structures of oppression in the
lives of women as well as providing an insular explanation for the killings.
In other ways, the discourse of globalism focuses a synoptic gaze primar-

ily on women outside domestic spaces — in work or leisure activities, as consequences of processes of globalization. Often its gaze is explicit; sometimes the focus proceeds by inference. But in each case, the subject of the discourse of globalism is an abject one: a subject in need of regulation; a subject as passive victim; or a subject as fetish of the masculinist gaze.

The documentary by Saul Landau and Sonia Angulo, *Maquila: A Tale of Two Mexicos* (2000), by linking feminicide to globalization, participates in this narrative. The film treats the issue of global justice, providing a critique of globalization as a "new world disorder."[35] Filmmakers provide a generally persuasive account of unfair labor practices, gender and labor exploitation, health and safety violations, and environmental degradation through the dumping of toxic waste, chemical emissions, and toxic leaks. The film renders the "story of the struggle of a nation, deep in the midst of globalization" — as the rap lyrics by Manny Martinez and Greg Landau put it. The documentary is notable for its attention to the growing unionization movement among maquiladora workers, especially in light of the claims made by certain researchers on the Left regarding the impossibility of organizing workers from export-processing zones into a "coherent oppositional politics to capitalism."[36] Even though the filmmakers emphasize the agency of transnational activists and labor organizers, in rendering feminicide intelligible to viewers, *Maquila: A Tale of Two Mexicos* adopts a masculinist point of view.

The maquila women are portrayed as alluring victims. The killings of women in Juárez are shown midway into the narrative, opening on the comments of local economist and member of the opposition party Victor Quintana, who characterizes "globalization" as a process that "tears apart the social fabric." It is women's visibility in public, nondomestic spaces — as laboring bodies and dead bodies — that provides the visual evidence for this "tear[ing] apart of the social fabric." A visual collage of women in various public sites follows Quintana's commentary: images of women in the maquila industry; images of women hanging out in discos and on the streets; images of women working in the sex industry. The accompanying sound track of "El Corrido de la Maquila," by Greg Landau and Francisco Herrera, directs viewers to interpret the images, which point to the dangers inherent in women's visibility and expression of nonnormativity, especially in spaces outside the private sphere of the home. "The dangers in the maquila," as the song's lyrics express it, demand parental (masculine) "protection" (regulation and surveillance) of young women outside the private sphere. And if viewers failed to grasp this message, the next segment in the film drives the point home: a graphic scene of police examining the body of a recently found murdered woman in Juárez. The segment ends with the words of Zapatista leader Subcomandante Marcos, who led the popular uprising in Chiapas in the 1990s, describing globalization as a project designed to "eliminate a part of that population; erase them from the face of the earth," — but this fails to undo the logic of association established in the film through the complementary visual images and song lyrics. Namely, women are killed for engaging in activities that exceed patriarchal gendered "norms": hanging out in bars or on the streets, working in the sex industry. In establishing this montage, *Maquila: A Tale of Two Mexicos* characterizes women not simply of as victims of globalization but as subjects in need of patriarchal regulation.

Early on, journalist Debbie Nathan also associated feminicide with forms of sexuality engendered under conditions of globalization. Drawing from ethnographic research on sexual practices in the maquiladora industry, Nathan wrote about instances of "a rigid version of femininity" and "the sexualization of factory life" in the maquilas. Evidence for the maquila industry's promotion of hypersexualization includes heavy flirting on assembly lines; Mexican male supervisors soliciting dates from assembly workers; competition among women for the supervisors' attention; the grooming of the youngest and prettiest girls for the "annual industrywide 'Señorita Maquiladora' beauty contest, complete with evening gown and swimsuit competition." Nathan further described the hyperfemininity of "maquila girls" in this manner: "Unlike their North American sisters, who dress for assembly line in no nonsense T-shirts and sneakers, most maquila girls don miniskirts, heels, gobs of lipstick and eye shadow" — a hypersexuality that according to Nathan spills over into the weekend and after-hours.[37]

Besides reporting on how maquila workers adopt the hyperfeminine forms of sexuality introduced into "traditional" societies like Mexico by global forces, Nathan uncritically embraces the state's framing of the victims as leading "la doble vida — the double life of assembly work by day and casual prostitution by night."[38] During the Burials on the Border conference, I was sitting in the audience with family members who were visibly distressed by Nathan's public remarks, in which she drew the following analogy (later published in *NACLA*) about their rapes: "Oddly, the Spanish word for 'double life,' *la doble vida,* sounds a good deal like *las dos vías,* sex per the vagina and anus."[39]

Nathan's discussion of the sexualization of maquila life is based on a selective and partial interpretation of the research of sociologist Leslie

Salzinger. Although Salzinger studies the "sexualization of factory life" in the maquiladora industry, this reference applies to only one of the three sites in her study; she concludes that representations of gender "vary between localized areas of domination, even those sharing elements of a common discursive framework."[40]

Specifically, Salzinger focuses on the "constitution of gendered meanings in a set of three work places" and on the ways in which gendered meanings and subjectivities conform or diverge from "public narratives" about the "archetypical nature of Mexican 'sex roles.'"[41] One of the factories, Panoptimex, exhibits an "objectifying modality of control" and reinforces "gendered meanings and subjectivities [that] appear to echo those crystallized in public discussions about maquilas . . ."[42] (the factory animating Nathan's argument). However, Nathan ignores Salzinger's findings about the shop floors in the other two factories (Anarchomex and Androgymex): "The differences that emerge here are particularly striking," Salzinger notes. Unlike in Panoptimex, gender in these two other examples is not a significant category, nor are women's identities "defined around objectification."[43] Salzinger's work on the maquiladora industry in Ciudad Juárez calls attention to "the palpable heterogeneity and fluctuating significance" of gender representations on the borderlands, especially in terms of how these differences are lived out in women's daily lives on the shop floors.

Ignoring this complex variability in gendered meanings and subjectivities, Nathan unwittingly echoes what is in fact the "managerial narrative" of the female Mexican employee, one that has served to describe the dress style of Mexican female workers through references to prostitution. In large measure, the stereotype of maquila workers as "prostitutes" is part of a much longer history of othering practices derived from colonialist fantasies about the border as a zone of "sexual excess" and border women as "culturally bound to sexual chaos."[44] It is an old colonialist (and now neocolonialist) narrative indeed, this construction of Mexicanas on the border in terms of sexual excess and chaos.

Nathan's reference to the "hyperfemininity" found on the Mexican shop floor and the differences in dress style between U.S. and Mexican factory workers is surely in part related to a narrative of objectification prevalent about workers in Mexican factories in general. But it is also symptomatic of a broader problem in public discourses on femininity that needs to be amended to include the role of national and global culture, for example, the role of Mexican cinema and television in circulating highly sexualized images of femininity, as well as the articulation of class and culture in elements of fashion and dress style. In a study of managers in the maquiladora industry, Melissa Wright observes: "Throughout the maquilas, attention to women's dress style is continually articulated as an American or Mexican affect, and often in reference to cultural representation rather than to a national divide. The difference is generally discussed as one of length; fit, in terms of degree of snugness; color (bright or subdued); shoe style; make-up applications and hairstyle."[45]

To a great extent, the links Nathan forges between dress style (what according to North American puritanical standards is highly sexualized) and "engaging in casual prostitution" echo managerial narratives about maquiladora workers on the border. As Wright notes, "When I asked one of the production managers, Roger, to describe the labor force, he said, 'Some of these girls have second jobs. You know, I've heard that some work the bars.' The message that you cannot tell the difference between a prostitute and a maquiladora worker was common in my interviews."[46]

The devaluation of border female sexuality, as Nathan has noted, is part of a more generalized narrative about the border as a place of excess, violence, prostitution, drugs, and contraband that circulates in the Mexican popular imaginary. Nathan dates these images of the border to the early twentieth century. One can also trace regional identity differentiation back to the colonial era, especially with metropolitan locations like Mexico City stigmatizing the northern (frontier) regions as sites of vice and degeneracy. Expressed in popular cultural forms such as corridos, canciones rancheras, and much later in films and telenovelas, the earlier stigma of the frontier and of its inhabitants contributes to the ongoing othering of border femininity within Mexico, to what Nathan calls "this demonized yet casual throw-away view of border women" within the national imaginary.[47]

The complexities of identity in Mexico have to do not only with the regional differences in constructions of border women as the other, according to Nathan, but also with patriarchal forms of domination, including "the fact that Juárez also registers the highest levels of reported domestic violence in México."[48] Nathan unfortunately lapses once again into uncritical acceptance of the narrative of nonnormative sexuality engendered by processes of globalization, positing a link "between maquila development, which has encouraged 'la doble vida,' and the sexualization of violence against women that appears to be a backlash against their changing economic and social roles on Mexico's northern border."[49]

A more nuanced understanding of the regulation of women's bodies under economic processes of globalization is offered by Ursula Biemenn's 1999 documentary *Performing the Border*. The film focuses on women's bodies, rendered through experimental techniques — nonsynchronized sound and images, time-lapse filming uncoupling the image from real time, image enhancement, and a meditative voice-over. The effect of these nonrealist techniques is to distance and disturb the viewer's relation to reality and to force us to contemplate the links between the exploitation and alienation of laboring bodies in various sites within global capitalism, as workers in the maquiladora industry and in the sex industry. Informed as it is by a committed feminist politics, *Performing the Border* portrays women not as being in need of regulation and surveillance, but rather as the very *objects* of regulation and surveillance — an emphasis supported by the interviews of journalist Isabel Velásquez and writer/filmmaker Bertha Jotar.

Ultimately, though, *Performing the Border* is unable to escape the logic of associating the murders of women in Juárez with their nonnormative practices. Like *Maquila: A Tale of Two Mexicos*, Biemenn's film equates exploited bodies with exterminated bodies visually through a linear sequence of narrative elements that creates a chain of associations: maquila workers–sex workers–victims of feminicide. The segment portraying female workers in the maquila industry is followed by the testimony of a Juárez sex worker and immediately afterward by a segment on the murdered women. In its metonymic association of globalization–nonnormative sexuality–feminicide, *Performing the Border* fails to disrupt the premise of the discourse of globalism, especially the notion that the extermination of women's bodies proceeds from the same logic as their exploitation: global capitalism. Like *Maquila: a Tale of Two Mexico*, *Performing the Border* is complicit with "Eurocentric victimology,"[50] a discourse that produces the murdered women of Ciudad Juárez solely as objects of global capitalism. In many ways, *Performing the Border* evidences an "imperially-charged agenda," the power of "First World" feminists to define "Third World" women as "objects of capital" and as "traces of patriarchy," failing to record the ways in which "women resist despite huge constraints and penalties."[51]

The aforementioned film and journalistic representations, though limited, are much less egregious than the literary writings of Charles Bowden. Crossing the line from "titillation and information," his essays warrant close examination for the discursive production of border woman as fetish.[52]

Bowden adopts the narrative of globalism to explain the realities of

Mexico in colonialist terms, claiming that "the only cheap thing in Mexico is flesh, human bodies you can fornicate with or work to death." His view of Ciudad Juárez as a "city woven out of violence" supports the emphasis on nonnormativity as the cause of feminicide as well. Bowden similarly reiterates the myth of maquiladora killings, focusing on the sexual behaviors of maquila workers, whom he describes as "mostly young, often living free of family, with their own money and desires."[53] For Bowden, feminicide represents the "blood price" the nation pays for globalization, and he attributes violence to male backlash. "Killing girls," Bowden argues, "has in effect become what men of Juárez do with the frustrations of living in a town with less than one percent unemployment but with abundant poverty. It is the local language of rage, a blood price exacted for what Juárez is: the world's largest border community, with 300 maquila plants, and the highest concentration of maquila workers in the country."[54]

Although there is no doubt that feminicide embodies the most deadly logic of masculinity, that its perpetrators are misogynist and racist killers, the focus on working-class men deflects attention away from the multiple structures of violence in the lives of women. However, Bowden's own explanatory logic is also in many ways a form of male rage, or symbolic violence against women. In his most recent essay on the murders of women in Ciudad Juárez, for example, Bowden borrows the title of a popular banda tune ("Quiero bailar con la niña fresa") allegorically, to stage his own desires and symbolic male rage, in his own "I Want to Dance with the Strawberry Girl." This is how he ends his article:

The faces with the darkened lips and highlighted eyes, the cool young faces all say the same thing: Every man in this building wants me. . . . Her blouse is rich with red, her long white skirt erupts with roses. Her hair rises on her head in the crown of a contessa and then trails down her slender back. Worship me. The face is blank, no smile. A few hours ago she was a cog in a machine for 40 bucks a week. Tomorrow morning she will be scurrying round El Centro for a week's supplies and then to the mercado publico, where cheap restaurants beckon and old men play the music of Chiapas. Outside, the city is spiked with painted poles and black crosses. El Paso glows across the river, as distant and cold as a star. But now, in here, hips smear against the bass line, the body heat rises.[55]

The masculine gaze this passage enacts is perverse and disturbing. Here Bowden assumes to know the desires of a working-class woman in Juárez ("Every man in this building wants me"). Bowden conjures up images about the border familiar to U.S. audiences, images that portray the border as a space of "excess." The female body and the territorial body of Juárez are libidinal in a hot-tempered, close-up way. El Paso is the icy, distant North American counterpart ("El Paso glows across the river, as distant and cold as a star. But now, in here, hips smear against the bass line, the body heat rises"). With his focus on border/sexual excess, Bowden does not simply reproduce globalism's emphasis on nonnormativity as an explanation for the murders; rather, he adopts a misogynist gaze, enacting the symbolic violence of male rage.

This is not the first instance of symbolic violence in the work of Charles Bowden. In *Juarez: The Laboratory of Our Future,* Bowden again crosses the line between titillation and information, recounting his fantasies about Adriana, a "whore" and former maquila worker with two children:

In my fantasy, Adriana and I do the right thing and follow the instructions of our time. We build a small casa by the sea. Actually, she has wrapped up her graduate studies at the National Autonomous University of Mexico, UNAM. She has an MA in romance languages and, of course an MBA, plus a doctorate in anthropology awarded for her groundbreaking study, "Sexual Surrogates: Free Trade, Multi-Culturalism and the Feminist Perspective." She is now preparing a dictionary of industrial argot in her own work for the journal of linguistics and is contemplating study of dialogues with clients using the full French critical apparatus. . . . The children will play on the beach. I'll keep an eye on them because the undertow here is terrific. Each morning she and I will jog up and down and the pounds will melt off and restore her girlish figure. We will live on locust, wild honey, young goat, fresh fruit, vitamin supplements, garlic tablets, and various hot salsas.[56]

I imagine myself as the interlocutor of this passage. Is Bowden anticipating the feminist, antiracist critique of his writing, explicitly mocking after constructing a feminist poststructuralist reading of his literary fantasy? I take the bait, for this brutally senseless parody of yuppie lifestyle á la mexicana heralds the by now classic "rescue fantasy" of Western masculinity — one fixated on saving Third World women from the excesses of their own cultures. Written in the context of his account of feminicide in Ciudad Juárez, Bowden's ironic humor affronts common civility, revealing the perverse logic of his racist and colonialist gaze. The abjection of poor and working women in Juárez is nowhere more flagrant than in the "intimacy" he conjures up with the young women on the border, for example, the "fresa" who animates his voyeuristic gaze; the "whore" who serves as muse for his literary fantasies. Bowden's perversity, his racist and colonialist gaze, constructs border women as abject. What's more,

Bowden links these abject bodies to a third one he summons in his text, the mimetic image of one of the murdered border women.

The photograph published on page 66 of *Juarez: The Laboratory of Our Future* depicts the body of a kidnapped, raped, and murdered sixteen-year-old girl found in a park that is located literally on the border between Ciudad Juárez and El Paso and that is "dedicated to friendship between both nations." The photographer, Jaime Bailleres, told Bowden that a newspaper refused to publish the image because, according to Bowden, "the lips of the girl pull back, revealing her white teeth. Sounds pour forth from her mouth. She is screaming and screaming and screaming."[57]

What logic would venture to further deface this image of a border woman's horrified expression — this face of terror that Bowden initially mistook for a "carved wooden mask." "Something," as he tells us, "made by one of those quaint tribes far away in the Mexican south?"[58] The mask, Benjamin asserts, allows us to "get ahold of an object at very close range by way of its likeness, its reproduction."[59] Bowden continues: "I keep a copy of it in a folder right next to where I work and from time to time I open the clean manila folder and look into her face. And then I close it like the lid of a coffin. She haunts me, and I deal with this fact by avoiding it."[60]

Bowden did not avoid the face/mask. In his first article published in *Harper's* and later in his book on Ciudad Juárez, Bowden published it.[61] By so doing, he defaced it, thereby unleashing the magical power of deface-ment, which is, according to Michael Taussig, "the most common form of magical art."[62] What if in actuality the editors of the newspaper understood the logic of mimesis? Perhaps in Mexican political culture they are well aware of the enchanting qualities of defacement, and their refusal to pub-lish (commodify) the image represents instead a refusal to practice a form of defacement, a disfiguration of the copy of her face because it would in all likelihood summon "a strange surplus of negative energy."[63]

In the hands of a literary writer/journalist from the United States, the face of horror belonging to the body of a woman on the border is aes-theticized and transformed into a fetish, "a horror made beautiful and primitivism exoticized."[64] Bowden's urge to get "ahold of an object at very close range by way of its likeness" grows stronger every day. "The skin is smooth, Bowden writes, "almost carved and sanded, but much too dark. And the screams are simply too deafening."[65] Perhaps in Mexico, ancient knowledges bespeak the mimetic magic of representation, its ability to animate what it is a copy of. In a "culture of masks," as Subcomandante Marcos refers to Mexican political culture, this face/mask may well trig-ger "a strange surplus of negative energy."

Rethinking State Terrorism

Cultural representations informed by the discourse of globalism have played a crucial role in deflecting attention away from the complicity of the state in creating a climate of violence. Although liberal and sympathetic to the murders of women in Juárez, often the discourse of globalism reifies the "global economy" as a "thing operating transhistorically and driven by its own laws and motion."[66] In other ways, globalism posits an isomorphism between the local and the global that has led to grand generalizations about the demise of the state.[67] This failure to provide a more nuanced approximation about the interplay of "global and transnational" *as well as* "national and local dynamics implod[ing] simultaneously into the everyday experiences of members of urban households"[68] has worked to absolve the state of its complicity and perhaps even direct involvement in the murders of poor and dark women in Ciudad Juárez.[69] As the master narrative on the Left, globalism generates a problem of interpretation that is unable to account for the consolidation of a new form of state-sanctioned terrorism in Mexico. However, the state is in many ways directly implicated in the culture of feminicide in the region. In February 2002, state agents ambushed and assassinated Mario César Escobedo Anaya, a defense attorney for one of the suspects in the killings who was leading charges against police for their use of torture in extracting confessions. There have been numerous death threats against activists and journalists in Ciudad Juárez, including Esther Chávez Cano, the head of the NGO Casa Amiga; Samira Izaguirre, radio journalist and founder of the NGO Luz y Justicia. And at least a dozen activists, including Izaguirre, have filed petitions for asylum in the United States.[70]

In order to broach the ways in which the problem of interpretation is complicit with state-sanctioned terrorism we need to first examine how "the state is implicated in the construction of gender regimes."[71] The *outdated* Roman and Napoleonic codes informing Mexico's legal system have in fact ratified and promoted violence against women, especially in the private sphere, where male violence is normalized as "a mechanism of punishment and control."[72] Mexico's regulatory and judicial system, strengthened by traditional cultural values, supports "the idea of masculine authority and ownership" over the lives of women and grants male impunity in the exercise of violence against women.[73] In fact few Latin American countries have legislation against violence in the private sphere. Under current Mexican law, if injuries inflicted during interfamilial violence heal before fifteen days, the woman cannot file charges against her domestic partner; if the injuries heal after fifteen days but are not permanent, the aggressor is simply fined.[74]

For years, feminist grassroots activists and NGOs have sought legal and judicial redress, aiming to extend full citizenship rights to women. Yet in the struggle to eliminate violence against women, activists are waging an uphill battle. Recently, members of the conservative party (PAN) in the Senate blocked ratification of the international human rights instrument CEDAW, the Convention to Eliminate all Forms of Discrimination against Women, a nonbinding document that would at least have signaled the state's support for the prevention of gender violence in Mexico.[75]

The movement to extend rights to women in Mexico is of utmost importance because, as in many other Latin American nations, "Violence against women and sexual assault are typified in law as crimes against the honor of the family, rather than as crimes against the personal, physical integrity and human rights of the woman victim."[76] This interpretation of gender violence as "crimes against the honor of the family" has lethal consequences for women, since Mexican laws "still consider the honesty, honor, and good name of the woman to be relevant to the characterization of certain sexual crimes and to determine their punishment."[77] The state in effect tolerates violence against women, especially in the legal and juridical realm, depoliticizing and relegating violence to the domestic private sphere and narrowly portraying it as personal in nature, rather than as a "systemic historical and political event."[78] This same dynamic also depoliticizes other forms of family violence, such as incest and pedophilia, which often go unreported and/or ignored. Reinforcing these manifestations of family violence is a discourse that discourages women from leaving the private sphere, the purported site of patriarchal protection and authority: public space is imagined as inherently dangerous.[79]

Given its failure to extend citizenship rights to women, Mexico's legal and judicial system is part of "the state machineries for the exercise of violence."[80] Recognizing state complicity, the United Nations Declaration on the Elimination of Violence against Women "points to areas of state negligence, as opposed to direct responsibility. It notes that states are obliged to exercise 'due diligence' in preventing all acts of violence against women."[81]

Much of the problem with the discourse of globalism stems from its portrayal of sexual violence as primarily an effect of global capitalism without accounting for the ways in which global manifestations of power differ from as much as they intensify earlier and more traditional forms of patriarchy within the nation-state. A more nuanced understanding of sexual violence in Juárez identifies the multiple sites where women experience violence, within domestic and public spaces that are local and national as well as global and transnational. And this leads us to another way in which globalism is complicitous with the state.

The meanings surrounding the deaths are elusive. Are they committed by a single or multiple sex serial killers? By the police- and state-sponsored paramilitary groups? By the "Juniors" (sons of the elite)? By traffickers of illegal human organs? By an underground economy of pornography and snuff-films? By a satanic cult? By narco-traffickers? By unemployed men envious of women workers? By men expressing rage against poverty? By men threatened by changing sex roles? By abusive spouses or boyfriends? There are so many contrary interpretations and competing narratives that they have created a "problem of interpretation" that is "decisive for terror, not only making effective counterdiscourse so difficult but also making the terribleness of death squads, disappearances, and torture all the more effective in crippling of people's capacity to resist."[82]

Fifty years ago, Walter Benjamin wrote: "The tradition of the oppressed teaches us that the 'state of emergency' is not the exception but the rule. We must attain to a conception of history that is in keeping with this insight."[83] These insights permit understanding about the role of the Mexican state in creating the "state of emergency." Mexico's neoliberal policies — its disinvestment in the public sphere, instituted by the shift from a welfare state to a state that facilitated globalization — has produced the very culture of violence that it purports to police.[84] As Agamben so aptly reminds us, "Power no longer has today any form of legitimation other than emergency . . . power everywhere and continuously refers and appeals to emergency as well as laboring secretly to produce it." In Mexico, the "state of exception . . . has now become the norm."[85]

It is thus important to recognize how violence — not only in Ciudad Juárez, but also in Mexico City — is not simply a problem *for* the state but is in fact endemic to it, a "state of exception" produced by an authoritarian government that has cultivated extreme forms of violence, corruption, and yes, even death, in order to cripple people's capacity to resist, to smother effective counterdiscourse and overpower the revitalized democratic opposition.

As the uprising of the Zapatistas in Chiapas has reminded us, the Mexican government has been waging a "dirty war" of terror, violence, and extermination against all forms of dissidence, including the poor, women, and indigenous communities. The state hides behind the mask of democracy, its appearance a subterfuge for the repressive, authoritarian government which, until the 2000 presidential election of PAN candidate Vicente Fox, had been dominated by a single ruling party, the PRI. We should consider feminicide in Ciudad Juárez a part of the scenario of state-sponsored terrorism because it is situated in the "space of death," which "is important in the creation of meaning and consciousness nowhere more so than in societies where torture is endemic and where the culture of terror flourishes."[86] As Taussig so poignantly writes about the complicity of the state in generating a climate of terror: "There is also the need to control massive populations, entire social classes, and even nations through the cultural elaboration of fear."[87]

If the subject "woman" under the patriarchal state figures as the embodiment of the nation, the "space of death" occupied by these poor and dark women, embodiments of the nation, creates "meaning and consciousness" around the role of the state in creating the conditions of possibility for feminicide. The fact that all of the victims were members of the most vulnerable and oppressed group in Mexican society — dark-skinned women — underscores the extent to which in Mexico "women's relationship to the state is racialized and ethnicized as well as gendered."[88] One way to politicize violence against women of intersecting identities is by highlighting the role of the patriarchal state in creating the conditions of possibility for the proliferation of gender violence.

Another way to politicize violence is to think about it in broader terms, not just as isolated or personal in nature, but as a form of state-sanctioned terrorism, a tool of political repression sanctioned by an undemocratic patriarchal state in its crusade against poor and racialized citizens: "The choice of particular women as targets of rape is almost inevitably determined by their identities . . . [as] members of an ethnic group, race or class."[89]

The murders of poor and dark women in Ciudad Juárez, situated as they are in a nexus of violence that spans from the state to the home, are thus connected to broader questions of power and gender inequality within a patriarchal state. The consideration of gender violence as "social feminicide" implicates "the role of an existing social order in practices that result in the death and devaluation of female lives."[90]

Transnational Activism on the Border

In March 1999, the crosses started appearing. Black crosses on pink backgrounds, painted in protest on electrical poles throughout Juárez, by Voces sin Eco (Voices without Echo), a grassroots group of families of the

FIGURE 1. Black cross on pink background painted on telephone pole in Ciudad Juárez. Photo by Celeste Carrasco, courtesy of Lourdes Portillo.

murdered women (figure 1). Eerily barren crosses, silent witnesses to symbolic and experiential instances of violence, suggestive of what local poet
Micaela Solís calls "the language of the abyss: the cries for help we never
heard/the screams of their voices."[91] The fusion of traditional secular and
religious iconography — pink for woman; cross for mourning — contra-
venes against epistemic and real violence. Women are the protagonists of
this grassroots movement.[92] In painting the crosses in public spaces,
Voces sin Eco forged a new public identity for women, claiming public
space for them as citizens of the nation.

As in other places in Latin America, the women of Juárez used religiosity subversively to stage a confrontation with the historical and social
trauma in the region. The use of religiosity — crosses, luminarias, vigils —
is a form of indirection and nonliteralness for healing the trauma of the
unrepresentable: death as the ultimate other. As a political and discursive
strategy, religiosity gives voice to a new consciousness, one that recog-
nizes the contradictions in the interface between woman's visibility as
abject subject (murder victim) and the invisibility of woman in the public sphere (citizen).

Woman's visibility as abject is a subject-effect produced by the intersection of experiential violence and symbolic violence: the violence of racist misogynists, the violence of state-sanctioned terrorism, the violence of discursive frameworks of interpretation, but also the violence of representation. The hypervisibility of the feminine body in audiovisual media, as in the commodification of gruesome photographs depicting tortured and dismembered bodies, heightens the invisibility of the disposable body of the poor, dark woman on the border.[93] Faced with such literalness and explicitness, religiosity is a mode for reimagining the murdered, violated body otherwise: as a subject undeserving of annihilation.[94] In other ways, the discursive strategies of religiosity contemplate visibility for a new subject: the cross marks the intersectional identities of the targeted feminine subject, the feminine body of the poor and dark woman.

As in other parts of Mexico, in this northern region, certain bodies (white) are held in higher esteem than others are.[95] Although the women were indeed targeted for their gender, perhaps even more significant are the racial and class hierarchies that constitute their identities as women. As one of the mothers, Mrs. González, so aptly phrases it: "For the poor there's no justice. If they'd murder a rich person's girl, they'd kill half the world to find the murderer. But since they've only murdered poor people, they treat us like dirt."[96]

Three years after the crosses were first painted on telephone poles, the local coalition of grassroots groups and NGOs extended its reach beyond Juárez, growing into a broad-based, national and international movement to end violence against women in Mexico. By early 2002, a new coalition of feminist activists from hundreds of organizations came together under the campaign Ni Una Más. In December 2001, thirty thousand protesters from both sides of the border gathered in Juárez. And in March 2002, hundreds of women dressed in black (elderly women, campesinas, housewives, factory workers, students, and professionals) marched for 370 kilometers, from Chihuahua City to the Juárez-El Paso border, in the Exodus for Life campaign. Staging demonstrations to publicize the murders, the transnational campaign Ni Una Más is working to extend citizenship rights to women in Mexico.

Horrific forms of violence against women have had an unintended and spiraling effect. In the wake of feminicide in Juárez, this emerging formation of feminist and cross-border activism is part of the new space of planetary civil society, of the movement for global justice, of the challenges to global capitalism, neoliberal state policies, and the rise of the global police state. Women's activism on the borderlands constitutes an identity formation that intersects with the transnational drive for women's human rights that gained momentum in the decade of the nineties after the United Nations World Conference of Human Rights in Vienna (1993).[97] However, this transnational movement for women's rights poses unique challenges. For example, is it possible to locate women's oppression within the human rights framework developed by feminists in the First World? Is it possible to evoke a transnational subject identity within a planetary civil society? The writings of Third World feminists provide a cautionary tale.

Claiming a singular transnational identity for women ignores the profound differences among women across the globe, but especially within specific national localities, as Vasuki Nesiah reminds us: "A discourse about universally shared oppression can obfuscate global contradictions."[98] Although First World feminists have contributed significantly to "the theoretical and practical revision of international rights law," especially in their redefinition of women's rights as human rights, the challenge today involves framing women's international human rights within very complex and specific cultural contexts. For this reason, Celina Romany writes, "an integrated and more coherent use of international instruments," such as the coupling of the Women's Convention with the Race Convention in international law, as has been accomplished in South Africa, is an important step in the right direction. "The constitutional agenda had to recognize how a gender-essentialist critique fell short and did not adequately conceptualize a regime of rights and protections responsive to the realities of Black women."[99] In this manner, Romany's "intersectional methodology directs us to ask the woman/race question" and, in the case of Juárez, the class question as well.

Grassroots activists in Juárez are well aware of the limitations of basing a human rights framework on a singular transnational identity or "shared international subject class." For as Mrs. González reminds us, it is their intersectional identities as specific class, race, and gender subjects which makes women in Mexico particularly vulnerable to feminicide and state terrorism.

In many ways, the murder and disappearance of women in Ciudad Juárez have strengthened the resolve of feminist and human rights in the campaign to eliminate multiple forms of violence in the lives of women and children. In the short term, women's rights groups are seeking legal and juridical redress, lobbying for reforms to the penal code, including a law covering violence in the private sphere.[100]

The eloquent *El silencio que la voz de todas quiebra,* written by a group of courageous journalists and creative writers, ends with these words: "What makes anyone (random or premeditated killer, individual or serial, alone or accompanied, Mexican or foreigner) think that in Ciudad Juárez one can rape or kill a woman without fear of retribution?"[101] A rhetorical question, no doubt, but its spirit of denunciation challenges public and private patriarchies in Mexico.

At the national level, the state continues to produce the very "state of exception" it aims to police, combining rhetoric with inaction and non-intervention in eliminating violence against women.[102] In November 2001, President Vicente Fox directed the attorney general of Mexico to assist in the investigation of feminicide. However, as of this writing, the cultural elaboration of fear continues in Chihuahua. So too does the struggle to eradicate all forms of violence in the lives of excluded citizens, disenfranchised subjects of the patriarchal state, women, indigenous people, dark and poor women, gays, the urban and rural poor, and children. In this newly constituted planetary civil society, human rights activists on the borderlands hold onto a vision of a future in which no person can "rape or kill a woman without fear of retribution."

Conclusion

This study of the cultural representations of feminicide grew out of my ongoing collaboration with filmmaker Lourdes Portillo. In September 1999 I joined Lourdes at the Burials on the Border conference after she had spent two harrowing weeks in Ciudad Juárez filming for a documentary that was eventually released as *Señorita extraviada* (2001). My current analysis of cultural discourses is informed by the dialogic relationship we cultivated in the course of the production of her documentary. Just as her investigation has influenced my thinking, so too has my study influenced her framing of feminicide in Juárez. In the course of our projects, both of us have constituted frameworks of intelligibility that are mutually influenced by our ongoing discussions about the continuing violence against women. I have listened to her theories about the murders and commented on several versions of the film; she has similarly impacted my study and clarified my understanding about the murders of women.

Lourdes maintained daily contact with the mothers and local women rights activists. I drew strength and inspiration from the generosity she exhibited toward family members and activists and from the passion and commitment that drove her documentation of the murder of their loved ones. In the months that followed the release of *Señorita extraviada,* I accompanied Lourdes on several occasions during screenings of the film throughout the United States and abroad. Often we spoke in public forums to audiences who were generally unaware of the murder and disappearance of women in Juárez.

During these public presentations, my work has been to provide a framework for the film and to discuss its political and aesthetic merits. I situate this film within its activist tradition, as a film that refuses to withdraw from political action, a film expressing a moral outrage and seizing terror through confrontation. *Señorita extraviada* is an activist film in large measure because of its crucial role in the formation of what I have termed a planetary civil society. Lourdes has made video copies of the film available to grassroots groups throughout the Southwest, the Mexico-U.S. border, and Mexico City, for raising public awareness and participating in fund-raising campaigns for families of the murdered women. The film has served women rights activists in their appeals beyond the state to international forums. It has also served to publicize the murders of women in European, U.S., and Latin American contexts through its exhibition at major international film festivals, where it has won numerous awards, including the prestigious "Nestor Almendros" award from Human Rights Watch.

As an activist film in the tradition of radical cinema, *Señorita extraviada* is driven by a project of social transformation and concientización, aiming to move its viewers into political action. The film poignantly echoes the strategies of grassroots activists, mothers, sisters, and relatives of the disappeared in their ongoing struggle against state-sanctioned terrorism, reflecting the struggle of those who continue to demand justice despite threats against their lives and the use of disappearance as a mechanism of social control. *Señorita extraviada* is undoubtedly an issue-oriented film, yet its mode of delivery is eloquent and groundbreaking.

Making a film about an event that is ongoing and continues to unfold is an inherently challenging undertaking — even more so if the subject matter is as horrid and terrifying as widespread violence, murder, and disappearances. Given the absolute abjection of women through death, as well as the desecration of their bodies in public discourse, Lourdes confronted an enormous problem of representation. In the course of several trips to Ciudad Juárez, Lourdes faced quite a challenge. Not only did she experience firsthand the social trauma that these murders have produced throughout the region, but she bears witness to the psychic trauma that family members were living under and that they continually re-live with each new report of a murder or disappearance. The film was thus motivated by these inextricably related conditions of the problem of representation and of social and psychic trauma. How does one represent the dead in a respectful manner, in a way that does not further sacrilize their bodies, but honors the memory of their former existence? How does one represent the dead in a way that is respectful of the families and that honors their grief?

Drawing from the discursive strategies of grassroots groups like Voces sin Eco, Lourdes employs religious symbolism and iconography subversively. She enshrouds her film in the discourse of religiosity. The strategic placement of images of crosses, montages of crucifixes and home altars, along with the musical score of Gregorian chants, including the solemn chant for the dead ("Kyrie Eleison"), all work to establish a meditative, hieratic rhythm in the film. Lourdes describes *Señorita extraviada* as a "requiem." She has in effect resignified the requiem into an artistic composition for the dead. To her credit, not a single dead body appears in the film; nonetheless the haunting presence of the victims is summoned both literally, through the placement of photographs, and figuratively, through her reworking of the requiem form.

Like her earlier film, *Las Madres, Señorita extraviada* emphasizes the process of radicalization rather than victimization. The narrative gives voice to women's agency, to the mothers and sisters who have emerged as protagonists in grassroots movements. Through their agency and determination, poor women have shouldered the work of detection and forensic investigation, searching for missing daughters or sisters, combing the desert for bodies, and identifying remains.

The film portrays women on the border neither as passive victims nor as hapless dependents of the patriarchal state, the family, or international human rights groups. Instead, the film underscores the agency of mothers and women activists on the border, women who affirm the continuity of life, grieving and mourning, while acting as politically motivated citizens demanding the rights of women within the nation-state. It is the mothers and women activists, and not secondary sources or experts, who are the film's ultimate guarantors of truth.

Informed as it is by a women's rights framework, *Señorita extraviada* avoids positing a singular identity for women in Mexico. It emphasizes an intersectional methodology which in my estimation has generated a new understanding of feminicide among Mexican intellectuals, not simply as class and gender motivated, but as *racially* motivated as well. Since the release of *Señorita extraviada* I have noticed references to the "racial" nature of the killings on the editorial pages of *La Jornada,* a national daily based in Mexico City, where emphasis on the "misogyny," "classism," and "racism" of the killings has now become common.[103]

Although Lourdes draws from experimental and realist techniques, unlike conventional documentaries, *Señorita extraviada* provides neither a singular cause for feminicide nor a contrived resolution. Lourdes draws attention to a confluence of intersecting and overlapping forces including but not limited to broader structural processes of economic globalization and the neoliberal policies of the patriarchal state, as well as more localized virulent forms of patriarchal domination. Ultimately, Lourdes turns her critical gaze onto the patriarchal state, a feature that some audience members have criticized for deemphasizing the role of global capitalism. But it is also clear from Lourdes's investigation that, in the words of one women's rights activist in the film, "The state is ultimately responsible." The film draws attention to the role of state agents as actual perpetrators of the murders, as well as to the state's role in creating the conditions of possibility (the state of exception) for the patriarchal expression of a sexual politics of extermination in the region. If Lourdes's critical gaze on the state bothers some audiences, what is even more disturbing is how the filmmaker ultimately turns the critical gaze back onto its viewers.

In this respect, I am indebted to my students in a film course I taught during the spring of 2002 at UCSC for their insights about how the film's powerfully unsettling and disturbing ending implicates the viewer in responsibility.[104] The film's ending points to our complicity, not as a literal implication or responsibility for the murders, but as an ethical one. The film ends on the tone of moral outrage and in so doing calls for our ethical political engagement, summoning us to take action. I also like to think about the film's ethics as summoning the "space of death," a space, to quote Jean Franco, "of immortality, communal memory, of connections between generations," a space "particularly important as a site of struggle in the colonized areas of the world, and this struggle is of necessity ethical."[105]

At the Burials on the Border conference I sat next to Guillermina González as she gazed intently at the postcard reproduction of the conference poster (figure 2). "These are my sister, Sagrario's, eyes," she said. "I took out the photo from my wallet and they are the same eyes." They in fact happened not to be Sagrario's eyes, according to conference organizers, but Guillermina's fixation overwhelmed me. She stared at the image of those almond-shaped indigenous eyes, belonging to a partial

FIGURE 2. "Burials on the Border" conference poster.

face, so photographically enlarged that the pixel dots were visible; a partial face staring through the pink outline of a cross which partially hid this
face — or did the cross deface the face? It wasn't Sagrario, but to
Guillermina it was. Was I witnessing what Taussig in another context calls
"a type of 'release' of the fetish powers of the face in a proliferation of fantasy and of identities, no less so than the very notion of identity itself, a
discharge of the powers of representation"?[106] And what charge did
those almond-shaped eyes with the quality of magic emit? Almond-
shaped indigenous eyes, both Sagrario's and not Sagrario's: eyes that

return the gaze, transform the object into the subject of the gaze, witnesses for her voice without an echo.

The ghostly barren black crosses on pink backgrounds, painstakingly emblazoned around Ciudad Juárez, as abrasions in public discourse, as embodiments less of Christ, the man made flesh, than of female flesh made human sacrifice. No literal images of the dead, no identifying names on tombstones, only the symbolism of a cross — the Christian cross, the cross of the Four Cardinal Points — superimposed on the traditional hue for femininity: representations of the unrepresentability of trauma. Hundreds of barren crosses in public spaces, crosses as rearticulations of discursive violence, as recodifications of femininity, as expressions of the inability to express terror and trauma: black-crosses-on-pink as figures for the "space of death," so "important in the creation of meaning and consciousness nowhere more so than in societies where torture is endemic and where the culture of terror flourishes." Crosses speaking for justice for eyes that cannot see, for women who can no longer speak, crosses marking the threshold of existence.

CHAPTER TWO

Cross-Border Feminist Solidarities

In their self-help book for Latinas, *The Maria Paradox,* Rosa Maria Gil and Carmen Inoa Vásquez outline the Ten Commandments of Marianismo, or the Latino patriarchy's do's and don't's for Latinas.[1] The ninth commandment is of particular interest for those of us who consistently break the silence and expose intracommunity problems. It states: "Do not discuss personal problems outside the home." While I am not an exponent of cultural truisms or essentialisms, this interdiction is one that many of us — Catholic Chicanas, Mexicanas, and Latinas — heard as we were growing up, and recently it has been employed to regulate the public discourse of Chicana feminists, especially when our discussion of "personal problems" touches upon the issue of gender violence within our communities.

As Gil and Vásquez intimate, the ninth commandment works implicitly as a "gag order" on women. "Personal problems belonged inside the closed doors of the home [and] taking them out into the world constituted a betrayal of the rules of familismo."[2] From my own experience, this gag order is often reinforced by the customary cultural dictum of *vergüenza,* or shame — "¿Qué dirá la gente?" (What will people say?) — a dictum that resonated for me recently as I read José Limón's *American Encounters,* a book dealing with "the sociocultural confrontation between Mexicans and Anglos in the United States." The chapter entitled

"Tex-Sex-Mex: Dirty Mexicans, Aztec Gods, Good Ole Boys and New Texas Women" attracted my attention not only because it deals with the issue of Chicano masculinity but just as significantly because it engages with the writings of Chicana feminists, including my own.[3]

Following in the tradition of Guillermo Flores and Américo Paredes, Limón contests the "rhetorical denigration" of Mexican men, which involves "an articulation of colonialism directed at the Mexican male body, which offered the greatest opposition to the colonialist project."[4] Limón is concerned with alternative images of Mexican masculinity — images which refute "all that the other side [Anglo-America] has always believed of us," in other words, alternatives to the "dirty Mexican," the "degenerate and menacing Mexican bandido" that has terrorized the cultural imaginary of the West since the early nineteenth century.[5] One such alternative image for Limón is the Tejano — and former Clinton cabinet member — Henry Cisneros. By exploring Chicano masculinity, Limón aligns himself with antiracist scholars whose research deconstructs racist iconography and contests the violence of colonialist representations. However, folded into his analysis of colonialist iconography is another implicit though not entirely occulted project: the naming and centering of those subjects whose (discursive) violation he deems worthy of contestation and redress. For Limón the "Mexican male body" is the privileged subject of antiracist analysis; in other words, what counts is the discursive violence perpetrated against Chicano masculinity. This analytic perspective is especially discernible in his efforts to discipline feminist writers like Sandra Cisneros who dare to transgress the ninth commandment and publicly give voice to "family" secrets. The section following his discussion of Henry Cisneros is entitled "The Other Cisneros . . . Sandra" — a heading that on its own furthers the othering process of woman so prevalent in antiracist discourse. In this case, Limón heavy-handedly critiques the short story "Woman Hollering Creek" because, according to Limón, Cisneros "lapses on the issue of Mexican immigrants."[6] Just what issue does she lapse on?

In this story, Cleofilas, a young, recently married Mexicana who with her husband has migrated from Mexico to Seguin, Texas, finds herself a victim of domestic violence. Cisneros's story is as much about a woman's disenchantment with romantic love as it is about cross-border solidarity between women confronting family violence. It is, after all, Felice, the boisterous, pickup-driving Chicana, who comes to Cleofilas's rescue and supports her refusal to be a victim of domestic violence. Cisneros tells the tale of survival as an alternative to all those instances of women who do

not make it out of abusive relationships, who never escape familial violence — those women whose destinies haunt Cleofilas:

Was Cleofilas just exaggerating as her husband always said? It seemed the newspapers were full of such stories. This woman found on the side of the interstate.
This one pushed from a moving car. This one's cadaver, this one unconscious, this
one beaten blue. Her ex-husband, her husband, her lover, her father, her brother,
her uncle, her friend, her co-worker. Always, the same grisly news in the pages of
the dailies. She dunked a glass under the soapy water for a moment — shivered.[7]

Limón is unmoved by Cisneros's efforts to politicize domestic violence. Instead he reproaches the writer for her unfavorable portrayal of
Cleofilas's husband, who, according to Limón, is represented "as the sordid degenerate portrait of a Mexican immigrant male, especially in his *animalistic sexuality*."[8] I highlight Limón's characterization in order to draw
attention to its hyperbolic quality, for the passage that follows is as
graphic as the violence in this story gets:

The first time she had been so surprised she didn't cry or try to defend herself. She
had always said she would strike back if a man, any man were to strike her.

But when the moment came and he slapped her once, and then again, and
again, until the lip split an orchid of blood, she didn't run away as she had imagined she might when she saw such things in the telenovelas.[9]

To be sure, the husband is brutal, but it is less clear that he displays
"animalistic sexuality." Limón's characterization is out of touch with the
reality rendered in the short story. And, if we gauge this critique against
the broader aim of his project — to contest colonialist constructions of
masculinity — then Limón's discursive strategy becomes transparent: he
exaggerates (and sensationalizes) Cisneros's portrayal in order to further
his project of salvaging the Mexican male body.

Unfortunately, his desire for alternative (humanized) portrayals of
Chicano masculinity involves imposing a gag order on Chicana feminists.
"One can only wonder," Limón laments, "what happens in the consciousness of Cisneros's *very many* Anglo-American lay readers as they
read this story in the context of a U.S. hysteria about unregulated — in
every way — Mexican immigration."[10] Here it is again, this discourse of
vergüenza (¿Qué dirá la gente?), coupled with the patriarchal disciplining of efforts on the part of Chicana feminists to break the silence — a discourse of shame and secrecy that overcompensates for colonialist representations of Mexican men as degenerate and violent.

Limón's critique is reminiscent of a mid-1980s controversy over the publication and film adaptation of *The Color Purple*, by Alice Walker. As in the case of Maxine Hong Kingston's *Woman Warrior*, the controversy over *The Color Purple* centered on "the political costs of exposing gender violence" within communities of color.[11] Feminist fictional writers have been chastised for airing "dirty laundry" because public talk of male violence is seen as furthering racist and colonialist stereotypes of men of color as well as perpetuating dominant culture's views about "blacks and other minority communities as pathologically violent."[12]

The policing of feminist public talk about intracommunity violence is also rooted in the hierarchical ranking of oppression — the notion that struggles against oppression based on class or race are more important than those against sexism and homophobia. This perspective privileges masculine definitions of violence and violation, in particular public, state violence over private (familial) forms of violence, and fails to recognize the role violence plays in reproducing all forms of hierarchies. The emphasis on public (state) violence directed against men in the community often obscures the domestic forms of violence against women, children, and the elderly.[13] Such a perspective depoliticizes the site where the most vulnerable members of the community experience violence (in the family sphere) and downplays the significance of familial forms of violence, including incest, pedophilia, and rape.

Masculinism's regulation and disciplining of Chicana feminist discourse is part of a more pervasive "'conspiracy of silence,'" as Valerie Smith puts it, "that constructs as disloyal or anti-male any black feminist who attempts to name the vulnerability of black women to abuse at the hands of black men."[14] As a survivor of domestic violence I know too well about the "conspiracy of silence" that devalues the bodies of women of color. Like other feminists of color, Chicanas are up against a heavy burden of representation: acknowledging colonialist constructions of Mexican/Chicano masculinity (i.e., the dirty, degenerate, and menacing Mexican bandido, gang member, immigrant) while denouncing sexual and physical assault on women and children by men in our communities.

My own antiracist formation in Chicano nationalism conspired against my better judgment as a woman, indoctrinating me to accept that one should not take violence personally, that it was our duty as women — wives, daughters, girlfriends, sisters — to tolerate male violence against us because it was in fact produced by the racist, imperialist system that dehumanized men of color. And, my Catholic upbringing condoned "familismo" — the belief in la familia as a sacred institution — an ideology readily embraced by my nationalist brothers and some young sisters, myself included, who in the late sixties had not yet developed a feminist consciousness. For five years I endured physical and mental abuse from my then-activist, Vietnam-veteran husband, ending up in a women's shelter in 1978 — the year that the National Coalition against Domestic Violence was founded. I endured this abuse not simply because I excused his "acting out" as an effect of the Vietnam War; the Chicano nationalist script absolved him of personal responsibility. According to its antiracist logic: His violence against me was justified on the grounds that he was a victim of the colonialist legacy of racism and had been denied male power by the "gringo imperialist system." My own experience twenty-five years ago reminds me of how wars are indeed waged on the bodies of women. Much later, when I shared my story of domestic violence with a Chicano couple in Santa Barbara, California, the man in the relationship repeated the nationalist rhetoric. This time the years of violence on my body turned to rage, for I had by then cultivated a feminist consciousness and thus comprehended the full weight of Kimberlé Crenshaw's poignant observation: "When violence is understood as an acting-out of being denied male power in other spheres, it seems counterproductive to embrace constructs that implicitly link the solution of domestic violence to the greater acquisition of male power."[15]

Politicizing family violence means that we should also frame our discussions within a historical framework. As multicultural feminists we need to recognize that most of the empirical evidence on sexual assault and domestic violence shows that Mexican and Chicano men are no more prone to commit violence against women than are those from any other national or racial group. Domestic violence is a leading cause of female injuries in nearly every country, cutting across the axes of race, class, religion, nationality, and ethnicity.[16] The difference that researchers have found among various social groups is related to the level of activism around sexual assault, especially in reporting of incidents of sexual and physical violence, where Latinas trail behind white women. Researchers attribute the disparities in Latina underreporting to several factors, including the lack of the availability of bicultural and bilingual social services; cultural differences in definitions of violence; community pressures "to cast police officials as outsiders, hostile to community"; and in the case of immigrant women (undocumented and documented alike), the fear of deportation by the U.S. Immigration and Naturalization Service.[17] I would also attribute these discrepancies to the power of the Ten Commandments of Marianismo, in particular the ninth (do not speak out), mentioned earlier, but also the seventh: "Don't be unhappy with your Man, no matter what he does to you" (my mother's response when I shared with her my own experience of domestic violence).

Given the legacy of anticolonialist nationalist discourse, within which structures of class inequality and racism have historically assumed precedence over gender and sexual forms of exploitation, it is striking that so few cultural representations (one is Cisneros's "Woman Hollering Creek") testify to la familia as a site where Chicanas experience sexual assault and domestic violence. One of the few Chicana films in distribution on the subject is *De mujer a mujer* (directed by Beverly Sánchez-Padilla, 1993), a film that bears witness to the psychic effects of sexual violence in the life of Chicanas in South Texas. Cisneros's fictional account of domestic violence is, despite Limón's characterization, careful not to demonize a class of men or to attribute cultural, genetic, or biological origins to violence, as colonialist discourse would do. After all, Cleofilas returns to Mexico, where "her parents had never raised a hand to each other or to their children."[18] Nor does the author treat domestic violence as an individual, isolated event, for as we have seen, the story's protagonist reads newspaper accounts of other women in similar circumstances.

Speaking out against efforts to pathologize Chicano and Latino men as excessively violent is a far cry from mandating silence about the violence that is perpetrated against women in our communities. The wars waged on the bodies of women are not simply effects of racist structures of domination (if that were the case, only racialized men would commit the crimes) or class inequalities (if that were the case, only working-class men would commit the crimes). Sexual and domestic violence against women is a serious problem worldwide, one that demands our careful attention to the racialized, gendered, sexualized, and class dynamics in women's lives, in the context of recognizing the multiple intersecting systems of domination manifesting in this era of global capitalism.

But, how can we mitigate the larger script that consistently portrays communities of color as pathologically violent? How can we forge an enabling politics around the issue of gender violence — one that does not perpetuate the stereotype of a "barbaric" and "uncivilized" Third World? One way to broach the issue is by examining the evolution of the human rights framework over the past two decades.

Early feminist intervention in the area of jurisprudence pushed for a redefinition of international law to include so-called private (domestic) forms of violence such as rape within the framework of human rights. Violations of women's rights within the family were excluded from the first generation of human rights legislation, where the focus was on violations within the public realm, or state violations against the individual. In other words, the framework of international law was historically designed to protect the rights of men, as defined by Western political liberalism, especially the state's "infringement of public civil rights, including the right to free expression, to political association, and to a free trial."[19] During the 1980s, feminist lawyers and women's rights activists began to challenge the masculine bias and universal claims in the first generation of human rights, arguing for a redefinition of human rights to include the private realm because "many human rights violations against women, including domestic violence, female genital mutilation, sexual slavery, forced pregnancies and sterilization, are committed within the family, and by private individuals and organizations."[20]

Given the naturalization of violence against women, feminist legal scholars and activists have aimed to expand the "equality provisions" of international rights law to include the "private realm," thereby dismantling the artificial distinction between these spheres.[21] As women's rights activists have noted, gender bias in international law extends across the social spectrum, excluding not only violations against women in the private realm but also other forms of violence against women in the public realm, including those within the context of war. According to the 1995 report on women's human rights the traditional definition of rights is inadequate in protecting women: "The fact that this assault is committed by men against women has contributed to its being narrowly portrayed as sexual or personal in nature, a characterization that depoliticized sexual abuse in conflicts and results in its being ignored as a crime."[22]

More recently, feminist activism in human rights law has had significant practical outcomes, including the "historic decision of [the] International War Crimes Tribunal for the Former Yugoslavia on 10 December 1998 to pass a sentence which included guilty on the grounds of rape."[23] The movement for women's human rights highlights the significance of politicizing violence against women, for "only when sexual violence is perceived as a political event, when it is made public and analyzed, can its causes and contexts be probed and strategies to overcome it be considered."[24] Undoubtedly the international campaign to eradicate gender violence has raised public awareness about women's human rights and enabled the expansion of the human rights framework. But from a feminist critical race perspective, the movement to redefine women's rights as human rights has been based on restrictive and problematic assumptions.

In the first place, human rights discourse is limited for its almost total emphasis on violations perpetrated outside of the Western capitalist context, that is to say, the neocolonized developing world. Most public discussions of human rights abuse highlight the most "extreme" forms of gender violence: female genital surgeries in Africa, infanticide in China, sexual slavery in Thailand, forced pregnancy in Mexico, dowry murder in India, and so forth. The emphasis on very extreme forms of human rights abuse taps into racist and colonialist constructions of the Third World as "brutal" and "uncivilized." In fact, the hypervisibility of masculine brutality in the Third World was recently deployed to justify United States military intervention on behalf of Muslim women, as evident in the cynical appropriation of the language of human rights to wage the war on Afghanistan. In the words of Secretary of State Colin Powell: "The rights of women in Afghanistan will not be negotiated."[25]

Although there is no denying the reality of violence against women in the developing world, the exclusive focus on non-Western contexts obscures the very reality of gender violence human rights abuses in the West: sexual slavery, household slavery, and sweatshop slavery in First World cities like London, New York, Los Angeles, Paris, and Zurich.[26] The rhetoric of human rights discourse is based on Western notions of the abstract subject and practices of individualism that ignore other, more fluid, definitions of rights and subjectivity, especially those rooted in the context of the Americas and derived from indigenous notions of identity and group/collective property rights.

As I noted in chapter one, Celina Romany's call for intersectionality in human rights law provides an epistemological alternative to the Western liberal definition of gender identity as universal. Besides complicating the First World notion of a singular transnational gender identity, Romany's intersectional methodology opens up the space for a more comprehensive definition of human rights abuses. An analysis of the ways in which race, gender, class, and sexuality intersect in the lives of women broadens the concept of gender violence to include instances of socioeconomic violence. In other words, intersectionality expands the framework of human rights to include socioeconomic rights to basic needs such as food, health care, a living wage, environmental safety, and shelter.

Within the context of global capitalism, this expanded definition of violence to include social, cultural, and economic concerns moves the focus away from the so-called Third World (and by extension, "Third World" men) as inherently "barbaric" and "uncivilized."[27] This new critical paradigm of women's human rights implicates the practices of transnational capital, the United States global empire, and European market economies in the violation of women's rights in all parts of the world.

This expanded definition of violence informs the practices of multicultural feminist writers and activists who refuse to isolate domestic rape and violence from a discussion of socioeconomic violence. Drawing from a new critical rights paradigm that refuses to locate violence against women within a single axis of domination, multicultural and Third World feminist thinkers are working to denaturalize and politicize violence against women within Third World and multicultural communities. Although today there indeed may be greater public awareness and media coverage about domestic violence, rape, and gender violence in the context of war, private forms of violence continue to be the "invisible," "shadow war" in the lives of many women.[28] Cultural representations play a crucial role in restoring to cultural memory the significance of sexual and gender violence as "systemic historical and political events."[29]

Paulina (1997) is the first U.S.-made film that represents the issue of sexual violence from an intersectional perspective, focusing on one of the most vulnerable and exploited women in Mexican society: la criada (the domestic/maid). A nonfiction feature directed by Vicky Funari and Jennifer Maytorena-Taylor and cowritten with Paulina Cruz Suárez, *Paulina,* which is set in the early 1950s, tells the story of Cruz Suárez, who, at the age of fifteen migrated from Puntilla Veracruz to Mexico City, where she has worked as a maid ever since. Violence haunts Paulina's memories: At the age of eight while bathing outdoors, Paulina slipped, injuring herself between her legs. As she lay bleeding, her mother screamed "rape," accusing the town's cacique (boss), Mauro de la Cruz, of raping Paulina. Paulina was subsequently hit by her mother and beaten by her father. She became estranged from her family, was expelled from school for allegedly losing her virginity, and was ostracized by her community. When Paulina turned thirteen, Don Mauro returned for her. Paulina's family traded her to him in exchange for some land. He took possession of her, raped her, and kept her under guard as one of his mistresses until Paulina managed to escape and flee to Mexico City.

Paulina Cruz Suárez's migration to the city was not unusual even in the early 1950s, when she joined the ranks of women in similar economic circumstances from rural Mexico. Mexico's export-oriented strategy for economic development led to declining job opportunities in the agricultural sector as well to the "destruction of artisanal production," creating a new pattern of gendered migration in which many young women like Paulina left rural communities for larger urban centers in search of work.[30] From the 1940s to the 1960s, female migration followed a rural to urban pattern, with women as young as ten to nineteen years old finding employment in the industrial sector as factory workers, although most poor and indigenous women worked as maids, often as live-in domestics for the growing Mexican middle class. By 1970, more than half of the immigrants to Mexico City were women.[31] Research has tended to emphasize a correlation between gendered migration and economic forces such as the structural transformation of rural and urban economies. Few researchers have investigated other equally significant factors forcing women to migrate, such as "the patterns and dynamics of abuse and coercive control to which women are subjected at the interpersonal and structural levels of everyday lives."[32]

For this reason, it is important to recognize the role "conflicts and inequality" play in the history of women's transnational migration, especially since "assault perpetrated by alcoholic husbands and the flight of women and children . . . as a form of survival, attest to an oppression which contests the idealized vision of indigenous life."[33] In their study of Latina transnational migration, Arguelles and Rivero address the blind spots in migration histories of Third World women, highlighting the need to look beyond "narrowly defined political and economic factors." Their ethnographic studies on Latina immigrants unveil "various combinations of violence that contributed to their decision to leave their homelands," including "issues of sexual violence, enforced sex and gender roles, sexual orientation, sexual abuse and assault, or coerced motherhood."[34] Like Sandra Cisneros in "Woman Hollering Creek," codirectors Funari and Maytorena-Taylor in *Paulina* broaden the discussion of gendered migration to include migration as "a strategy for managing or escaping from gender and sexual abuse."[35]

Paulina clearly brings an articulated cross-border feminist politics to bear thematically and aesthetically on the representation of violence against women. The film follows in the tradition of feminist avant-garde filmmakers Barbara Hammer and Carole Sheeman, among others, who in the early seventies first explored the connection between touch and sight. Hammer, for example, theorized the erotics of the female body through touch in *Dyketactics* (1974), coining a style she termed "experiential cinema." The filmmaker favored the experiential aesthetic of touching over the Western "privileging of sight," which she found limiting because, as Hammer notes, "It was Aldous Huxley who pointed out that children know the world through touching before they can ever see."[36]

Paulina's opening sequence is highly sensual, or experiential, emphasizing touching and its sensual connection to sight through the portrayal
of hands. The sequence intercuts nine times between the hands of Paulina
at different ages: the hands of an older working woman doing various
domestic chores like sweeping, peeling mangoes, washing dishes; the
hands of an eight-year-old touching stems of grass, caressing leaves on
trees; and finally a pair of young, bloodied hands digging into mud.[37] The
image of the bloodied hands accentuates the erotics of the female body,
with its allusion to menses and coming of age, which in turn foreshadows
the protagonist's development as she rethreads the discontinuities in her
life, finding her voice and place in the world as a woman. The blood in
this sequence (and in other parts of the film) also alludes to the sexual violence that Paula experienced as a young woman.

It took Funari and Maytorena-Taylor ten years to make this trans-bor-
der film, primarily because few people deemed its subject matter — violence in the life of a Mexican maid — worthy of funding. Time worked in
the filmmakers' favor, however, for it allowed documentation of Paulina's
transformation and coming into voice. What gradually emerges from
multiple interviews is a nonlinear tale of Paulina's experiences of resistance, survival, and empowerment. Credited as cowriter, Paulina played an
active role in shaping the film's dramatic structure. In fact, in order to
visually interpret her "actual" memories of the event, several scenes are
filmed from her point of view in a subversive style known as "theatricality" (figure 3).

This stylistic strategy is most effectively realized in the second scene of
the film, which begins with Paulina's voice-over narrating events in her
past while the events that she describes are visually depicted on the
screen — a technique used frequently in documentary reenactments.
Paulina is shown as a young woman riding on a bus, sitting next to a man,
while the older Paulina's voice-over tells us: "I remember when I was
eighteen years old. I was on my way to town. It was the first time I went
back there after being in Mexico City. I was going to confront the
cacique, the town boss." Suddenly something happens to break the frame
and alter the relationship between film and spectator: the young actress
playing Paulina turns and looks directly into the camera (at us), holds up
a script and begins to read, repeating verbatim the older Paulina's previous narration: "I remember when I was eighteen years old. I was on my
way to town. It was the first time I went back there after being in Mexico
City. I was going to confront the cacique, the town boss." This formal
technique subverts conventional film narrative, stressing theatricality, a

FIGURE 3. Two actors from *Paulina:* Mathysclene Heredia (left), who played the eighteen-year-old Paulina, and Erika Isabel de la Cruz Ramírez, who played Paulina at age thirteen. Courtesy of Vicky Funari and Jennifer Maytorena-Taylor.

reenactment strategy that positions the film within a mode that Sylvie Thouard (following Bill Nichols) calls the "performative" documentary. Characteristic of recent films and videos by Third World and queer producers in postcolonial and global culture, performative documentaries of the 1990s combine the formal aspects of "referentiality mixed with expressiveness and reflexivity."[38]

While *Paulina* does in fact recount the experiences of violence in the life of a poor rural woman, it is not a documentary account of those experiences or of the personal life of its protagonist. In fact *Paulina* stresses theatricality in order to unsettle our perceptions of reality. Just as this experimental style is designed to capture how Paulina *reimagines* past events — as opposed to mimetically copying them — so too is it used to depict the way she imagines how others perceived her. For example, the reenactment of Paulina's trip on the bus continues with the man who sits next to her attempting to fondle her, and to his surprise, the young Paulina grabs his hand, biting his finger. As he screams the bus comes to a halt and its passengers turn to look at Paulina, whose face is covered with blood from the wound she inflicted on her assailant. It is at this point that the filmmakers stretch the conventions of realist reenactment further, imaginatively layering Paulina's point of view with those of four other passengers on the bus. From the point of view of a teenage boy, the young Paulina appears as a menacing, crazed witch with disheveled hair, laughing as blood runs out of her mouth; from the point of view of a young girl, Paulina is a heroine, dressed in the traditional wrestling costume of Mexico's popular superheroes; from the perspective of an older, conservative woman, Paulina turns into a shameless floozy; and finally, from the perspective the young white photographer on the bus (played by filmmaker Vicky Funari), Paulina appears as a feminist icon, an Aztec goddess holding up a heart after completing the ritual of human sacrifice.

By rendering multiple points of view through experimental techniques, Funari's performative film straddles the border between fiction and nonfiction, documentary and dramatic cinema. One of the film's major effects is to call into question the claim of nonfiction film to represent reality, especially in places where it ritualizes the process of recollection and imaginatively portrays the Kafkaesque dimension of memory work. In this regard, *Paulina*'s subversion of a singular truth based on subjective recollection is further accomplished through its juxtaposition of interviews shot within the conventions of a realist aesthetic ("talking heads") against the dramatic scenes depicting the multiple points of view of different characters. This Rashomonian dramatic structure and fractured storytelling device are most effectively deployed in the narrative reenactments of Cruz Suárez's initial accident. The fact that Paulina fell and injured herself is not contested; what is contested is how the event took place, the ways in which the family reacted and interpreted the event, and, most significantly, the effects of the accident on Paulina's psyche.

In the dramatic reenactment of the accident from Paulina's point of view, she is accompanied by her sister into the woods for a bath; Paulina slips, injures herself; the sister runs for help and returns with the mother, who is screaming that Paulina has been raped by Don Mauro, while a group of townspeople gather around Paulina making demeaning remarks, including "Eso pasa por andar de coqueta" (That's what happens for being such a flirt). Paulina recalls lying in bed and overhearing her father talking to the town cacique, who agrees to return for her when she is older. The mother's account differs radically: Paulina falls while the mother is bathing her; no one learns of the accident because the mother quietly carries the daughter home and cares for her injuries in private — a version corroborated in the next scene by Paulina's father.

To some extent, these dramatic reconstructions from multiple perspectives work to challenge the veracity of individual memory and call

FIGURE 4. Eight-year-old Paulina as played by Mariám Manzano Durán. Courtesy of Vicky Funari and Jennifer Maytorena-Taylor.

into question the truth of testimony. Rather than attempting to render the past as it actually happened — as realist documentaries attempt to do — the filmmaker utilizes reenactments inventively, as a means for disclosing the limits of memory, its partiality and selectivity, as well as to foreground the film's own ideological point of view. For example, Paulina's parents remember that she fell in love with the cacique and left with him willingly; Paulina remembers that she was kidnapped, repeatedly raped, and physically and psychologically assaulted. Yet these contradictory versions are not given equal weight either in terms of screen time (Paulina's account is longer) or within the dramatic structure; Paulina's account is privileged. In one of the most lyrical and memorable scenes, a young Paulina looks back with saddened eyes at the father (figure 4) while he ends his own version of the accident with a disclaimer: "Hasta el día no puede uno platicar lo que no debe uno de platicar. Hay cosas que se pueden platicar y hay cosas que no. . . . Para no hacer buya, para no hacer escándalo." (Even today, one cannot speak of things that one should not speak of. There are things you can speak of and things you can't. . . . To avoid a scandal, to avoid an uproar.).

The "things one cannot speak of" or "should not speak of"; the "things" that would cause an "uproar" are those having to do with violence in the domestic sphere, including incest, pedophilia, rape, and child slavery. And it is the haunting memory-image of a young Paulina glancing back at us (at her father) through time that reminds us of the damage caused by harboring these family secrets.

With this singular dramatic juxtaposition of images — a young girl's doubting gaze directed at her father's image — the film delivers its most scathing critique of the intersecting private and public forms of patriarchy in Mexico. Contesting intracommunity silences around sexual assault, *Paulina* restores to cultural memory an event in Paulina's life that her family preferred to keep secret. Yet, exposing violence against women within a rural Mexican community is but one of the film's objectives, for by politicizing sexual violence through its creative exposé of Paulina's life, the film had a significant effect on the real-life Paulina.

The multiple and often contrary points of view mobilized in the narrative work to document a complicated web of psychic dislocation and fragmentation impinging on Paulina (figure 5). And the film goes one step further: it stages a spatial journey toward her psychic integration, embodiment, and, ultimately, healing. During one of the first interviews, Paulina expresses her feelings of dislocation, fragmentation, and disembodiment: "Yo tengo como un rompecabezas, mi cuerpo" (My body is like a jigsaw puzzle). Later in the film she responds with a cracking voice to the interviewer's question ("How do you define yourself?") in these terms: "When you were hurt as a child . . . and you were neither a girl nor a woman. I feel I can't define myself as a complete woman" — a response shrewdly augmented by the image of a Polaroid shot being snapped; as it develops, a corporeal absence is rendered in the photograph.

This visual play on invisibility/visibility through Paulina's absent photographic image lays bare her psychic fragmentation and disembodiment, which in turn resonates with the feelings expressed by other victims of sexual assault. As an act of sexual subordination and control, rape not only devalorizes and dehumanizes women, but also represents "a violent invasion of the interiors of one's body . . . the most severe attack imaginable upon the intimate self and dignity of a human being: by any means it is a measure of severe torture."[39] Sexual violence is a form of "spirit injury," with multiple effects on the individual, especially "the slow death of psyche, of soul and of the identity of the individual."[40] Paulina's desire to heal the "spirit injury" is expressed in terms of a search for wholeness, psychic integration, and embodiment.

The film's documentation of Paulina's healing process compounds our

FIGURE 5. Graphic depiction from *Paulina* of the young Paulina's psychic fragmentation after having been beaten and raped. Courtesy of Vicky Funari and Jennifer Maytorena-Taylor.

(viewers') relationship to the text and positions us simultaneously as spectators and witnesses. My use of the concept "witnessing" is inspired by Kelly Oliver, who broadens its secular meaning of "observing" and "testifying" (as in a court of law) to include the notion of "bearing witness," that is to say, testifying "to something that cannot be observed."[41] As spectators we bear witness to Paulina's (literal and metaphoric) journey through memory; however, our ability to witness is limited by Paulina's mediation: "I came to Puntilla to see if I can kill Paula . . . the image of Paula, so that Paulina can be born. Paulina the servant."

At first glance, Paulina's desire to "kill Paula . . . the image of Paula, so that Paulina can be born" seems to confirm the violent rupture with the self as described in psychoanalytic theories of subject formation. Yet, as Paulina proceeds in her journey, her encounter with difference and otherness shifts away from "hostility" and toward "welcoming and loving"[42] relations: "And now it is like telling everyone, 'I'm doing this for the little girl who stayed in Puntilla. I want to rescue that girl because that girl is me.'" This concept of identity situated within "welcoming and loving" relations of difference supplements secular psychoanalytic notions of identity formation with a spiritual element. For it is here, in the realm of the spirit, that Paulina's desire for wholeness, centeredness, and unified subjectivity is located: "It's like I'm putting my body back together, like a jigsaw puzzle. Some said one version, others said another. One part was in Mexico City and the other part was in Puntilla. In Puntilla I was Paula and in the city I was Paulina. I was in pieces. Now I think I am whole. I'm finally Paulina."

The film *Paulina* represents a unique blend of political, artistic, and epistemological strategies. As part of the new genre of performative documentaries, *Paulina* combines a feminist aesthetic, experimental techniques, and spirituality to give voice to "something that cannot be seen" (as in the spiritual component of identity). The film gives visibility to the silences around sexual assault and domestic violence and ultimately politicizes gender violence by testifying to its dehumanizing effects.

The film is notable for its refusal to invoke the notion of "shared oppression of women"; it deliberately avoids a First World "rescue narrative" and power relations rooted in the construction of "'Third World' women — typically as passive victims of male oppression."[43] Although both Funari and Maytorena-Taylor controlled some elements of the production process, including fund-raising and the technical aspects of filming, Paulina contributed significantly to production decisions as well. Her participation in the making of the film played a significant role in the formation of her identity, both on screen and off; she was the coproducer of her own cultural script. The cinematic portrayal of her struggle against violence is complemented by other, equally empowering, examples of Paulina's agency in the "real world" (figure 6). Her advocacy on behalf of women's rights includes joining the movement of denunciation against gender violence in Mexico and participating in audience discussions during the film screenings in Mexico and abroad.

In delicate and indirect ways, *Paulina* directs our attention to the "false universalism" of liberal political theory, the limitations in the concept of the "abstract subject," and the masculinism behind the human rights emphasis on public/state violence. The film also goes beyond the gender essentialist framework, opening up a space for the articulation of a new critical paradigm on women's rights. The film's focus on the intersection of gender, race, and class contributes to the intersectional perspective called for by Romany: "Women who experience multiple forms of discrimination in their public and private lives need to participate in a redefinition of human rights law. Both race and ethnic subordination compound the ways women experience devaluation and invisibility in society."[44]

FIGURE 6. The real-life Paulina Cruz Suárez at age fifty-five. Courtesy of Vicky Funari and Jennifer Maytorena-Taylor.

In documenting the overlapping structures of class, ethnicity, and culture, *Paulina* shows the range of social differences that shape Paulina's gender identity as well as the ways in which women's invisibility and vulnerability are effects of "different axes of domination: capitalism, patriarchy and the processes of racialization that take place through colonialism and immigration."[45]

As an expression of cultural citizenship, *Paulina* gives visibility to new gendered subjects within the nation-state as much as it contributes to new, alternative formulations of rights for women. Like other cultural representations by multicultural and Third World feminists, the film is part of a new identity formation of cross-border feminisms, as well as the intersectional paradigm of women's human rights — a theoretical understanding that moves beyond gender essentialism and looks "beyond the state as the sole guarantor of 'rights.'"[46] The film *Paulina* is at once a poignant testimonial to the highly textured differences among women and a cogent analysis of the overlapping structures of domination that engender violence in the lives of women around the globe.

CHAPTER THREE

Gender, Multiculturalism, and the Missionary Position on the Borderlands

In *Playing in the Dark,* Toni Morrison writes: "The imaginative and historical terrain upon which American writers journeyed is in large measure shaped by the presence of the racial other."[1] There is no denying what Morrison calls the "Africanist presence" in U.S. culture. Until very recently, however, the "Mexicanist presence" was rarely acknowledged as also shaping "the imaginative and historical terrain upon which American writers" [and, I would add, artists, musicians, and filmmakers] journeyed." In fact, *Lone Star* (directed by John Sayles, 1996) figures as one of those rare instances in the history of U.S. cinema in which the Mexicanist presence occupies center stage.

In sharp contrast to other films dealing with the Mexico-U.S. borderlands, *Lone Star* portrays the region as a multicultural symbolic and material landscape, and features Chicanas and Chicanos as central players in the history of the region.[2] For this reason, John Sayles's portrait of race relations in the multicultural borderlands undermines the black/white racial binary that has historically informed in undeniable and prevailing ways the texture of U.S. culture. Unlike other racial melodramas, for example, *Lone Star* features the entwinement of Anglos and Mexicans as central to the filmmaker's revision of national identity.[3] More importantly for my own study of cultural representations, the filmmaker seems to accomplish his project by centering Pilar Cruz (Elizabeth Peña), a

Chicana, as the female subject of this new multicultural nation. But on closer inspection, I found that the process of racial and gender othering so common in national formations continues to inform the new multicultural nation in the film's universe.

Although subtly and indirectly, *Lone Star* affirms racial hierarchies, often obliquely filtering its vision of the multicultural nation through a white, benevolent, patriarchal gaze. The film's richly textured and complex narrative structure of multiple story lines and shifting points of view hides this contradictory impulse: on the one hand enabling or opening up a space for Chicana subjectivity and historical agency to emerge; yet on the other, subsuming Chicana identity within a masculinist logic. In the following pages I hope to make visible the cinematic strategies by which prevailing racial and patriarchal structures are reinforced in relation to Chicana and Mexicana representation. My point of departure for exploring the construction of female identity and subjectivity is an autobiographical insertion into the text; I begin where *Lone Star* ends, when its lead female character, Pilar, utters the film's final words: "Forget the Alamo."

Personal Memories

I first heard the phrase "Forget the Alamo" more than three decades ago. It was my father's antidote to the official versions of Texas history taught in the public schools of Corpus Christi. Although we faced prejudice on a daily basis, it was in those required eighth-grade Texas history courses that we Tejanas and Tejanos (Mexicans native to Texas) confronted an officially sanctioned symbolic violence perpetrated against us. Sitting in Oakland's Grand Lake Theater in 1996, next to my thirteen-year-old son, who is disturbed by the film's incest theme and critical of its "too many plot lines," I found myself transported back to my own childhood in Texas as I listened to a history lesson in the eighth grade, in a classroom adorned with the six flags over Texas and haunted by the legacy of the battle of the Alamo.

For weeks, I was captivated by the teacher's petite hourglass shape, her crimson hair, and those red dots speckling her flesh and framing her marble-blue eyes. Mrs. Roy gave interminable, heart-wrenching lectures, reenacting with melodramatic detail the Anglo-Mexican struggles leading to Texas independence. Today, I imagine her to be a devotee of the historian Walter Prescott Webb, passionately propagating his views about the "cruel streak in the Mexican nature." She had mastered the skill of counterpoint pedagogy, detailing history in terms of binary opposition: the noble letter-writing campaign of Stephen F. Austin versus the "bloody dictator" Santa Ana's wrath; the memorable deeds and bravery of Travis, Crockett, and Bowie versus the atrocities of the "treacherous" Mexicans; the high-powered artillery rifles and canons of the "villainous" Mexicans versus the handful of muskets, revolvers, and the bowie knife of the heroic Anglos. I can still see her there pacing excitedly before us, diligently pointing at the screaming map of Texas, its multicolored flags and charts. She gazed at me, the only Tejana in the class, and I felt her whiteness overpowering me each time she mentioned "the cruel streak in the Mexican nature."

Thirty years later, when I understood the subjugating power of symbolic violence, the shame I felt back then would turn to anger as I screened the 1915 film *Martyrs of the Alamo* during a research trip to the Library of Congress film and video collection. Directed by W. Christy Cabanne, *Martyrs of the Alamo* was supervised by the infamous race filmmaker D. W. Griffith, whose unmistakable imprint is etched in the narrative. The five-reel racial melodrama is shot in 35 mm and replicates Griffith's "system of narrative integration," especially in its liberal use of "stylistic techniques — from composition to editing — to articulate an ideology of race that positions 'whites' as superior and 'non-whites' as deviant and inferior."[4] According to the film's intertitle, Mexicans, under the command of Santa Ana, figure as the invaders in a world of "liberty loving Texans who had built the Texas colony."

The articulation of style and race in the story is reinforced through characterization and cinematic techniques such as mise-en-scène, editing, and shot composition, featuring crosscutting and parallel action to render racial differences between Anglos and Mexicans. Mexicans are caricatured as dark, ominous, and physically aggressive. Medium and close shots depict the psychological depth of Anglo characters, whereas the camera remains distant from the Mexican characters. Filmed mostly outdoors and framed through distant and long shots, Mexicans are portrayed as a mass of bodies whose faces are indistinguishable from each other. And Mexican females fare no better, playing folkloric "cantina girls" entirely preoccupied with dancing for Mexican men. Yet, the most disturbing aspect of *Martyrs of the Alamo* is the way filmmakers reroute the historical conflicts in Texas through the discourse of sexual degeneracy.

The intertitle keeps looping through my head: "Under the dictator's rule, the honor and life of American women was held in contempt." This racial melodrama is informed by an exceedingly disparaging though entirely predictable racial narrative, namely, the colonialist fantasy of white womanhood under siege. *Martyrs* is, as Herman Gray writes of *Birth of a Nation,* a "scandalous representation" of nonwhite masculinity, an expression of white anxieties about miscegenation.[5] Following in the tradition of Griffith's racialized family melodrama, *Martyrs of the Alamo* recasts late-nineteenth-century pseudoscientific theories of degeneracy and miscegenation. The film portrays Mexicans as sexually hungry subaltern men, predators devouring the angelic female with their looks, teasing a white mother with baby, touching white women's blond locks. In so doing, the film draws from a repertoire of racial and imperial metaphors to construct the view of Mexican sexual degeneracy as a threat to the virtue of white femininity and racial purity. Santa Ana epitomizes Mexican degeneracy in the final segment of the film, which creates the myth about his out-of-control libido. The intertitle, "An inveterate drug fiend, the Dictator of Mexico was also famous for his shameful orgies," is followed by a scene depicting Santa Ana, in a drunken stupor, surrounded by four Mexican prostitutes dressed exotically in dark mantillas, vests, and skirts, dancing for him. Narrative resolution around Santa Ana's capture rewrites the political struggle over Texas as a defense of white femininity and by extension the white nation, thereby rationalizing the Anglo takeover of Texas. By the end of this film, I am furious. Now, many years after sitting in that eighth-grade classroom in South Texas, I can dismiss *Martyrs of the Alamo* as the most extremist, xenophobic account of the Texas conflict I have ever seen; I am furious on behalf of that thirteen-year-old girl, sitting in that Texas history class.

I return to that classroom, listening anxiously to Mrs. Roy. It is 1967. I imagine the harshness in the looks of my Anglo classmates, burning my flesh. By the time my Texas history teacher delivered her final soliloquy, reciting the climactic battle for Texas independence — the primal scene that has so obsessed Anglo-racist imaginary and that is reenacted in countless colonialist films, including *Martyrs of the Alamo* — I had been interpellated into her historically distorted, chromatically tainted uni verse, inside the walls of the Alamo, inside the Anglo-Texas fantasy of racial mastery: the purely "white" side of the line. I would later buy a "bowie knife" from a mail-order catalogue. By the eighth grade, I had internalized the elision of Tejanos and the racist-colonialist gaze — a self-hatred equal to the hatred Anglo teachers of Texas history felt for Mexican Texans.

In the same year, 1967, my father gave me a book to temper my fulmination against the Mexican oppressors of Anglo "freedom fighters." I still own that copy of Rafael Trujillo Herrera's *Olvídate del Alamo* (Forget the Alamo), published in 1965.[6] As the title makes evident, *Olvídate del Alamo* is a diametrically opposed version of the battle for Texas. Told from a Mexican point of view, it renders the struggle in Texas less in terms of liberation and more from the perspective of conquest. Like Mrs. Roy's history lessons, Trujillo's text failed to account for the political intricacies of nineteenth-century Tejas, including the important fact that Tejano landowners joined Anglos in the fight against the centralist government of Santa Ana, or that some Tejanos died alongside the Anglos inside the Alamo. Even so, I read *Olvídate del Alamo* eagerly, and the book ignited a lifelong passion for oppositional discourse and counterknowledges. In addition to giving me this introduction to Mexican nationalist discourse, my father would further dis-order my Texas history teacher's lessons. "Just imagine," he said, "that one day you invite a guest into your home and you allow them to live in your home on the condition that they follow certain rules. Then one day, your houseguests decide that they don't agree with your rules and so they decide to take your house and kick you out. That's how it happened in Tejas."

I now grasp that while symbolic violence produced, marked, and incised my body as a historically specific racialized and gendered subject of Texas, an oppositional force, metaphorized in the phrase "olvídate del Alamo," reoriented the terms of my inscription. This is the counter-memory of Tejas that Pilar Cruz's final words in *Lone Star* — "Forget the Alamo" — enable, putting me in touch with a long tradition of opposition to racist discourse — through popular forms of knowledge, transgressive tales of resistance, subaltern practices of suspicion toward official versions of history. It is through these social practices and counterdiscourses that I, as an actual, historical spectator, negotiate my reception of the film. Pilar speaks to that thirteen-year-old; Pilar stands up with her against the white history of Mrs. Roy. Pilar represents a new breed of Texas history teachers — a Tejana on the borderlands, contributing to a cultural formation that refuses the absolutism of binaries. Together with other schoolteachers depicted in the film, Pilar complicates the ethnocentric version of the war for Texas independence; she recounts the stories of the Texas conflict in terms of their profound ambivalences, in tales of complicity, resistance, and domination. It is this cultural formation that I embrace, for it enables my own spectator position, as much as it informs my critical reading and my own profound ambivalences toward *Lone Star*.

Multicultural Fantasies

Lone Star is set in Frontera (literally, Border), Texas, and details the story of Rio County Sheriff Sam Deeds's (Chris Cooper) investigation after the discovery of skeletal remains on the outskirts of town. The remains are believed to belong to Charley Wade (Kris Kristofferson), a racist and corrupt sheriff who mysteriously disappeared in 1957 after waging a campaign of bigotry and terror against the local Mexicana/o and black communities. Sam Deeds's father, the legendary Sheriff Buddy Deeds, one of Charley Wade's former deputies, becomes Sam's prime suspect. In the course of his investigation, Sam rekindles an interracial romance with his teenage sweetheart, Pilar.

Shot in Eagle Pass, Texas, the film captures the "feel" of Texas visually, its super 35 mm film conveying the wide-screen look of the South Texas landscape. The murder mystery provides the major plot line, but Sayles also portrays a multigenerational drama, rendered through the life histories of an Anglo sheriff, a Chicana teacher, and an African American colonel. *Lone Star* is in the hybrid category of a "blurred genre," combining elements from the Western, mystery, thriller, and romance. The film is also the latest in a long line of border films, for the border functions in an iconically significant way.[7]

Since the early days of silent cinema, U.S. filmmakers have made hundreds of films about the Mexico-U.S. border.[8] In fact, an obsession with borderlands is not the sole purview of U.S. cinema. Since the 1930s, the border has also captured the imagination of Mexico's film industry, which, in one decade alone, released over 147 films in the border genre.[9] In the cultural imaginary of both the United States and Mexico, the border figures as the trope for absolute alterity, a "no-man's land" symbolizing eroticized underdevelopment — an untamed breeding ground for otherness and the site of unrepressed libidinal energies. Its inhabitants are coded as outcasts, degenerates, sexually hungry subalterns, and outlaws. In both Mexican and U.S. cinemas, the representation of the border as a no-man's land is symptomatic of a colonialist and racist imaginary. The product of an ethnocentric gaze, this representation of frontier territories as abject serves both to define the United States and metropolitan Mexico and to shape their respective national identities.

In contrast, Sayles's portrait of the borderlands captures the complexity, nuances, and multidimensionality of the terrain. At first glance, *Lone Star* reads like an application of Chicana/o borderlands theory, especially evident when Sayles invokes the Mexico-U.S. border as a paradigm for his own analysis of U.S. social relations: "There's a kind of racial and ethnic war that has continued. That continuing conflict comes into the clearest focus around the border between Texas and Mexico." For John Sayles, *Lone Star* is a "film about borders," and the border operates as the signifier for the borders of everyday life: "In a personal sense . . . a border is where you draw a line and say 'This is where I end and someone else begins.' In a metaphorical sense, it can be any of the symbols that we erect between one another — sex, class, race, age."[10]

And Sayles did his homework on Chicana/o studies cultural critiques and border theories, reading Américo Paredes's *With a Pistol in His Hand,* screening Robert Young's filmic adaptation *The Ballad of Gregorio Cortez,* listening to border corridos, and studying their lyrics closely.[11] Like many border narratives written by Chicanos/as, *Lone Star* is set on the borderlands region — the two-thousand-mile strip of land, roughly twenty miles wide, separating Mexico from the United States. Sayles portrays the region as a heterogeneous contact zone, a third space, neither Anglo nor Mexican, but rather multilingual, intercultural, and multiracial. And, the film thematizes literal and figurative border crossings, cultural and social relations of accommodation and negotiation within and between the inhabitants on the borderlands. Exploring the racial, cultural, economic, and familial conflicts on the borderland, *Lone Star* candidly depicts tensions between Texans and Tejana/os, Anglos and blacks, and Mexicanos on both sides of the border, as well as the relations of complicity between the Texan-Anglo and the Tejano-Mexicana power elite. For example, Pilar's mother, Mercedes Cruz (Miriam Colón), is a successful restaurant owner who calls the Border Patrol upon seeing desperate Mexican immigrants run across her yard, and in another scene requests that her immigrant employee speak English: "In English, Enrique. This is the United States. We speak English." Another Chicano, Jorge, forms part of the Frontera elite, while Ray is a Tejano deputy who plans to run for sheriff in the next election with the support of the local (Anglo and Mexican American) power structure. Thus, throughout the film, relations of power and privilege are nuanced, figuring centrally in both individual and group transactions. In this respect, *Lone Star* renders the experiences of continuity and discontinuity that mark daily life — ongoing and conflictual encounters between various social groups, reference codes, beliefs, and linguistic and cultural systems. The film indeed reads like an alternative lesson in Texas history.

The filmmaker attempts to situate the figure of the border/borderlands as a central element in a historical revisionist project as well as in efforts to reclaim an alternative racial memory of the borderlands. In this way, Sayles is able to challenge the prevailing historical amnesia and U.S. ideology of "presentism," evident especially in his efforts to illuminate how past histories weigh incessantly on present circumstances and how the mythic legacy of the past clouds the present's truths. Sayles underscores the political project of showing the bearing of the past on the individual's present through an effective use of the cinematic techniques of seamless editing in the flashback sequences.[12]

Contesting exclusionary formulations of monocultural Texas history, *Lone Star*'s racial memory differs from the two extremes represented on the one hand by the Anglo colonialist erasure of Tejana/o subjects in Texas history (e.g., eighth-grade Texas history class and *Martyrs of the Alamo*) and on the other by Chicano nationalism's reversal of that exclusion: Tejanos as the victims of conquest, the "good guys" in a "them versus us" binary revision of Texas history. Sayles portrays race relations in terms of an exercise of race and class power, showing interconnections as well as singularities. Anglos and Mexicanos, Tejanos and Texans figure as both agents and subjects of domination and complicity. And, the film's revision of Texas history goes beyond its documentation of Anglo-Mexicano relations of negotiation and accommodation, for *Lone Star* also reflects the filmmaker's "need to document" the history of multiculturalism in this country:[13] "As I said, [the United States is] not increasingly multicultural, it's always been so. If you go back and turn over a rock you find out, for example, that maybe a third or more of African Americans are also Native Americans and a much higher percentage of African Americans are also white Americans."[14]

My profound ambivalence toward this film has something to do with Sayles's willingness to complicate the nation's racial imaginary. The filmmaker seems to celebrate a new social order, painting a tapestry of interracial, postcolonial Texas, reviving a textured story of racial entwinement and complexity on the borderlands — a pluricultural transborder contact zone comprised of Native Americans, blacks, Tejanos, and Anglos. The Mexico-U.S. borderlands in Sayles's universe is hybrid and multilingual; his is a tutored and refined view that diverges substantially from the prevalent "black-and-white" paradigm about race relations in the United States. In skirting the explicitness and literalness of racialized and gendered othering, the filmmaker appears to modulate the subjugating power of symbolic violence. After all, this story brings out the occulted history of a multicultural United States. Despite the film's critique of monocultural and ethnocentric constructions of the nation, however,

Lone Star's overture to multiculturalism is driven by a deeply colonialist and phallocentric project.

Genuine multiculturalism involves the redefinition of the nation, a rearrangement of center-margin power relations, insisting upon the interplay of multiple and plural identities. An earnest subversion of the border requires that one interrogate the boundary markers of race, class, gender, and sexuality, for in recasting the nation as multicultural, its center is no longer defined by the myth of racial purity, sameness, and singularity, but rather by hybridity, difference, and plural identifications. If Sayles's multiculturalist project is to truly represent a new social order and make a dent in the predominant monocultural, ethnocentric vision of society, it must decenter whiteness and masculinity. Even though multiculturalism always involves relations of power, no one category of membership can serve as the universal to which all others are subordinate: not whiteness, maleness, heterosexuality, or European-ness.

However, as Sayles's words make evident, maleness is the key, privileged signifier of the narrative: "For me, very often the best metaphor for history is fathers and sons. Inheriting your cultural history, your hatreds and your alliances and all that kind of stuff, is what you're supposed to get from your father in a patriarchal society."[15] A masculine-centeredness mirroring this sentiment permeates the film. Although the border figures as the symbol for multiculturalism, crossings, intercultural exchanges, and hybridity, history is metaphorized in patriarchal terms. On the surface, *Lone Star* attempts to rewrite the social order to encompass difference for a multicultural nation, but the white father–white son structure keeps the center intact and multiplicity at the margins of the story world. By reinscribing the centrality of the oedipal narrative and the voice of white racial privilege, the film reaffirms the masculinist borders of whiteness, containing difference and regulating the disruptive aspect of otherness.

The plot is driven by the son's search for truth, and the son is motivated by a repressed hatred for his father, the legendary, benevolent patriarch of Rio County, Sheriff Buddy Deeds. Like Westerns and border genre films, *Lone Star* renders the symbolic structure of the "Law" literally in its portrayal of the father-son dyad as the embodiments of "civil law": both are county sheriffs. The narrative reproduction of patrimony pivots around the oedipal structure insofar as the son, Sam, assumes the place of the father, Buddy, literally as the sheriff of Rio County, but also symbolically, in the order of the phallus, the law of the father. This usual oedipal scenario is accentuated even more in the text by the father-son conflict generated within the film: the son is driven by symbolic patricide, a desire to kill the father — not literally since Buddy is already dead — but figuratively, for he is the prime suspect in the murder investigation. In other words, rather than honor his father's name, the son's investigation camouflages an obsessive desire to prove his father's culpability, to taint his father's reputation, thereby destroying his name.

As in the best mystery thriller, the plot twists and suspense of *Lone Star* yield a surprise and unexpected resolution to the murder investigation. Whereas all the evidence pointed to the father as the prime suspect, Sam discovers that the murder was in fact committed by Hollis Pogue, the current mayor of Frontera, who was not only the fledging deputy of the notorious Wade but also the horrified witness to Wade's racist atrocities. Narrated in a seamlessly edited flashback, the murder of Charley Wade plays a pivotal role in the film's revisionist project: Wade is murdered by the young deputy Hollis to prevent the murder of Otis Payne, the black owner of Big O's Roadhouse and Mayor of Darktown. Emblematic of white benevolence on the Texas frontier, the murder of one white man by another white man to save a black man's life rewrites race relations in Texas, positioning black-white cooperation on center stage as resistance to white racism. Despite this revisionist endeavor, narrative closure around the son's discovery of the father's innocence further reinforces and consolidates whiteness as well as the enduring centrality of the father-son dyad.

The extent to which this film is driven by the symbolic oedipal structure is even more apparent in the plot's secondary father-son antagonism between Otis Payne and his son, Colonel Payne. José Limón has argued that this racialized twist on the classic oedipal drama actually decenters "the otherwise 'white' paradigm" of masculinity.[16] I would counter that blackness in fact "colors" the oedipal drama while ultimately leaving white patriarchy intact.[17] The film's subplot of intergenerational conflicts — those involving male characters (young and old; black and white) — in fact consolidates patriarchy throughout the film. In contrast to the "resolved" masculine conflicts, those implicating the female characters, Mercedes and Pilar, remain unresolved — a major dramatic elision that, as I will later discuss, helps to confirm the masculinist, oedipal undertones of the film. Both white and black masculinity resolve the oedipal conflicts in favorable terms, and overcoming patricide enables Sam, as son, to assume his rightful place: the place of the father in the symbolic order, thus guaranteeing the reproduction of patriarchy.

It is precisely this patriarchal structure of the oedipal narrative that contains as much as it facilitates the emergence of Tejana and Tejano subjectivities and points of view. Although the structuring of information within the film positions Sam Deeds as the center of consciousness and the filter for narrative information, in other ways the filmmaker provides characters with psychological depth through the flashback — a technique used for stitching present events with past memories. The subjectivities of female characters such as Pilar and Mercedes are constructed through this mode, but only Mercedes's memories remain autonomous; through seamless editing, Pilar's are linked to Sam's flashback about their teenage rendezvous. Thus, with the exception of Mercedes's flashback, each of the seven flashback sequences is mediated by the presence of the main white hero, forcing the memories of interracial conflict to be structurally folded into the son's desires. The unearthing of Texas's racist past and the revision of a multicultural social order are always already subsumed and contained within the *point of view* of whiteness and masculinity, which is privileged in the narrative. Ultimately it is the son's desire for symbolic patricide that grants authority to other points of view.

As the main vehicle for racial discourse, the white masculine subject further circumscribes the parameters of racial memories of conflict and collusion, thus marking the impossibility of a Tejana and Tejano psychical interiority and points of view outside of the framework of an oedipalized white masculinity. For example, whiteness represents the mediating term for interracial contacts, both between people of color and between the sexes. Whites have meaningful interactions with blacks, and whites interact with Mexicans, but contact between members of racialized groups does not exist apart from white mediation. Even though the whiteness privileged in *Lone Star* is no longer the white racist masculinity that dominated race relations in a previous era, a new benevolent patron, *amigo* of Mexicans and blacks, is figured in the personas of Buddy and Sam Deeds.

In many ways it is the sharp contrast between the images of Mexicans in *Lone Star* and those portrayed in *Martyrs of the Alamo* eight decades earlier that animates my profound ambivalence toward Sayles's border-crossing narrative. I know that my viewing of the film exists in the context of the near total absence of Chicana/o representation in public discourse, an absence that can disable one's critical vigilance toward those indirect, less obvious, and less implicit forms of racial/gender othering. In my initial enthusiasm for *Lone Star* I found myself in the company of other Chicana and Chicano scholars, seduced by the film's avowedly utopian multiculturalism.[18]

A case in point is the exuberant appraisal of *Lone Star* written by my

Tejano paisano José Limón, who celebrates the film's novel and distinctive iconography and downplays its sexist overtones. Apart from the heterosexual bias in Limón's definition of citizenship, his study positions the biracial (Mexican-Anglo) couple as an allegory for race relations in this country. Limón is interested in exploring "the emergence of a new social order" through what he postulates as the "good marriage" between Anglos (usually males) and Mexicans (in most cases females): a "politics of negotiation and conflict" which is "beyond domination, inequality, iconographies and ambivalences."[19] According to Limón, the film exemplifies the degree to which things have changed in postcolonial Texas, inasmuch as it demonstrates the "transformation of traditional iconography" and a reconciliation between Mexicans and Anglos: "The expressive events I have discussed here may be evidence of what historian David Montejano first identified as a developing rapprochement between Anglos and Mexicans in Texas — the genesis of a new mestizo mainstream, if you will — a rapprochement that works in part in transformational relation to a series of images that in the past have ratified Anglo domination."[20]

I do not want to quibble with the class origins of this positive assessment of the "new mestizo mainstream," for the violently savage murder in Jasper, Texas, as well as the growth of the punishment industry paint a less favorable "rapprochement" for the Mexican and black working class of Texas.[21] Even so, the relationship between film and social reality is just not as transparent as Limón makes it out to be. Part of the problem with his analysis stems from the fact that Limón utilizes film as empirical evidence for social transformations and fails to acknowledge the mechanisms that have historically structured vision in general, and more specifically, his own way of seeing.

Missing from Limón's analysis is a more nuanced and complicated rendering of the narrative economy of cinema. Limón takes issue with a previously published articulation of my earlier statement: "The unearthing of Texas' racist past and the revision of a multicultural order are always already subsumed and contained within the point of view of whiteness and masculinity which is privileged in the narrative." Limón disagrees, noting that "it does not follow that there is a singular 'whiteness' which is uniformly privileged and by extension underwrites the unchanging social order."[22] While I do, in fact, make a distinction between the forms of whiteness articulated by the film, my reference to the "point of view of whiteness" does not refer to the experiential realm. Rather, I am referring to the realm of the symbolic, where, in the case of this film, point of view is indeed overwhelmingly circumscribed by whiteness and masculinity.

In places, Limón appears to recognize that he is dealing with the level of the discursive or with the symbolic realm of social reality. Yet often he slips back into a naive view of film as a transparent reflection of the "real world." A long debate in film theory and history has already established film as neither a simple representation of social reality nor a transparent reflection of the social world. With this in mind, it is difficult to use *Lone Star* as ethnographic evidence for progress in turn-of-the-millennium Texas, as Limón attempts to do. The film is first and foremost a cinematic text, a cultural representation, someone's (John Sayles's) reconstruction and vision of the social world. Like most artistic texts, it is intersected by multiple cultural discourses, various competing histories, and representational traditions, and, at this level, is organized by the cinematic apparatus, including institutionally and historically determined codes, conventions, modes of address, mechanisms of vision, viewing subjects, and points of view.

In this light, my use of "point of view of whiteness" refers to the perspective that is constructed by the film and through the process of viewing this film. As even Limón (contradicting his earlier position) later acknowledges, this point of view happens to be that of Sam Deeds, who is the white masculine subject in the film. Proving my point, Limón makes the following observation: "Through his discovery of both the Oedipal conflict in his life and the true history of his town, he — and we — are able to bracket, deconstruct, and ultimately reject the Texas, truly 'white' and racist 'heroic' father figure."[23] Limón does not explain, however, just how the "he" and the "we" happen to converge in discourse. He does reveal his complicity with dominant mechanisms of visibility through which a white, heterosexual male subject comes into being. Just as significant, these words hint at Limón's uncritical assimilation of the cinematic apparatus as well as his lack of engagement with spectatorship in cinema.

From the perspective of feminist film theory, questions of female representation revolve around the cinematic mechanisms of spectatorship and identification. There are two, often conflated, notions of spectatorship relevant to my analysis of the white patriarchal gaze in the cinematic discourse of *Lone Star*. The first involves what feminist film critics refer to as the "hypothetical" or "textual" spectator — a concept used to signal the textually inscribed position in the text: the film's "ideal" viewing position. The second notion of spectatorship is often called the "historical" or the "empirical" spectator, that is, the spectator as an "actual" social subject who views the film at a particular moment in history. While the spectator in the text (the "hypothetical" spectator) represents the "ideal" or favored position for reading the film, the "historical" spectator is more variable, determined by her social identity and location, as well as by intersecting social discourses.[24] As Kaplan notes, "There is a delicate negotiation in any textual reception between the hypothetical spectator offered by the novel/film and the reading formations of the reader/viewer . . . Depending on the social practice through which this reader/viewer is constructed, she or he will be more or less receptive to the hypothetical spectator position of the novel/film."[25]

However, in his reading of *Lone Star,* Limón ignores the distinction between these forms of spectatorship available to viewers, and he further fails to consider the fact that the "we" is not a subject position preexisting the moment of enunciation. The "we" is a subject position constructed through the film's strategies: it is the site of the "hypothetical spectator," that is, the viewing position the film offers. Through formal, cinematic mechanisms the film constructs the "we" and positions "us" to identify as spectators with the camera's gaze, which is in turn aligned with Sam Deeds's point of view. As a historical spectator, namely a specific Tejano male spectator, Limón is "receptive to the hypothetical spectator position" the film offers and is unable to resist the film's mechanisms, identifying unproblematically with the character Sam Deeds and his point of view.

And, herein lies the fundamental difference between our readings. What is at stake with our opposing views is much more than matters of contrary interpretations of the film. As a historical spectator, formed by a critical feminist antiracist consciousness, I refuse to participate in the patriarchal and racial structures of vision that inform this film. I refuse the spectator positioning the film offers me: an identification with Sam Deeds. On the contrary and despite Limón's critical consciousness, he remains seduced by the white patriarchal visual economy of the film.

The Missionary Position

The film ends with Pilar's final comment: "We start from scratch — ? Everything that went before, all that stuff, that history — the hell with it, right? Forget the Alamo." Even as this story comes to its final resolution, the film's colonial and patriarchal structures of knowing and seeing remain firmly in place. Narrative resolution takes place in an abandoned drive-in theater, reminiscent of *The Last Picture Show* (1971). It is at the eroticized site of the Vaquero Drive-In — that weathered relic to the fifties, now overtaken by Johnson grass and the turbulent memories of Pilar and Sam's adolescent rendezvous — where Sam divulges the truth of his and her existence, namely, that they share the same father. Pilar's final remarks give the film its radical aura, for this climactic scene is a tribute to the petrified remains of a bygone social order that resurrects a repressed interracial narrative lodged deep within the national imaginary, unmasking further the legacy of disavowal on the borderlands.

Since the nineteenth century, the Texas myth of origins has been saturated with the racial politics of exclusion and a discourse of racial purity that has denied social relations between the races. In fact, the identity of Texas is shaped by a deliberate repression of interracial political, social, and sexual relations. Interestingly, the final revelation about Buddy's long-term illicit affair with Pilar's mother disrupts a major racial fantasy, namely the white Texan disavowal of Mexican and Anglo entwinement on the borderlands. In the process, *Lone Star* makes evident the ways in which sexuality is as much a transfer point of power as it is of history and social relations. And we are ultimately left with the deep realization that "contact zones" — zones of crossings and mixings — are not simply linguistic, cultural, and social, but sexual as well.

By unearthing the hidden history of miscegenation, a repressed history of interracial social and sexual relations, *Lone Star* appears to rewrite the new social order on the borderlands as racially mixed at its core, differing substantially from the Anglo-Texan fantasy that constructs citizenship and/or membership in the Texas "nation" in terms of racially pure subjects. Nevertheless, Sayles's commitment to a new, more enlightened vision of race relations is superficial. And the revelation of an illicit love affair between and an Anglo male and a Mexican female fails to call into question the "cultural totality of the ruling order."[26] Given that the plot is structured around a very old racial narrative, namely the story of miscegenation as a model of social inscription whereby the white man's access to the brown woman's body is naturalized and the nation grafted and etched onto the body of a woman, *Lone Star* further reaffirms colonialist masculinity.

There is a long tradition in Western thought of fixing the body of woman as allegory for land and nation, and it is by reading the motif of "forbidden love" in the film through this form of embodiment that we can gauge the significance of interracial love and sibling incest for cultural politics. The notion of the nation as "mother country" engenders the nation as female, further naturalizing woman in her reproductive role as mother.[27] In the nation-building project, women's bodies mark the allusive boundaries of the nation, the race, and the family, especially since the patriarchal imaginary utilizes women's bodies symbolically and literally to shape national, racial, and familial identities. *Lone Star,* however, dramatically alters feminine representation, supplanting white femininity's role as embodiment with a new mestiza. *Lone Star* follows in the patriarchal tradition of engendering the nation as female, in this instance with a twist: the film projects the cultural imaginary of the new multicultural nation onto the body of a mixed-race mestiza. Just as significant, the film also extends its symbolic fantasy to encompass racialized sexual relations: just as the body of woman figures as allegory for the nation, so too does sibling incest function as allegory for race relations in Texas.

Even as the reunited lovers symbolize Mexican and Anglo race relations, the reality of Pilar and Sam's common paternity (as opposed to maternity) recodifies race relations in Texas yet again in patriarchal terms. The siblings derive the truth of their existence from the same paternal lineage, from a history metaphorized in patrimony. Although the film attempts to render the truth of the entwinement of Mexicans and Anglos through this allegorical brother-sister relationship, it is a partial and mystifying truth, privileging the father while rendering the mother invisible in the reproduction of Texas history.

In so doing the film envisions sexuality as a transfer point of phallocentric power, grounding miscegenation in a masculinist colonial fantasy that authorizes and privileges the white man's access to brown female bodies. The white man in this story occupies the missionary position, for he remains on top of the racial hierarchy, able to cross the racialized borders of gender (Buddy's illicit affair with Mercedes). Women in this narrative universe are the primary objects of hybridity: mixing and sexual crossings on the borderland.

In a recycling of a very old racist, colonialist fantasy of interracial sexual relations, namely the portrayal of white male access to a brown woman's body as normal and natural, the film placates white anxieties around miscegenation. To the degree that *Lone Star*'s story excludes and denies the history of other forms of sexual relations, namely those outside of the white male/woman of color paradigm, *Lone Star* reaffirms white supremacy's interdiction against interracial sex and marriage. Antimiscegenation laws were designed to ensure the racial purity of the nation, embodied in white womanhood. As we know from the history of race relations, antimiscegenation laws targeted mostly black and other nonwhite males who were constructed in social discourse as sexual predators, lusting after white women.

Although the portrayal of Sam as a racially pure subject minimizes the types of mixed-race identities in the new multicultural nation, Sayles's discovery that "maybe a third or more African Americans are also Native Americans and a much higher percentage of African Americans are also white Americans" is curious for what it omits: the racial mixed-ness of white Americans. Sayles affirms both the white supremacist myth of racial purity and its anxieties around miscegenation. The film in fact reproduces the othering process prevalent in national formations, especially because the nation is inscribed onto the body of multiracial Pilar, who harbors the social "stigma" of miscegenation. As the sole object of mixed-race parentage, Pilar embodies the borderlands and allegorizes hybridity, racial crossing and mixing across a new terrain in which white male access to the multicultural nation takes place through the body of a brown woman.

At best, *Lone Star*'s overture to multiculturalism is superficial, privileging white masculinity as the mediating term, potent enough to cross racial and sexual boundaries while erecting the mythic borders of its own racially pure masculinity. Despite its enthusiastic reception, *Lone Star* contributes to the maintenance of gendered and racialized power relations and consolidates longstanding hegemonic regimes of knowing and seeing within a new multicultural nation. By uncritically accepting the terms of the film's logic, critics like Limón continue to, as Norma Alarcón has argued in a different context, "recodify a family romance, an oedipal drama in which the woman of color of the Americas has no 'designated' place."[28] And nowhere is this erasure of the identity and subjectivity of women of color more evident that in the film's representation of motherhood.

Chicana/Mexicana Motherhood

In sharp contrast to *Lone Star*'s hyperinvestment in patrilineage, there is only a veiled discourse on motherhood that is submerged within the narrative. The film portrays motherhood in racial asymmetries, as represented by the binary between the absent (white) angelic, pure mother (embodied in Sam's mother) and the overshadowing, haunting presence of the Mexican/Tejana mother (Pilar's mother). The subordination of women of color in history is further accentuated by the heated tensions and unresolved conflicts between the Mexicana mother and Chicana daughter.

I was not so much disturbed by the rift between mother and daughter since their estrangement triggered memories of my own conflictual relation in the motherline. I have had similar experiences on both sides of the chain — as the daughter of an assertive, strong-willed, vocal, and independent mother, and as the mother of an equally assertive, strong-willed, vocal, and independent daughter. Relationships between mothers and daughters who share close personality traits are often riddled with conflicts and contradictions. Brown-Guillory writes about the mother-daughter relationship in the lives of women of color in these terms: "Studies . . . suggest that when a mother looks at her daughter, she sees herself. She is constantly reminded of her mistakes, yearnings, dreams, successes and failures. When a daughter looks at her mother she often sees herself and rejects the image in the mirror."[29] And if both mother and daughter are fortunate enough to weather the frictions and work through some of the resentment, blame, ill-feeling, guilt, and judgment, their relationship can blossom into a lifelong, indissoluble bond.

And this is what troubled me most about Mercedes and Pilar's relationship: the fact that the filmmaker/scriptwriter made no effort to resolve their conflicts, heal their wounds, or even formulate an ending that would leave us with the lingering impression of a more compassionate outcome. I longed for at least some semblance of closure between mother and daughter, an inkling of some future reconciliation. I would have liked to have left the theater with the sensation that, in the not so distant future, Pilar and Mercedes — as in the case with the fathers and sons in the film — would somehow work things out, just like I did several years ago with my own mother.

This ending is particularly disappointing given the film's potential for a fully developed portrayal of the mother-daughter relationship. The materials were there, but not realized. There are striking similarities between mother and daughter. Both are independent and assertive. Mercedes excels in the private sector as a successful restaurateur and as a public official in her role as a city council member. Pilar, likewise, is a prominent public figure, a teacher and leader in public debates regarding the school curriculum. Both are single parents, widows of Mexican men who later in life are both romantically involved with Anglo men. Perhaps Mercedes looks at Pilar and "sees herself" or "is constantly reminded of her mistakes, yearnings, dreams, successes and failures." Or maybe Pilar looks at Mercedes and "often sees herself and rejects the image in the mirror." Are these the wedges separating them? The sources of their mutual disenchantment? Because Sayles suppressed the point of view of women of color, we will never know.

And, although the male and female lead characters (Sam and Pilar) are portrayed as social equals in their respective roles as sheriff and teacher, the mechanisms of character identification and positioning create an inequality that transcends the fictional universe, reproducing and reaffirming racial and gender inequality beyond the frame. Alarcón's observations from another context resonate with the film's strategies, the notion that woman "is simultaneously presence/absence in the configurations of the nation state and textual representation."[30] Earlier I noted how the body of a mixed-race woman marks the allegorical boundaries of race and embodies the fantasy of a multicultural nation. In other words, Chicana identity is "present" as embodiment (object) of the nation but absent as its speaking subject. The key to this contradiction lies primarily in the alienation of the maternal presence from the mixed-race woman's genealogy.

Attempting to dislodge the concept of "mother" from its patriarchal straightjacket, Kristeva writes: "I am only a mother in relation to my child, not outside of that relation. It is precisely patriarchal culture that has essentialized and fixed the concept of 'Mother' to my being-in-the-world instead of permitting it to be a mobile part of my being that comes and goes depending on whether I am in relation or not to the child."[31]

In *Lone Star*, the maternal body on the borderlands, this "mobile part" of female subjectivity, the part "that comes and goes depending on whether [she is] in relation or not to the child," is present as characterization, in other words, by virtue of the fact that for both Mercedes and Pilar, motherhood is but one aspect of their identities as women. But in the film the maternal presence also drives a wedge between women of color. The film represents motherhood in binary terms, linking its positive aspects with white identity (Sam's absent mother) and its negative aspects with Chicana identity (Mercedes). More specific to the issue of mother-daughter relations, motherhood appears as a relationship riddled with negativity, turning against both Mercedes and Pilar.

In places, *Lone Star* seems to reject the essentialized, fixed concept of motherhood, representing the Mexicana mother, Mercedes, as mobile in relation to her various identities: lover, mother, business owner, boss, and public official, although in relation to her daughter, Mercedes is neither a friend nor a confidant, but is fixed and essentialized as a being-in-the-world, in the paradigm of the "over-indulgent, phallic mother."[32] In contrast to the film's focus on masculine triangular (grandfather-father-grandson) relationships, there is no equivalent representation available for Chicana/Mexicana identities. There is some degree of complexity to Mercedes' character treatment, places in the text where she is not simply a one-dimensional character, but ultimately she is contained by the demands of the text.

The Mexicana mother's discursive power is mediated primarily through character development. First of all, Mercedes's evolution and transformation is directly accessible to viewers. For example, Mercedes is the only other character, besides Sam, actively engaged in "memory work," in remembering and producing links to the past through the seamless editing techniques of the flashback. And it is precisely the production of Mercedes's personal memory that renders visible her interiority. As spectators, we recall how the sins of Mercedes include racial amnesia: denial of her national, racial, and class origins. She claims a Spanish (white) rather than a Mexican (mestizo) heritage; she insists that in the United States "we speak English"; she refuses to travel with her daughter to Mexico; and in the end, she disavows her own clandestine border crossing years ago.

In her final performance on screen, Mercedes recovers from this racial amnesia, resurrecting a repressed racial memory — the shadow haunting her present-day existence. She remembers the symbolic (primal) scene engendering her as a racialized subject. It is the scene of a young Mercedes Gonzales Ruíz crossing the border without documents and meeting her future husband, Eladio Cruz, whose extended hand welcomes her with the words: "Bienvenida a Tejas." This border crossing transforms a former citizen of one nation (México) into an undocumented immigrant of another (the United States). Apart from remaking a legal subject into an "illegal" one, the border crossing is also primal insofar as it marks her body as a racialized subject. Lone Star works to dislodge this primal scene of border crossings from the site of the repressed and, in the process, kindles an alliance between Mercedes and the Mexican immigrants she employs. A transformed Mercedes comes to the aid of Enrique and his undocumented fiancée. In this manner, the filmmaker portrays a character who is redeemed by her own volition, that is, by her active involvement in recalling things buried deep in her past and long forgotten.

The portrayal of Mercedes's metamorphosis works as an effective mechanism for furthering character identification with viewers, but it fails to transform mother-daughter relations within the text. If the story had elaborated on Mercedes's subjectivity in process, Lone Star would have effectively decentered the point of view of white masculinity and opened up a space for an engagement with various spectators and multiple identity positions. Unfortunately, narrative closure recuperates yet again the symbolic violence of the "Oedipal family romance," especially since the brother and sister's conflict with the all-powerful father is resolved, whereas the maternal presence is alienated from Chicana subjectivity, thereby furthering the erasure of any meaningful mother-daughter identification.

With the exception of commercially unsuccessful women's films, the motherhood genre rarely explores women's identification with the mother figure. And when female/female bonding is examined, it is "usually subordinated to patriarchal demands by the text's end."[33] *Lone Star* is no exception to this model of female inscription.

As I have noted, in sharp contrast to the manner in which each and every father-son relationships is portrayed, the conflicts between Mercedes and Pilar as mother-daughter remain unresolved by the film's ending. As noted earlier, the film's visual language reinforces women's estrangement, emphasizing Mercedes's critical gaze at her daughter and Pilar's judgmental outlook toward the mother. Resentments and conflicts between women sustain a patriarchal discourse that renders inevitable the abjection of the mother. And even though both Mercedes and Buddy are blamed for Pilar and Sam's predicament, Buddy is, in the words of his own son, "a goddam legend" who can "handle" such incriminations. The same does not hold true for Mercedes, who is portrayed as neither mythic nor grand but as much more "ordinary" and whose precarious vulnerability is reinforced through the negative interactions she maintains with other characters. Unlike the father in *Lone Star,* the mother is a character who cannot bear the burden of her incrimination.

Lone Star is not alone in its representation of motherhood, for "in many films the mother is blamed for her transgressions and the ills she visited upon her offspring."[34] Mercedes's ultimate transgression is not just her illicit love affair with a white Texan; it is her deceit. According to the narrative logic, Pilar has fallen in love with her half-brother because the mother has lied and hidden her past. While Mercedes attempts to prevent incest on the part of the siblings, she does so dishonestly and in the end, fails. Her failure is ultimately the film's success, for not even the incest taboo can prevent the romantic demands of the plot. But the film is ambiguous in this regard, seemingly condoning a "love that conquers all," even incest, while blaming the mother for the daughter's transgressions. In the end, the film portrays a daughter who follows in the mother's footsteps ("like mother, like daughter"), reproducing "the nefarious duplication between mother and daughter."[35]

Patriarchal discourse tends to incriminate the mother as "a figure in the design, out of focus; or if in focus then the blunt of an attack, a criticism, a complaint usually in the discourse of a child (male or female) or in that of an adult (male or female) concerned to attribute all ills to the mother."[36] Along with the film's portrayal of a predominantly hostile and venomous mother-daughter interaction, the lack of closure around Mercedes and Pilar's bonding in effect recodifies a cultural discourse of matriphobia, a hatred for the mother traced to Freudian psychoanalytic theories that were popularized in the United States during the 1940s and that remain with us to this day.

Given the centrality of intergenerational conflict as a major subtext of *Lone Star,* this failed resolution around female identification consolidates the oedipal family romance that critical feminist discourses and oppositional practices have for so long attempted to rupture. Unfortunately, the absence of a female counterpart to the father-son theme of reconciliation reverberates beyond the fictional universe of the film and into the cultural and social spheres of our own historical moment. Therefore, much more is at stake than the symbolic production of an estrangement between mother and daughter, for in the end these two women have no meaningful interaction.

In *Of Woman Born,* Adrienne Rich writes: "The quality of the mother's life — however embattled and unprotected — is her primary bequest to her daughter because a woman who can believe in herself, who is a fighter, is demonstrating to her daughter that these possibilities exist."[37] Mercedes's life was certainly embattled, and not simply by her own internal demons. Unbeknownst to Pilar, but not to the rest of the town, Mercedes carried on an illicit love affair during a time when interracial liaisons were frowned upon. Undoubtedly Mercedes lived an unprotected and difficult life, both as the "other woman" of a white man in segregated South Texas and as a single, working mother. However, the tragic figure in this story is not the mother, but the daughter: Pilar is the film's bastard child. Pilar's corporal estrangement is total, encompassing not just her matrilineage, as I have argued, but also her patrilineage.[38] And, it is this "illegitimate" child, bereft of a maternal presence, deprived of paternity, who represents the new subject of the multicultural nation.

Although *Lone Star* is the first film to represent the complexities of postcolonial Texas with some verisimilitude, much more is at stake than the film's agreement with a preexisting truth. The film ostensibly engages in historical revisionism, allegedly rewrites the primal myth of the nation, outwardly rejects the absolutism of the myth of pure and authentic culture and racial binarism. However, the film's serious limitations are evident insofar as the patriarchal and colonialist structures of knowing and seeing undermine the fictional representation of multiculturalism and a new social order. This "new social order" that critics celebrated as the "genesis of a new mestizo mainstream" positions racialized women in a troubling location. The abjection of the mother creates the corporal estrangement of the mixed-race Chicana from history: her history is rendered invisible through practices of repression and incorporation within patriarchy.

Yet, the work of creating a more just and humane future demands, not a denial or an erasure of the past, but its reimagination. While the film works to re-vision and reconstruct the white man's past so that he may enter a multicultural present and future, the Chicana enters history as a bastard child. Ultimately Pilar, as the embodiment of the new multicultural nation filtered through white patriarchy, is left without her matrilineage, paternity, and, most significantly, without the history lessons necessary to guide her into the future. At this moment in history, when the violence of racist patriarchy reasserts its power and domination over the multicultural nation, she (we) cannot simply afford to "forget the Alamo."

CHAPTER FOUR

The Chicano Familia Romance

"I remember mi familia" are the final words spoken by Paco Sánchez, the maudlin narrator in the film *My Family* (1995). This is not just his own particular familia that Paco is remembering. The trailing resonance in his voice, heightened by deliberate guitar strumming in the style of El Trio Los Panchos ringing over the L.A. sunset, suggests that Paco's familia, the Sánchez familia, are *our* familia, the familia of la raza, the people of Mexican origin in the United States. Overshadowed by the "theme of remembrance,"[1] *My Family* is a Chicano family romance, an epic composed of memory traces triggered by familiar historical tropes and desires: indigenous music and iconography, circular migrations, Californio territorial claims, service workers, repatriation during the thirties, state repression, pachuco resistance, political activism, and incarceration. These dominant tropes and desires provide the narrative threads for an alternative Chicano revisionist history and give voice to the film's veiled discourse on the nation. The Sánchez protagonists in the film evoke Oscar Lewis's Sánchez family of Mexico City — not just in terms of their appellation, but more in terms of what both signify for a social group. Like Lewis's "Children of Sánchez," Gregory Nava's "familia Sánchez" is paradigmatic for a nation. The familia of José and María Sánchez are designed to stand for the familia of Chicanas and Chicanos.

My Family was released at the height of this nation's "all out war over family values."[2] The New Right sought to cultivate the "Hispanic vote" during this moral panic, emphasizing the compatibility between the Republican social agenda and the strong family and religious values they perceived in Latino/a communities. And, films like *My Family* seem to confirm the New Right's speculations; even in its choice of title, the film champions the value of "la familia" to the self-identity of Chicanas/os as a people. Yet, although "there is no universally shared definition of family," the image of la familia represented in *My Family* is more in line with that of the "'centrist' neo-family values movement": the family defined in terms of heterosexual marriage, nuclear bloodlines, and gender hierarchies.[3]

In some respects the film anticipates the "marriage movement" of the new century, embodied in the politics of the Republican administration of George W. Bush, or, as María Sánchez, the mother of the Sánchez clan, puts it to her son, Jimmy: "There are some things in life that are sacred — sagradas — and we don't spit on them because without them it doesn't matter if we live or die. Marriage is something we don't spit on."[4] How could a film that purports to offer an alternative vision of Chicano history conform so closely to the mainstream ideology of family values? How could it mimic the Western concept of the family system? The answer to this paradox rests squarely in *My Family*'s cultural nationalist orientation.

In this chapter I will trace the trajectory of family ideology to early Chicano Movement politics as a way of exploring the gendered hierarchies found in such cultural representations. Recent portrayals of la familia in film include ... *and the Earth Did Not Swallow Him* (1994), *A Walk in the Clouds* (1993), *Selena* (1997), and *Spy Kids* (2001), which respond in many ways to the family values rhetoric of the nineties by reviving the myth of a singular, ideal familia. Instead of providing meaningful alternatives to right-wing ideology on the family, Chicano/Latino screen familias are complicitous with the "rampant nostalgia for the modern family system."[5] For, even as the idealized screen familia has contributed to the strong family values image of Chicanas/os, traditional images of la familia ignore the diversity of actual familia life in most Chicano/a households.

The ideology of la familia fails to acknowledge the complexity of sentiments and relationships within actual familias: the fact that familias are riddled with contradiction — objects of nostalgia and remorse, beloved and yet blamed for our shortcomings. Many of us, through consciousness-raising, psychotherapy, or "revived memories," have had to confront our experiences in oppressive biological familias: instances in which women and children were victims of incest, child abuse, rape, spousal battering, and beatings. Others grew up in nontraditional familias that departed significantly from the reigning model of la familia in cultural discourse. Like Chicana feminists who, to quote Norma Alarcón, are "making familia from scratch," some of us have been raised in blended familias, among multiple, nonbiological parents, with extended kin, between several households, in female-headed homes, or with lesbian and gay parents. Countless others have criticized the ideology of la familia because it is based on patriarchal kinship; they have thereby spoken outside the family, against the familia romance and its code of family loyalty and solidarity.[6] Thus, what Chicano mainstream images fail to capture is the deep fissures within Chicano/a communities over la familia.

In the following pages, my aim will not be to judge visual and literary records of la familia for their failure to represent some ontological "true" familia. Rather, I seek to question the salience of the ideology of la familia in Chicana/o cultural discourse and politics and to meditate on the effects of its monolithic representation for women's identities.

Gendering the National Imaginary

"Nations," as Anne McClintock reminds us, "are frequently figured through the iconography of familial and domestic space."[7] Chicano nationalist thought was no exception. From the inception of the Chicano Movement, Chicano/a activists mobilized around the one institution over which they exercised control, championing la familia as a "righteous causa":[8] "A guiding principle of the Chicano Movement which cuts across specific organization goals and tactics is the preservation of family loyalty. Ideologically, this principle is expressed by two concepts: la familia de la raza and carnalismo. La familia de la raza unites Chicanos to struggle as a family tied together by carnalismo, the spirit of brotherhood."[9] Early movement activists thus envisioned la familia in both political and cultural terms, as an indispensable support system capable not only of meeting the needs of its members but also of sheltering them from the violence, exploitation, racism, and abuse perpetrated in the external, public sphere of the Anglo capitalist world.[10] "Political familism" was the term used to characterize what Maxine Baca Zinn calls the "fusing of cultural and political resistance," as well as to theorize or speak about the links between family and nation. "Political familism," Baca Zinn continues, "is a phenomenon in which the continuity of family groups and the adherence to family ideology provide the basis for struggle. El

Movimiento has gone into the Chicano home."[11] Or, as another early activist, Rodolfo "Corky" González, succinctly puts it: "The key common denominator is nationalism . . . nationalism becomes la familia."[12]

It is worth noting that the breakdown of the boundaries between the public and the private implicit in political familism was due in large part to the influence of the United Farmworkers' Union, whose campaign "encouraged participation in the union by the entire family."[13] Mobilizing through the institution of la familia and adhering to family ideology as the basis for the nation depended on the exercise of gender power. As the guiding principle of "family loyalty" as expressed through "carnalismo" (the spirit of brotherhood) makes evident, women's relation to the Chicano nation was represented in unequal terms, particularly since, as Sonia Saldívar-Hull reminds us, "The code of family loyalty begins with the assumption that men can claim possession of female sexuality."[14] And nowhere is the representation of gender hierarchies more obvious than in the symbolic iconography used to represent the nation.

Widely circulating in movement publications during the sixties and early seventies, the visual expression of this image of la familia originally appeared in a 1968 Los Angeles issue of *La Raza*. Entitled "La Raza" by its author, the muralist Walter Baca, the drawing was recently brought to my attention by the historian Lorena Oropeza, whose analysis sparked my own early memories of this image, which in poster form hung on the wall of the Mexican American Youth Organization's headquarters in Corpus Christi in the early seventies. Oropeza's reading of "La Raza," which depicts a mother, father, and son, focuses on its portrayal of gender differences: "The man is at the top of the frame facing forward," she writes. "The woman, sheltered not just in a shawl but in the man's embrace, occupies the middle section of the picture. But she faces inward, toward the man."[15] The image in fact draws from the Catholic iconographic tradition of renditions of Saint Joseph, the Virgin Mary, and the Child Jesus. Occupying the symbolic place of the Virgin Mary, the Chicana mother is enshrined in motherhood and domesticity; her subordination is thus understood as a "divine" fact. The caption accompanying the image, Oropeza explains, completes the metaphoric chain linking family to nation: la familia = la raza = the community = the Chicano nation.

Feminist writers have drawn our attention to the fact that "nationalisms have 'typically sprung from masculinized memory, masculinized humiliation and masculinized hope."[16] And these three vestiges of early Chicano nationalism's orientation — masculinized memory, masculinized humiliation, and masculinized hope — are revived as key ingredients motivating the plot and driving desire in the film *My Family*.

"Inspired by Nava's family and based on his research of other Mexican-American families in East Los Angeles,"[17] *My Family* tells the story of social and family conflict mainly through the experiences of masculinity, providing "male characters with the 'space' to frolic in patriarchal bonding, violence, and the histrionics of the wounded macho."[18] Although the filmmaker sought to offer mainstream audiences an understanding of the "concept of the Latino family," the film downplays the significance of female voices within la familia, depriving women of significant agency through its overarching emphasis on masculinized memory, masculinized humiliation, and masculinized hope. As the "collective voice of the family," its narrator, Paco, embodies a "masculinized memory" who serves as witness for other male-centered stories of "masculinized humiliation," signified by Chucho and Jimmy (Paco's brothers), and for a new masculinity or "masculinized hope," embodied in the characters Jimmy and Carlitos (Paco's nephew/Jimmy's son).[19]

One of the sites in which masculinized hope is rendered intelligible in the film is its reworking of the classic oedipal crisis. By emphasizing the oedipal conflicts between fathers and sons (José and Chucho; Jimmy and Carlitos), the filmmaker attempts to render a more complicated and nuanced alternative to the "Leave It to Beaver" image of the family. Despite the film's portrayal of a broader range of subjectivities for male characters, the filmmaker fails to provide an alternative psychic scenario to male authority and subjectivity. In the end, *My Family* fails to disrupt classic Western oedipal structures; rather, it symbolically resolves masculine conflicts in favor of patriarchal authority. As Huaco Nuzum puts it, "*Mi Familia* is centered on male discourse that emphasizes and reinforces male positions of power within the structure of culture, nation, and the dynamics of the Mexican-American family."[20] In so doing, its narrative follows the masculinized plot of identifying the needs of the nation (family) with the "frustrations and aspirations of men."[21] What is additionally disconcerting about the revival of nationalist portrayals of la familia is the extent to which a film like *My Family* and the drawing "La Raza" mirror Western, patriarchal, definitions of the family.

The Chicano familia has been portrayed as "a critical force in [the] opposition to internal colonialism"[22] and as such an alternative to the white, European-American (colonialist) family. Yet the idealized familia of Chicano cultural politics looks conspicuously like the "singular ideal family" of the West. "In most of Europe and North America," Judith

Stacey writes, "the family has become nearly synonymous with a nuclear heterosexual couple and their biological or adopted children."[23] In the writings of Chicano activists, the family was claimed by Chicano nationalists as this space of pure culture, uncontaminated by colonialism, as this example from Alfredo Mirandé's 1977 essay exemplifies: "In an environment where Chicano institutions have been rendered subordinate and dependent, the family has been the only institution to escape colonial intrusion."[24] What early nationalist claims surrounding the familia as a "site of resistance" failed to recognize is the extent to which the private sphere was itself implicated in Western patriarchy: "Discourses valorizing the 'private' as the site of resistance against repressive states, or as the ultimate repository of cultural identity should not let us overlook the fact that, in most instances, the integrity of the so-called 'private' is predicated upon the unfiltered operations of patriarchy."[25] Baca's "La Raza," for example, reveals the deep influence of Western culture on the construction of Chicana/o family identity. Despite nationalist desires for a space of uncontaminated culture, the family form depicted in "La Raza" conforms to the Western family ideology of the nuclear heterosexual family as "natural and universal."[26]

And, when we add to this one-dimensional family form the reigning orthodoxy of political familism, we can begin to dissect other influences of Western culture, especially the modern construction of the nation and its use of gendered power relations within the family as the basis for the nationalist order/ideology. In writing about nineteenth-century nationalisms, McClintock explains: "The image of the family was projected onto these nationalisms as their shadowy, naturalized form. Because the subordination of woman to man and child to adult was deemed a natural fact, hierarchies within the nation could be depicted in familial terms to guarantee social difference as a category of nature."[27]

There are several points to extrapolate from McClintock's observations. First, the influence of Catholicism on Chicano culture compounded the largely secular, Modernist vision of familial hierarchies for, in religious tradition, gender subordination was also deemed to be sacred, divinely ordained in scripture as a timeless universal. The Catholic holy family in fact served as the model for the familia in not just Baca's "La Raza" but also in Nava's *My Family*. The parents of the Sánchez familia are named José and María, and the metaphor of Jesus Christ as the "lamb of God" guides certain narrative choices, as this voice-over by the film's narrator, Paco, illustrates: "Jimmy [the youngest son] represents the family, the *sacrificial lamb* who contains within his being all the pain, hate, suffering, racial persecution, and impotence of the family" (my emphasis).[28]

A further example of this profound Catholic influence is found in the research of social scientists David Alvirez and Frank Bean, writing about Mexican American family structure in the 1970s. Explaining gender roles within the familia, the authors naturalize the mother's (Virgin Mary) subordination to both the father (God) and the son (Jesus): "During the father's absence, the older son assumes authority and he is expected to be obeyed as if he were the father. Sometimes the range of his authority includes the mother, particularly when the son is close to manhood."[29]

Although I recognize that the use of the qualifier "sometimes" is deployed as a tactic for avoiding generalizations, Alvirez and Bean's infantilization of the mother within the father-son-mother triangle is reminiscent of Catholicism's depiction of the divine jurisdiction of "God the Father" and "God the Son" over the Virgin Mary. In fact, the Catholic holy family serves as the backdrop, providing sacred legitimacy for the researchers' one-dimensional and reductive account of Chicano family structure. By failing to mention the actual diversity of family forms within Chicana/o culture, Alvirez and Bean in fact perpetuate and normalize commonsense thinking about gender hierarchies within la familia.

Chicana/o family ideology also draws from Anglo-American norms around heterosexuality and consanguinity, especially in its assumptions about very particular roles for women as wives, mothers, economic dependents, nurturers, and cultural transmitters. One of the most effective mechanisms for consolidating/securing women's association with tradition is through "the contradiction in the representation of time as a natural division of gender." In nationalist discourse, "women are represented as the atavistic and authentic body of national tradition (inert, backward-looking and natural) embodying nationalism's conservative principles of continuity. Men, by contrast, represent the progressive agent of national modernity (forward-thrusting, potent, and historic), embodying nationalism's progressive, or revolutionary principle of discontinuity."[30] This paradox in Chicana representation — her marginality in relation to history yet centrality in culture — forms the basis for the revivalism of familia ideology in several cultural texts of the nineties, including *My Family*.

In keeping with the nationalist trope of the "mother as the center of Chicano culture,"[31] *My Family* positions María Sánchez at the center of its familia. At the same time, the absence of her narrative agency reinforces gender inequality within the family structure as much as it freezes her in time, within the biologically inscribed role of motherhood. Two other Chicano texts, . . . *and the Earth Did Not Swallow Him,* a familia melodrama by independent filmmaker Severo Pérez, and the memoir *Places Left Unfinished at the Time of Creation* (1999), written by John Phillip Santos, also conform to nationalism's gender-specific renditions of time.

Perez's remarkable adaptation of Tomás Rivera's literary classic by the same name, . . . *and the Earth Did Not Swallow Him,* tells the coming-of-age story of a young Chicano, Marcos, who remembers the year of hardships faced by his migrant farmworker familia (the Gonzales family) as they follow the crops from Texas to Minnesota. Noteworthy for its heartrending portrayal of the dignity and humanity of this familia as well as its veracious chronicling of the discrimination confronting farmworkers during the 1950s, . . . *and the Earth Did Not Swallow Him* often subscribes to masculinist depictions of stark gender differences in temporal terms. In the course of narrative, Marcos, the twelve-year-old male protagonist, experiences a change in consciousness that transforms him into the film's voice of reason, "the progressive agent of national modernity." On the other hand, the mother of the Gonzales familia figures as the "inert, backward-looking and natural" force of culture, emphasized by the filmmaker's framing of spiritual practices as blindly religious and superstitious, rather than as practices of resistance. In the scene where the mother lights a candle to pray over the ailing father, the rational son ridicules her form of healing practice: "What good is that candle going to do? It didn't help Tía Lupita. We are always sick . . . God doesn't care about us. Look at how we're living."

In his memoir about the "generation with a living memory of the deep family bonds into Mexico's past," John Phillip Santos takes gender difference in temporality to a new level, positioning the elder women of the Santos clan as natural and motionless embodiments of tradition; this is especially evident in the title of the first chapter, "Tierra de viejitas" (Land of the little old ladies), whereas the Santos men symbolize history, as in the chapter title "Codices de los abuelos" (Grandfather codices). Although the memoir's mythopoetic tone cuts across this gender divide, the emphasis on premodern female lineage predominates, as the following characterization of the women exemplifies:

> *Las Viejitas* were born in the Virgin's magic.
>
> They grew up in a twilight time and geography, poised between those ancient Indio origins from the south, Spain's grand utopian designs, and our Mestizo future in the north. The world they remember from their youth is not the modern Mexico ruled over by a rough-trade priestly elite of Ivy league, pedigreed

technocrats, orchestrating Mexico's extreme slow-motion collapse. Their legacy is from the time that the Spanish language, theology and science were first thrown across the Mexican geography like an enormous net, from a vision of the land enmeshed within the cosmos. That vision, with all of its mystical powers, has been almost lost.[32]

By envisioning the women in his familia within the space of the pre-modern, Santos anchors them in the natural world of the past, before history, as embodiments of the "conservative principle of continuity" rather than of rupture or the forward-thrusting movement of male history.

The revivalism of familia ideology during the nineties is noteworthy for its strategy of freezing women in mythological time, which in earlier Chicano nationalist thought also served as a mechanism for the construction of women as markers of cultural identity. In the words of Alfredo Mirandé: "The *macho* as the titular head of the family is usually seen as actively combating acculturation and assimilation but the woman resists equally via her own traditional way. As the center of the family and the mainstay of the culture and its traditions the Chicana has helped to counter the encroachment of colonialism. She perpetuates the language and values of Chicanos."[33]

Like patriarchal nationalisms elsewhere, Chicano nationalist discourse constructed Chicanas as "mothers of the nation." Deniz Kandiyoti explains that "the control of women and sexuality is central to national and ethnic processes," adding, "Women have the burden of being 'mothers of the nation' (a duty that gets ideologically defined to suit official priorities) as well as being those who reproduce the boundaries of ethnic/national groups, who transmit the culture and who are privileged signifiers of national difference."[34]

Thus, despite nationalist claims around the purity and authenticity of Chicano cultural institutions, gender power relations within la familia reveal other influences on the very construction of tradition. The Chicana/o familia was very much a hybrid cultural form produced in and through its encounter not only with dominant Anglo-American culture but also with Catholicism and nationalist discourses from other contexts. Indeed, even the claim around the uniqueness of la familia as the basis of Chicano activism — the ideology of political familism as intrinsically Chicano — is rendered problematic in light of feminist research about the foundational role of family ideology within other nationalist formations in Europe and Africa.

If the familia of the Chicano nation is a hybrid cultural form, sharing with other cultures the status of being "one of the principle sites of women's oppression,"[35] how was the ideology of familism normalized as the foundational principle of Chicano thought and cultural politics? Why do Chicana and Chicano scholars continue to insist on the centrality of familism as the basis of political activism? And, why is the ideology of la familia so engrained in cultural politics to this day? A partial explanation can be found in how the familia emerges as an object of knowledge in Chicana/o studies.

In Defense of la Familia

> Spy work. That's easy. Keeping a family together, that's difficult. And that's a mission worth fighting for.
>
> Carmen, in *Spy Kids* (2001)

While I was writing this chapter, Chicano filmmaker Robert Rodriguez released the action-adventure familia movie *Spy Kids*. The film is worth mentioning in this context not because it was one of the highest grossing films by a Latino filmmaker, but because the film's closing words, spoken by the girl-spy Carmen, recapitulate what I would like to characterize as one of the central *missions* in Chicano cultural politics around la familia: the defense of la familia. In a 1989 essay on Chicana feminist discourse, Pat Zavella writes: "Thus during a time when white feminists were recognizing the tyranny of the traditional family, Chicana activists were celebrating the unity of traditional Chicano families."[36] Chief among its celebrants was a group of Chicana and Chicano social scientists who, in contesting colonialist (or "functionalist," as Zavella terms them) fantasies about the Chicano family, inadvertently kindled a new mythology of la familia.

To a large extent their defense and celebration of la familia responded to the "scientific" production of knowledge about Chicana/o culture. Throughout the twentieth century, social scientists had played a key role in marking the parameters of Mexicanness (mexicanidad) and interpreting as well as defining Mexican — and by extension Chicana/o — culture to the "outside" world. The earliest ethnographic studies of Mexicans living in the United States were conducted in the 1920s and 1930s during the heyday of the eugenics movement. In many ways, the pseudoscientific "doctrine of race improvement" in eugenicist orthodoxy informed these early colonialist accounts about Mexican immigrant families, who were chastised for their "foreign habits" and "immorality" by researchers who emphasized "the need to Americanize Mexicans by teaching them appropriate family standards."[37]

A few decades later, the culture of poverty framework that came to dominate the social sciences led to even more pernicious interpretations of Mexicans in academic literature. Terms like "dysfunctional," "pathological," "authoritarian," and "fatalistic" were common adjectives used to define Chicana/o culture. This renewed assault on the Chicano familia was emboldened by the writings of Oscar Lewis, an anthropologist who first introduced his culture of poverty thesis in studies of Puerto Rican and Mexican working-class and indigenous families.[38]

Lewis considered working-class culture to be a product of the structural and institutional effects of capitalism, a symbolic response to the barriers erected by an economic system that disempowered and disenfranchised the working poor, but the terms of his argument were often reversed. Lewis's association of social and economic factors fueled the writings of more conservative culture of poverty exponents, whose work attributed the socioeconomic condition of Chicanos/as (and other racialized groups) to their culture or cultural values.[39] Celia Heller, for example, writes about Chicano youth: "This type of upbringing creates stumbling blocks for future advancement by stressing values that hinder mobility, family ties, honor, masculinity and living in the present — and by neglecting values that are conducive to it — achievement, independence and deferred gratification."[40]

The conservative appropriation of Lewis's culture of poverty thesis, especially the attribution of poverty to the interconnection between cultural tradition (familism), rigid gender/generational hierarchies (machismo), and individual character (fatalism) would subsequently be challenged by a group of progressive social scientists in Chicana/o studies. However, the culture of poverty framework posed a special burden of representation for Chicanos/as.

Culture of poverty arguments served to stigmatize the so-called underclass in general, but they proved especially damaging for Chicanas/os and other U.S. Latinas/os because the very objects of knowledge in Lewis's anthropological observations were from their own racial/ethnic group: Mexicans and Puerto Ricans.[41] Given the colonialist tradition in social scientific studies of racialized groups, it is not surprising that the Lewis's findings about very particular and contextually specific anthropological subjects in Mexico City would turn into essential and universal truths about Mexicans of every class and racial background, in every context, including those in the diaspora. In fact, Lewis's anthropological gaze ended up perpetuating the enduring, essentialist image of the Mexican familia as a cultural monolith. Beginning in the 1970s, Chicana/o revisionists proceeded to dismantle the colonialist paradigm on the Mexican and Chicano familia. The historical significance of their efforts cannot be underestimated, for conservative social science confabulations about the Mexican familia continue to this date.

In the summer of 2001, I attended a lecture entitled "Mythology and the Mexican Family" at the Biblioteca Pública de San Miguel de Allende, Guanajuato.[42] Speaking to an audience of U.S. tourists and expatriates (mostly retirees), Dr. Morton Stith, Karen Karabasz, and Marc Taylor recapitulated some of the most enduring stereotypes about Mexican family pathologies — its authoritarianism, fatalism, hypermachismo, Spanish "tradition of chivalry still here today," and female passivity and subordination. Parroting the colonialist fantasies I assumed had long been discredited, these three experts imparted their knowledge of the ancient, esoteric origins of contemporary Mexican family structure. Not surprisingly, the eldest of the three, Dr. Stith, summoned the ethnographic fascination with the Day of the Dead ("the most significant holiday in Mexico," he told us) as the backdrop for his tale of the immutable Mexican family. We were told of the yearly gathering for the feast of the Day of the Dead, of this Antlantean family comprised of more than five hundred individuals, a conglomeration of all generations deep into the prehistoric past, prior to the Conquest. He located the persistence of highly differentiated gender roles in the archaic and primitive ritual of burying the female's umbilical chord underneath the hearth; the male's outside in the fields. And, although I was hoping for a feminist — or at the very least, a gender-based — interpretation from Karen Karabasz's discussion of gender roles, she instead recounted the Aztec legend of Coatlicue and the fatal sibling rivalry between her daughter, Coyoxauhqui, and son, Huitzilopochtli, the Aztec god of war, for rendering intelligible contemporary sexual power relations within the family. So much for decades of critical research on the Mexican family.

For here once again were echoes of the labyrinthine discourse on Mexican cultural identity rooted in the work of Octavio Paz and Oscar Ramos, whose writings attributed Mexican pathology to the "exploitation of Indian women by Spanish men, thus producing the hybrid Mexican people having an inferiority complex based on the mentality of a conquered people," — views that Miguel Montiel had already in 1970 dismissed as "philosophical and ideological speculations."[43] It is as if the challenges put forth by Chicana/o revisionists had not made a dent on dominant interpretations of the Mexican familia.

Chicano researchers were impelled precisely by the inaccuracy of these types of ahistorical, essentialist speculations. They countered with their own counternarratives, deconstructing the theories and methods of scientific discourse, reinterpreting "negative" cultural values, and ultimately producing new knowledges about la familia. Their most enduring accounts of la familia were guided by an attention to "structure" as the explanatory framework for understanding cultural difference. In other words, rather than attributing the cultural distinctiveness of the Chicano/a familia to Mexican myth, tradition, or influence — as the presenters in San Miguel were apt to do — Chicana and Chicano revisionists sought to explain the familia model of extended kinship households, gender and generational hierarchies, and strong family ideology as a necessary adaptation to racial and economic inequality, as a survival strategy for confronting racism and poverty. In various ways Chicana/o revisionists responded to the culture of poverty discourse.

Writing in 1976, Alvirez and Bean explained "familism" and "the occurrence of extended family patterns" as "an adaptive response to social and physical environment," rather than in terms of "a cultural prescription."[44] And a few years later, Baca Zinn wrote: "Extended Chicano families might also represent a model of adaptation to the lack of support systems available to Chicanos in American society."[45] In an even earlier essay, Baca Zinn also wrote about the ideology of familism in structural terms: "Adherence to strong family ties and to a pattern of familial organization with distinct sex role differentiation has not indicated a mere passive acceptance of tradition. This adherence has afforded protection, security and comfort in the face of the adversities of oppression: it has expressed Chicano cultural identity in a society that destroys cultural distinctions."[46]

Even the rigid sexual hierarchies emanating from the "cult of masculinity" that so engrossed white American and Mexican (non-Chicano) social scientists were uprooted from their biological and genetic underpinnings and recast in structural terms by Chicano/a revisionists such as Baca Zinn:

This oppression may enable us to ask questions which would lead to an understanding of male dominance and aggression of the oppressed as a *calculated* response to hostility, exclusion and racial dominance in a colonized society. It is possible that the aggressive behavior of Chicano males has been both an affirmation of Mexican cultural identity and an expression of dominant society's definition of Mexicans as passive, lazy and indifferent.[47]

Although Chicana and Chicano researchers produced a rich body of literature confirming the heterogeneity of Chicana/o familias or the existence of a variety of family models, ranging from traditional family arrangements to egalitarian conjugal roles, from nuclear to extended family patterns, to differences by region, class immigrant, or native origins, the emphasis on structural explanations fostered an alternative but equally monolithic image of the Chicano family and shaped a defensive posture around Chicano culture. Structuralism had become a new orthodoxy, replacing early "functionalist" arguments that had asserted the pathology of Chicano culture.

Aspects of Chicano familias that had been described as negative in the earlier studies (i.e., male dominance and gender hierarchies) were now reinterpreted as positive. For example, some researchers attempted to nuance the term "machismo" by recuperating its semantic specificity, as in the case of Alvirez and Bean: "An important prescriptive aspect of the machismo role encourages the use of authority within the family in a just and fair manner."[48] And, about the regulation of women within Chicano familias, Mirandé writes: "The daughter's confinement to the home gives rise to a closely knit group of a mother and her daughters."[49]

Yet, informed as it was by this logic of reversal, by the transformation of the negative into the positive, the new orthodoxy of structuralism set into motion an equally myopic logic of valorization: an uncritical celebration of the Chicano familia with a singular focus on only the "positive" aspects of culture. Structuralist interpretations shifted the paradigm in the other extreme and absolved the individual, since anything that was wrong within la familia could now be explained in terms of structure rather than agency. Moreover, the fortress that structuralism constructed around the familia hindered internal criticism of Chicano familia and culture.

Against the Familia Romance

La familia as experienced by some Chicanas was not the reigning symbol of unity and struggle for all Chicana and Chicano activists. There was some apprehension about its masculinism, but its overinvestment in the mythology of family loyalty and solidarity hindered development of a systematic analysis of the underside of familism. Already in 1975, for example, Baca Zinn would identify the masculinist bent in Chicano/a research on the family but stopped short of pinpointing the ways in which its nationalist framework was rooted in male domination and gender hierarchy.[50] Ultimately, it was "the fervor of nationalist ideology guiding the Chicano Movement," as Pat Zavella succinctly observes, that "precluded attempts by Chicana activists to denounce sexism within the Movement or to point out Chicanas' subordination within Chicano families."[51] Not only did the masculinist equation of family with nation inhibit feminist critiques of la familia, but the rigid binaries of "them" versus "us" fostered by Chicano nationalists meant that any insurgent voices within the movement had to be positioned outside the familia romance, on the side of the colonialist enemies of the Chicano nation.

Chicana feminist Ana Nieto-Gómez was among the first writers to have documented the disciplining power of patriarchal nationalism, especially its framing of women's critical voices outside the nation: "Loyalists saw the Chicana feminist movement as an 'anti-family, anti-cultural, anti-man,' and therefore anti-Chicano Movement."[52] In fact, during this early period of "nationalist fervor," the family was often invoked to discipline, exclude, and silence women's oppositional voices, as this condemnation of Chicana feminists underscores: "The familia has always been our strength in our culture. But it seems evident . . . that you [Chicana feminists] are not concerned with the familia, but are influenced by the Anglo woman's movement."[53]

Although the family was hailed as the "spiritual sanctuary" for Chicano culture, even in this early period la familia emerges as an intensely contested terrain. As Dionne Espinoza's research on Chicana Brown Berets so ably demonstrates, early Chicana activists openly contested the contradictions that shaped and constituted their role as women in la familia — as mothers, sisters, aunts, and daughters — reconfiguring Chicano nationalism's one-dimensional representation of a putatively homogeneous familia. In their refusal to separate the struggle for "racial justice and gender justice," Chicana activists, according to Espinoza, "re-defined the family — framed in the movement as the pairing of a man and a woman — as a 'family of sisters,'" and reworked "carnalismo or 'brotherhood,' which referred to the kinship of men in cultural terms, into a kinship of women — that is, sisterhood."[54]

In subsequent years, Chicana writers and visual artists dedicated their creative efforts to cultivating the "collective identity" formulated earlier by Las Adelitas de Aztlan as "la familia de hermanas."[55] Writers like María Helena Viramontes, Sandra Cisneros, Cherríe Moraga, and Gloria Anzaldúa, as Sonia Saldívar-Hull explains, created alternative spaces for women's communities that disrupted "the static notion of a monolithic familia as a refuge from outside racism and class exploitation."[56] Often accused of "betraying" the Chicano nation and "destroying" la familia, visual artists like Judith Baca, according to Catherine Ramirez, reconfigured new forms of identification for Chicanas, a new form of familia "not based on patriarchal kinship, but on solidarity among women."[57] Far from seeking to destroy la familia, "border feminism's rebellion against the sacrifice of women for the sake of family unity" sought to unravel the myth of the familia romance and unsettle its cookie-cutter image.[58]

For it is clear that the one-dimensional image of the Chicano familia romance ignores masculinism and patriarchal privilege, as well as the constructedness of patriarchal kinship and the heterosexual nuclear family. The Chicano familia romance is uncritical of heterosexism and repression of queer sexualities; of intrafamilia violence, incest, pedophilia, rape. The familia romance's mythic image of la familia remains impervious to the "sociological fact" — as real today as it was more than a hundred years ago — of female workers as heads of households, which during the late nineteenth century accounted for 25 percent of "Spanish-surnamed" households in major cities throughout the Southwest.[59]

Many of us fail to see ourselves represented in the nostalgic familia romance of recent Chicano (and Latino) commercial films because they are so saturated with nationalism's hierarchical and masculinist ideology. Those "who sought to look critically at the family, its strengths and weaknesses, its advantages and disadvantages" have often been accused of "betraying" the community (nation), but in reality it is Chicano nationalism's familia that is the "story of betrayal."[60] It is a story of betrayal in large measure because patriarchal nationalism's definition of familia as central to the cultural identity of Chicana/os as a people is based on excluding many from its fold, and because it silences oppositional voices and alternative images of la familia.

Despite the hegemony of nationalist representations in cinema, new critical voices are emerging — voices that provide viewers with powerful screen alternatives to the nostalgic familia romance. Miguel Arteta's *Star Maps* (1997) merits consideration as the counterpoint to Nava's bucolic portrait of la familia, providing a more complicated analysis of familia dynamics within urban settings and under conditions of racism and capitalist domination. The film tells the story of Carlos Amaro's struggle to land a role in Hollywood against the backdrop of a disturbing account of domestic violence perpetrated by a father who has physically, emotionally, and psychically brutalized the family. Carlos's father, Pepe, runs a teenage male prostitution ring whose clientele is the white Hollywood elite. In exchange for his father's contacts in the movie industry, Carlos is coerced into working in the underground economy of child and youth prostitution.

Thus, familial relations as portrayed in this film are far from idyllic, nor is the private sphere of la familia a sanctuary from external forces of racism and class exploitation. Arteta characterizes la familia as the site of multiple forms of violence engendered by patriarchal authority and domination. *Star Maps* dramatizes a range of types of private violence, a pattern of physical, psychic, and emotional brutality inflicted by the father onto his wife and children. For example, the film dramatizes what Yvette Flores-Ortiz terms "the parentification of children," a "dysfunctional pattern in physically abusive Latino families" that "involves saddling children with the responsibilities of the parents."[61] In the film, the daughter María is the symbol of "parentification" insofar as she functions as surrogate mother/wife of the familia, the one responsible for the household and emotional work, the preparation of meals, and the physical care of a mentally ill mother and a mentally challenged brother who dresses like a Mexican masked wrestler and masturbates at the dinner table.

Another disturbing example of the dysfunctional familia is exemplified through the portrayal of the psychic effects of physical and emotional violence on the mother. Attributing her madness/delirium to Pepe's physical, emotional, and sexual terror, the filmmaker provides a scathing critique of patriarchal authority and domination and indicts Latino patriarchy for the crisis within la familia. The mother's mental breakdown takes an extreme form. She is bedridden and helpless, often escaping into a fantasy world of romance with the Mexican film star Cantinflas. Her one lucid moment in the film comes right before she commits suicide, when she advises María: "Don't do what I did. Leave while you can." Even though the mother's suicide offers a pessimistic portrayal of the mother as "victim" rather than "survivor" of patriarchal domination, the film does stress the agency and radicalization of a younger generation of Chicanas as embodied in the daughter, María.

Star Maps ends in a replay of the oedipal scenario, with Carlos beating his father not just for trying to upstage his acting role, but for the years of enduring physical and psychological violence, as illustrated in a carefully crafted flashback sequence. In contrast to a film like *My Family,* where the oedipal drama is resolved in favor of patriarchal authority, *Star Maps* is noteworthy for its disruption of Chicano oedipal structures.

Despite the film's focus on internal familia pathology, *Star Maps* is not a return to the culture of poverty thesis of the pre–Chicano Movement era, to the stereotypic images of the pathological Mexican family prevalent in racist, colonialist discourse that attributed family dysfunction solely to internal (cultural) factors. The filmmaker self-consciously analyzes the intersection of structural and cultural dynamics that contribute to a crisis in the "Latino family structure," dynamics that, as Arturo Aldama so aptly indicates, involve both "external forces (racism, the state, and colonialist consumption patterns) and internal factors (machismo, Americanization, active complicity) which take the longstanding sexist structures and processes of gender socialization to a grotesque extreme."[62] Like other recent films and videos in shorter formats, *Star Maps* provides a much needed counterpoint to the idyllic familia romance so prevalent in mainstream Chicano films.

Another such counterpoint is the short film *Loaves and Fishes* (2001), by the team of writer/actor Amparo Garcia Crow and Austin-based cinematographer/documentarian Nancy Schiesari. Set against the backdrop of the demolition of the forty-year-old San Jose Motel in Austin, Texas, this docudrama tells the story of María Elena, a young, pregnant, single mother of two who cleans the motel owned by her father and stepmother, which serves a clientele of mostly Latino immigrant workers. María Elena provides the narrative voice and perspective of the film. After conveying her father's prejudice against Latino day laborers ("My father would kill me if he knew I had any contact" with them), she develops a friendship with Javier, an immigrant from Chiapas, which seems destined for romance. Every evening, María Elena secretly delivers a plate from the family's supper to Javier, until the stepmother discovers her transgression. The film ends on a tragic note, with a confrontation between María Elena's father and Javier; Javier's subsequent arrest and deportation; and María Elena left alone holding her new-born baby while she laments the loss of Javier.

Besides subverting viewer expectations for a happy and romantic ending, Garcia Crow and Schiesari provide a thoughtful and nuanced meditation on the contradictions within a Chicano familia. Their densely packed narrative, with its layering of political themes like immigration, gentrification, and the intra-ethnic prejudice of Chicanos toward Latino immigrants within a main story line of tragic romance, is thus noteworthy for its efforts to unsettle the cookie-cutter image of Chicano familias. *Loaves and Fishes* is remarkable both for its sympathetic portrayal of a single mother's subjectivity and for its nuanced depiction of her family situation as riddled with contradictions. The father and stepmother provide María Elena and her children with food and shelter, but she is forced to work as the hotel's cleaning woman, despite her visibly advanced stage in pregnancy. And, María Elena is also subjected to an overbearing and mercurial father and a stereotypically sinister and envious stepmother. One memorable scene in the film portrays a family dinner that is far from idyllic: María Elena's disabled son taunts the grandfather, who storms out of the room, while her rebellious teenage daughter calls the stepmother a "bitch."

The short film *Sex Drunk*, by Richard Castaneiro, also delivers a formidable critique of la familia, in this instance by tackling the issue of Chicano masculinity. Most of the action takes place during the by now clichéd Chicano/a intergenerational "familia gathering" (with its much touted mariachis, piñatas, outdoor dining, drinking, and dancing), but the filmmaker focuses on rarely mentioned aspects of familia gatherings — the underside of Chicano fiestas rarely seen on film. Excessive drinking exacerbates familia conflicts and tensions. The young protagonist, Alex, becomes uncontrollably jealous and abuses his young wife during the party. They fight and leave the party. Once at home, the young wife expresses her intent to leave their abusive relationship. In the end, the theme of Chicano masculinity in crisis is emphasized with the final image of Alex alone, reflecting on his violent and obsessive behavior.

Another recent short, *By Her Side*, directed by Ana Rosa Ramos, offers an engaging reflection on woman-to-woman bonds within la familia. The film's emphasis on a separate female sphere of mother and daughter relationship provides a glimpse into the genuine connections of love between a daughter and her mother. However, Ramos's portrayal of their relationship is far from idyllic; rather, it open-heartedly conveys mother-daughter conflicts and codependency, and it candidly interrogates the disappointments and limitations in the Chicano cultural script of "sacrificial motherhood."

The independent film *Luminarias* (1999), directed by José Luis Valenzuela and written by Evelina Fernández, is unrivaled for its reworking of la familia into a kinship of women. Emphasizing Chicana solidarity, interiority, and female-to-female relationships, the film constructs an alternative vision of la familia that dramatizes the bonds among four Chicanas who support each other through the ups and downs of heterosexual romance. Although its primary emphasis is on the romantic lives of urban, middle-class Chicana professionals living in Los Angeles, in significant ways, *Luminarias* extends a gendered perspective on the familia/nation.

In the first place, its narrative rejects the notion of female sacrifice for the sake of family unity through its subplot of Andrea's divorce. Rather than remain with an unfaithful husband, Andrea shuns the distorted view of marriage (i.e., "the family staying together for the kids"), and decides to divorce Joe. *Luminarias* further deconstructs the idealized, romantic image of la familia as a "safe haven" for Chicanas by rendering the theme of gender violence and child abuse through the story of Cindy's custody battle with her batterer-husband.

Counternarratives such as these independent films reveal the extent to which speaking against the familia romance is not about destroying "familia" or being "anti-familia." As a new genre of familia films make evident, deconstructing the familia romance is the first step in an arduous process of constructing meaningful alternatives to la familia's basis in male domination. Alternative films and videos help us to reimagine a new kind of familia, one that is not modeled on patriarchal kinship or based exclusively on heterosexual pairing. There are in fact other models of kinship within Chicano/a culture — models that rework and subvert the power of masculinity and male dominance. "Comadrazgo" is one such alternative.

Based on Catholicism's godparent kinship system, comadrazgo is a female-inflected model of reciprocity or, in the words of Keta Miranda, a "form of feminine Chicana solidarity" encompassing familial as well as political ties of friendship and intimacy.[63] Although largely absent from mainstream images of la familia, for decades comadrazgo has served as a kinship system crucial to women's survival in the absence of males. In light of large numbers of Chicana/Mexicana female-headed households, comadrazgo developed historically as a woman-centered alternative to the patriarchal kinship basis of familia, as a form for appropriating la familia "for women's communities."[64] Like the Chicana Brown Berets, who thirty years ago "recast the concept of 'familia' in constitutively egalitarian and woman-identified terms," a film like *Luminarias* reminds us of the historic basis and relevance of comadrazgo, and thus opens an alternative space for acknowledging the complexity of sentiments and relationships within Chicana/o culture.[65]

CHAPTER FIVE

Familia Matters

As a young girl growing up in South Texas, I remember my fascination with "pachucas." Precursors to today's "homegirls," the pachucas of my youth embodied adolescent rebellion, sexuality, and deviance — an urban toughness and coolness usually associated with masculine behavior. Walking to Catholic school wearing a navy-blue pleated uniform and two-toned Oxfords, I admired their hipster fashion: tight, short skirts and fitted sweaters/blouses, kaleidoscopic makeup and, extravagant beehives. They were my mythic figures, outspoken and confrontational, fighting and smoking cigarettes on street corners and outside tienditas (barrio grocery stores) and thus carving their presence in the public sphere. It was their transgression of gender and sexual norms, their rejection of Mexican American propriety *(buenos modales)*, that rattled my family's middle-class aspirations.

Although in some Chicano familias, mothers warned their daughters about lesbians, mine was more threatened by pachucas: *"por ser muchachas corrientes y callejeras"* (for being cheap, street-roaming girls). Pachucas physically and verbally defended themselves, fighting like their male counterparts, but also, just as importantly, these young women exhibited a mastery over the urban, masculinized territory of the streets. Indeed it is on the streets where pachucas subverted expected gender roles and negotiated a presence for themselves as women in public life. A contested semiotic terrain, the street is often riddled with contradictions, functioning both as a site in which young girls are transformed into "street roamers" (callejeras) from the perspective of Chicana/o parents, but also as a space that engenders new subjectivities for women. By refusing to occupy the gendered place assigned to them within the home, pachucas violated the boundaries of Chicana femininity, transgressing physical and social boundaries and creating a "distinctive style that defied middle-class ethics and expectations."[1] In so doing, pachucas marked the limits of la familia and introduced disorder into its patriarchal project.

In broaching the significance of the pachuca as a subject for feminist oppositional discourse, I found it useful to explore the ways in which feminist theory has dealt with the myth that the public and private spheres are separate, discrete domains. The social division of the private and public spheres into gendered spaces is not restricted to Chicano familias, but is endemic in modern patriarchal societies. Women's subordination within the family is in part premised on the artificial division of the social world into separate realms, but it is also based on the separation of the economic sphere of production from the domestic sphere of reproduction and the "enclaving of childrearing from the rest of social labor."[2] Nancy Fraser's work on contemporary social theory is particularly useful for exploring the creation of social identities within the public sphere. Taking issue with the tendency in feminist scholarship to collapse the entire arena outside the home into the single concept of the "public sphere," Fraser asks us to consider classic capitalist societies as comprised of two levels of interrelated public/private separations: "systems" and "lifeworld spheres." At the level of systems, she underlines the division between the state (public) system and the capitalist economic (private) system of market relations. At the level of lifeworld spheres, Fraser separates the private family sphere from the public sphere, defining the latter as a "space of political opinion formation and participation."[3] In so doing, Fraser takes issue with writers who define the private realm solely in terms of the home or the family. For Fraser, the private realm is more than the domestic sphere since it encompasses both the official economy of paid employment (the private system of market relations) and the family (the private lifeworld sphere). Within this framework, the public sphere would not be considered an "arena of market relations," but is instead constituted by both the state and the public lifeworld sphere, which Fraser characterizes elsewhere as an arena of "discursive relations": The public sphere "designates a theater in modern societies in which political participation is enacted through the medium of talk. It is the space in which citizens deliberate about their common affairs, hence, an institutionalized arena of discursive interaction."[4]

Jean Franco writes about the many contradictory meanings in the term "private," noting that "in classic political thinking, it refers to the feminine space of reproduction as against the masculine space of production . . . to private life as the space of the self as against social space, to private enterprise against the state, domesticity as against action in the world, a household or private space as against the public sphere."[5] These contradictory meanings have a direct bearing on Chicanas' relation to domesticity.

Unlike white middle-class women, Chicanas and other working-class women have historically worked outside (as well as inside) the home, and thus have not simply been confined to the role of housewife. Under modern capitalism, women of color and white working-class women have operated in both levels of the private sphere — in both market relations and the family, as both workers (producers) and mothers/wives (reproducers). Therefore, when I discuss Chicana confinement to domesticity I do not mean women's presence outside the home in the labor force, but rather the regulation of their access to the public sphere of the "streets" and "discursive relations."[6] Because the street is a central space where pachucas "deliberate about their common affairs," it functions as an informal "institutionalized arena of discursive relations."

In the case of Chicanas, domesticity derives from the structure of gender relations in premodern, Catholic Spain, as opposed to the more general case, where women's subordination within the domestic realm originates in the modern division of labor under capitalism. In fact, the "immobility" of middle-class women in Latin American society, their "territoriality," as Jean Franco explains, can be traced directly to Spanish pre-cortesian culture and Catholic hegemony over family structures: "Here we should keep in mind the privatized and inward looking Hispanic house and the fact that the virtual confinement of married women to the home had not only been required by the Church but was also intended to insure the purity of blood that Spanish society had imposed after the war against the Moors."[7] In this respect, the confinement or territoriality of women within the home has been strengthened by the syncretic blend of Catholic orthodoxy around the proper place of women in the social order and the Spanish crown's anxieties around *pureza de sangre* (purity of blood) — prohibitions that resurface in the contemporary era to confront other perceived threats to patriarchal order. In the five hundred years since the Conquest, Spain's anxiety about and fear of racial mixing have reappeared in sublimated form as a concern for girls' and women's safety.

Although there is no denying the very real dangers women face on the streets, the fact that, as Keta Miranda notes, the street is "a setting for intimidation of women, from low-level harassment to assault and rape," most of the violence against women happens inside the home. As an element in the structure of power, the street has been designated as masculine territory, a "zone of occupation by men."[8] Even though there are social allowances granted for women's work outside the home, young Chicanas, as potential wives/mothers, are socialized to view the home in gendered terms as their safe haven.

Given the genealogical status of Catholicism and premodern Spain in women's territoriality and immobility, Chicanas subordination is directly linked to masculinist and racist prohibitions around miscegenation. Masked as a concern for their safety, the confinement of Chicana young women to the home is first and foremost about protecting sexual property and policing sexuality. And this is precisely the masculine familial project that pachucas interrupted and disrupted insofar as they refused to be contained by domesticity or to be limited by the prevailing orthodoxy of appropriate female behavior.

In the cultural politics of Chicano nationalism, pachucos (the male counterpart to pachucas) have been celebrated as Chicano heroes, equals in the struggles against domination and conquest to the likes of Aztec warriors and Mexican revolutionaries such as Cuauhtémoc and Emiliano Zapata. Since the 1960s, Chicano writers and artists have redefined pachucos as "race rebels" in opposition to middle-class Mexican American and white masculinities.[9] One of the principle sites for the proliferation of the image of pachucos as race rebels has been in the sphere of popular culture, especially cinema and theater. "On the eve of the premier of *Zoot Suit,* a play [and film] that features the pachuco as its protagonist," Catherine Ramirez writes, "Luis Valdez declared the pachuco a 'Chicano folk hero' and credited him with giving 'impetus to the Chicano Movement of the 1960s.'"[10]

Until very recently, the pachuca rarely figured as an agent of cultural and political oppositional practices, even within Chicana feminist discourse. There are a few early poetic and literary works by Chicanas that nonetheless acknowledge the significance of pachucas for the creation of alternative, oppositional female identities. For example, Tejana poet and performance artist Carmen Tafolla wrote one of the first movement poems on pachucas in 1975 as part of her "Los Corts" (Five voices). Four

years later, in the poem, "and when I dream dreams," Tafolla conveys the
heartfelt testimony of a young pachuca whose self-reflexive voice
denounces the ways young Chicanas are persecuted and criminalized in
public schools:

> I never graduated to a
> Cafeteria Guard,
> who knows how they were picked
> We thought it had something to do
> with the FBI
> or maybe the principal's office.
> So we got frisked,
> Boys in one line,
> Girls in another,
> twice every day
> entering lunch and leaving
> Check — no knives on boys.
> Check — no dangerous weapons on girls
> (like mirrors,
>   perfume bottles,
>   deodorant bottles,
>   or teased hair.)
> So we wandered the halls
>   cool chuca style
>   "no se sale"
>   and unawares,
>   never knowing
>   other junior highs were never frisked
>   never knowing
>   what the teachers said in the teacher's lounge
>   never knowing we were (s'posed to be)
>   the toughest junior high in town[11]

The novel *Maravilla*, by Laura del Fuego, is another site of pachuca
oppositional femininity. Set in Los Angeles during the 1960s, *Maravilla*
tells the coming-of-age story of Cece, a young member of Las Belltones
East LA girls' gang. Through the voice of a young pachuca, del Fuego
transgresses Chicano Catholic prohibitions around the "sins of the flesh":

According to the Catholic church, there are two categories of sin — venial and
mortal. Venial being less serious of the two, sort of like a misdemeanor, with mortal sin being more like a felony.
I used to lie in bed wondering what category the sin of masturbation fell
into . . . especially after having brought myself to orgasm, with my hand rigid
from applying constant friction to my clitoris. I began to think that, if I only

played with myself and stopped before reaching that little, gratifying explosion, it might be classified as a venial instead of the deadly mortal.[12]

Besides breaking the silences around female sexuality, which are so engrained in traditional Chicano familias, del Fuego deliberately subverts its dominant heterosexual norms, portraying Cece's homosexual desires for another young Chicana: "There was a quick, sarcastic ring to her voice, and she had the greatest tits in the world, which she accented whenever she had the chance. But the reason I fell in love with Gerry wasn't because of her tits but because of her laugh. I loved her laugh, raucous and daring."[13]

During the late 1990s, a new generation of Chicana feminist scholars began to trace the import of pachucas (female zootsuiters) and homegirls (girls' gangs) on the feminine construction of oppositional race and gender identities.[14] Keta Miranda's superb and perceptive ethnography of girl gangs in Oakland, California, examines the ways in which girls in gangs challenge "cultural nationalist concepts of community" by re-creating "forms of feminine Chicana solidarity" through "bonds of friendship," "solidarity," and "mutual trust."[15] Catherine Ramirez, for example, analyzes the role of "pachuca style" and "Chicana style politics" in the formation of alternative national identities.[16] This unprecedented scholarship has unearthed the ways in which pachuca and homegirl identities deliberately challenge sexual and gender norms, transgress gender roles, thwart behaviors and expectations, and defy dominant (Chicana/o and mainstream) boundaries of domesticity and femininity. However, the significance of these identities as symbols of defiant and contestatory femininity has had limited resonance in terms of how pachucas and homegirls are portrayed in popular culture forms like film.

In cinema, images of pachucas and homegirls have tended to emphasize their nonnormative sexuality. For example, in *Zoot Suit* (directed by Luis Valdez, 1981), the mother reacts to her daughter's pachuca dress style by saying, "Pareces puta . . . pachuca" (You look like a whore . . . a pachuca) — an association that I heard repeatedly during my childhood. The pachuca Berta is portrayed as a promiscuous, sexually dangerous female delinquent. The sexual subtext of the film *Colors* (directed by Dennis Hopper, 1988) goes even further in linking the pachuca with excessive sexuality, particularly through the use of the trope of miscegenation in portraying the romance between Luisa, a Chicana character played by the Cuban actress María Conchita Alonzo, and a white police officer, Danny (Sean Penn). In the first part of the film, Luisa appears as the nice, subservient, sexy-but-not-too-promiscuous girl from the barrio. Toward the end of the film, Luisa is transformed into a hypersexualized femme fatale.

In other films, pachuca subjectivity is occulted through a strategy of containment that denies her narrative voice on screen. In the film *American Me* (directed by Edward James Olmos, 1992), for instance, Julie's (Evelina Fernández) identity as a rehabilitated pachuca is rendered intelligible in the domestic space of her bedroom, the only place where we see the insignia (cross tattoo) of her previous membership in a girls' gang. In other words, not until the final montage sequence in the film is her earlier pachuca identity made known to viewers. The film's containment of pachuca subjectivity through the act of hiding the inscribed symbol of pachuca identity on Julie's body betrays the filmmaker's anxieties and fears around the performance of pachuca social identity in the public sphere as well as the extent to which this alternative femininity threatens patriarchal norms.

In 1993 I characterized the erasure of pachuca subjectivity as a "strategy of containment" used in cinematic representation:

Who is this new subject, this Chicana whom Edward James Olmos claims is the heroine of *American Me,* the hope in our barrios? His story ends before hers can begin. In the final close-up shot of a cross tattooed on Julie's hand resides her untold story. It is the history of Chicana membership in gangs that unfolds not on the screen, but in my mind. The final weathered look in Julie's eyes sparks the painful silent memory of the female gang members I have known: Chicanas surviving and resisting la vida dura (the hard life). I often wonder why the story of Julie's oppression and resistance, why the pain of her rape is not up there, on the Hollywood screen, looking at me.[17]

That story of Chicanas surviving la vida dura would appear on screen in 1994. Three decades after Herbert Biberman's *Salt of the Earth* (1954) positioned a Mexican American woman as a central protagonist of history, another white director attempted a similar project. *Mi vida loca* (directed by Alison Anders, 1994) tells the story of young Chicana gang members, homegirls with names like Mousie, Sad Girl, and Whisper, who live in Echo Park, LA. As I have written elsewhere, *Mi vida loca* is a splendid contradiction.[18] The first commercial film to focus entirely on Chicana gang members, *Mi vida loca* faithfully conveys the style, stance, posture, gestures, mannerisms, and speech of so many pachucas-cholas-homegirls I have known throughout the years. Yet its daring and gritty realism is so partial in its one-sided view of la vida loca, or what I prefer to call la vida dura.

Reviews of the film were mixed.[19] Professional film critics criticized *Mi vida loca* on political and ideological grounds, as confirming negative stereotypes of Chicana welfare mothers; reproducing mainstream stereotypes about inner-city gangs; perpetuating nihilism among urban youth; and depicting teenagers without ambition, leading dead-end lives.[20]

I am less concerned with these types of objections: hopelessness and helplessness are in fact pervasive among inner-city youth. Unless we deal directly with the very serious social, economic, and structural problems of the inner city, a positive or uplifting ending to a gang film will make no difference in the lives of young gang members. Even though I too desire the production of films that show Chicanas and Chicanos as characters other than gang members, filmmakers such as Anders cannot be held responsible for the widespread dissemination of these images in popular culture. While it is true that in choosing her subject, Anders took advantage of the 1990s fascination and commodification of the "gangsta style" in mainstream popular culture, *Mi vida loca* is not the usual gangxploitation film.

In fact, *Mi vida loca* is the first Hollywood film to take homegirls seriously, detailing the gangsta life of the Echo Park Locas. At first glance, it seems as though the story is told from a homegirl point of view. The film opens with frames of the iconography of a vibrant barrio. It portrays homegirls who are fiercely independent, struggling as single teenage mothers whose boyfriends or husbands have ended up dead or in prison. In terms of the politics of representation, especially in the context of other portrayals of Chicana homegirls, *Mi vida loca* appears to have all of the essential ingredients.

In the first place, through its exclusive focus on relations among teenage girls, the film enables a Chicana homosocial perspective to emerge for the first time on the big screen. The film begins by telling the story of two childhood friends, Sad Girl and Mousie (Angie Aviles and Seidy Lopez). The girls are lifelong friends whose friendship is momentarily interrupted when they both end up pregnant by the same homeboy, Ernesto (Jacob Vargas). Mousie and Sad Girl's fatal showdown at a vacant barrio lot has a surprise resolution when Ernesto is gunned down by one of his despised customers, a white female druggie. This ironic twist in the plot propels the story in a different direction and opens up a space for narrating a tale of female bonding and collectivity, not just between Sad Girl and Mousie, but among the homegirls in general.

It is Giggles, a veterana just released from prison, who utters the words about female unity that consolidate the homosocial space created in the film. On their trip home after picking up Giggles from prison, the Echo Park Locas stop for a bite to eat. Inside the diner, as the homegirls share news about their lives, an argument about Ernesto erupts between Sad Girl and Mousie. Giggles interrupts them with the following words: "Girls, you don't ever throw down with a homegirl over a guy. Guys come and go. They ain't worth it." From this point on, *Mi vida loca* unfolds as a sisterhood saga, portraying young Chicanas whose lives are marked by camaraderie, affection, struggle, and survival.

The film is shot in a style Anders calls "romantic realism," with camera movement following characters' emotions. The film's cinematographer, Rodrigo García (son of writer Gabriel García Márquez) effectively mixes low-angle close-ups with opalescent and luminous shots. Structurally, the film disrupts conventional narrative coherence. Rather than presenting a single unifying thread, *Mi vida loca* features three interlocking stories, giving the film its episodic quality. One of the minor plots features an epistolary romance between La Blue Eyes and El Duran, who is in prison; another plotline revolves around Ernesto's obsession with a lowrider truck.

The voice-over narration in the film is often self-reflexive, exhibiting a subjective quality; other times the narration is informational and descriptive, further accentuating the film's ethnographic-documentary character. The film's ethnographic-documentary texture derives from its use of six different narrators; the use of multiple narrators, framed by shifting points of view, effectively disrupts spectator identification with a single cinematic position. The film opens with a voice-over representing Sad Girl's point of view, shifts to Mousie's voice, and then Ernesto's voice and point of view — a strategy that enables shifts in viewer's identification from one character to another. Thus in contrast to the single narration, point of view, and/or character identification typical of most mainstream films, *Mi vida loca* constructs multiple positions from which viewers can identify with its narrative reality, positing a collective subjectivity that destabilizes and challenges the individualism usually seen in Chicano gang films. In the end, the film's depiction of subject formation through shifting perspectives enables a space for collective Chicana urban identities often neglected in other films about gangs.

As Keta Miranda's ethnographic study makes evident, *Mi vida loca* succeeded in eliciting meaningful identifications with "real" historical subjects — with actual homegirls who expressed pleasure at seeing "themselves" on the screen and represented with such fidelity.[21] The film's circulation of alternative images of girls in gangs fulfills Chicana desire for representation in the public space of culture and opens up a discursive space in which homegirls may reclaim and affirm their authority as subjects in history and producers of meaning. At the San Francisco Film Festival's screening of the film in 1994, during the question-and-answer session, the following comments by a member of Oakland's Da Crew girls' gang were directed at Anders: "The movie was really down . . . Why didn't you show the girls really throwing down? And why did they throw down over a boy? You know, we wouldn't throw down over a guy."

Even as Chicana gang members welcomed and celebrated their arrival on the screen as subjects of cinematic discourse, they objected forcefully to some of the details in the film's multiple plots. Members of Da Crew took issue with the filmmaker's claims to authenticity or realism, asserting that (1) homegirls don't get pregnant by the same guy because they have more respect than that; (2) a homeboy would not become obsessed over a lowrider truck at the expense of his kids' welfare; and (3) rival gangs fight over turf, never over a car.[22] And, despite the film's feminist politics, its aesthetic and narrative innovations, *Mi vida loca* succumbs in some respects to conventional film antics. Sad Girl's final statement — "Women don't use weapons to prove a point; women use weapons for love" — has the melodramatic flavor of a Mexican soap opera.

In light of these objections it is important to emphasize that three of the film's interlocking stories actually reflect autobiographical experiences from the life of the filmmaker. Herself a victim of unrequited love, Anders transformed a romantic episode in her past into the epistolary affair between La Blue Eyes and El Duran. A short script written by her former boyfriend, Kurt Voss, inspired the lowrider truck segment. And, the subplot in which the two homegirls discover that they both have become pregnant after having intercourse with the same man is adapted from a story that Anders's daughter heard on the streets.

In *Mi vida loca,* Chicana homegirls are portrayed as independent and self-sufficient young women whose survival depends on a bond and camaraderie with their cohorts. For them, the familial contract is not an option; the Chicano family is portrayed as either dysfunctional or nonexistent in their lives. An important point that Anders misses is that although the heteronormative nuclear family may not figure prominently in the lives of these women, alternative forms of family support systems exist in the barrio. The sisterhood so eloquently captured in the film is not created in a vacuum. Often, stories and films about Chicanas fail to recognize how girls' survival in the barrio depends heavily on what Miranda terms the "tradition of *comadrazgo,*" a kinship between younger women and older, compassionate and understanding women who have also resisted and survived la vida dura.[23] For reasons that are unclear, Anders chose to portray Chicana teenagers as self-sufficient, having little interaction with adults. Untold is the story of the elaborate extended family of mothers, grandmothers, and aunts who visit them in jail, bail them out, help deliver, feed, and take care of their babies. At the San Francisco Film Festival's screening of the film, Anders told the audience: "My goal was to humanize people who don't get represented on the screen." And, although Anders misses crucial elements of Chicana homegirl reality, *Mi vida loca* nonetheless serves as an effective vehicle for my discussion of the significance of pachuca/homegirl identity for feminist oppositional discourse, because the film opens up a space for the refashioning of Chicana urban subjectivities.

What is the nature of the space that *Mi Vida Loca* enables? As we know, social identities are both produced and constituted experientially both in the public/private spheres and within and through representational forms. In cultural discourse, the making of identities is also depicted for us artistically through narratives. *Mi Vida Loca* makes visible these discursive processes, especially through the forms of viewership that the film enables and constitutes. As the images on the screen demonstrate, the film challenges the artificial division between the public and private spheres, where men and women are assigned their respective gendered terrains. In the film, the production of Chicana urban identities takes place simultaneously on the "streets" and in the domestic site of the "home," thereby positing the body of the homegirl as a disruption of gender-circumscribed space.

One scene in the film in particular obliterates the public/private split completely: the interior domestic scene in which Giggles organizes the Echo Park Locas. At this meeting, a dozen or so homegirls sit around the living room smoking, drinking beer, and discussing the main issue before them: what should be done with Ernesto's truck. While the Echo Park Locas are meeting in the feminized territory of the home, their male counterparts conduct a meeting on the same issue in the masculinized territory of the streets. Yet, in this instance the home is not linked to women's subordination and containment, but is a space of "discursive interaction." In contrast to the typical portrayal of "home" in Chicano films, in *Mi vida loca* the home functions as the arena where homegirls construct their agency, voice their concerns, and act as citizens in their communities. By organizing the homegirls, Giggles has enabled the emergence of new forms of visibility for women in the public sphere.

Although the homegirls are young, single mothers, they refuse to be confined by, or contained in, domesticity.

In reflecting upon the cultural representations of the Chicana homegirl-chola-pachuca I have underscored the ways in which her body contributes to Chicana feminist discourse, and how her very presence disrupts the patriarchal familia. Pachuca-homegirl-chola invisibility as subject in Chicano cultural representations, the discursive emphasis on her otherness, is rooted in how her image symbolically threatens the Chicano "family romance." Her comportment registers the outer boundaries of Chicana femininity; her body marks the limits of la familia; her masquerade accentuates her deviance from the culture's normative domestic place for women. And perhaps, pachuca-homegirl-chola agency has not been exalted by those who venerate the pachuco because her body defies, provokes, and challenges as much as it interrogates the traditional familial basis of the Chicano nation.

CHAPTER SIX

"Fantasy Heritage"

Tracking Latina Bloodlines

Carey McWilliams first coined the term "fantasy heritage" during the 1940s in his trenchant deconstruction of the Mission myth.[1] Most often attributed to Helen Hunt Jackson's *Ramona* (1884), the Mission myth entailed reinventing a romantic Spanish history for California—a fictionalized past exploited by Los Angeles "Boosters" bent on transforming the region into the cultural and economic capital of the West.[2] "Discovered as a tourist promotion in the 1880s," McWilliams writes, "the Spanish mission background in Southern California was inflated to mythical proportions."[3] "Fantasy heritage" named the selective appropriation of historical fact, the transformation of selected elements of history (e.g., the economic system of missions and haciendas) into a romantic, idyllic past that repressed the history of race and class relations in the region. "Any intimation of the brutality inherent in the forced labor system of the missions and haciendas, not to speak of the racial terrorism and lynching that made early Anglo-ruled Los Angeles the most violent town in the West during the 1860s and 1870s, was suppressed."[4]

It seems fitting that McWilliams would coin the term "fantasy heritage" in the context of Los Angeles' Mission Revivalism. After all, Los Angeles (or in the words of Mike Davis, its "alter-ego, Hollywood") is the palisade of the fantasy dream machine: cinema. As several film adaptations of *Ramona* and dozens of films about the so-called Spanish pastoral era so forcefully illustrate, cinema played a key role in reworking California history in the popular imaginary, thereby helping to construct a fantasy heritage for the region.

An early example of fantasy heritage in the making is found in the film *Fiesta de Santa Barbara* (1935). Documenting the enduring legacy of "supremacist pseudo-history" in official public culture, the film depicts the annual "fiesta" or tribute to the "Spanish" (as opposed to "Mexican") ancestry of the city, with a cast of characters, including Hollywood actors and a mostly white Santa Barbara elite, living the "imagined knightly lifestyles of the dons," riding Palominos alongside mantilla-draped doncellas.[5]

As this discussion makes evident, the "fantasy" in my title does not refer to psychoanalysis, or the notion of fantasy as a psychic process, even though I will argue that fantasy is "directly involved in the constitution of a subject's identity," much as it is in its psychoanalytic inflection.[6] Fantasy, as McWilliams deploys the term, is opposed to reality, and like the imagination, represents the other of reason and rationality.

McWilliams was part of the realist generation who subscribed to a cult of science grounded in the principles of empirical observation.[7] For McWilliams, fantasy heritage undermined the "reinforcement of factuality" that served as modernity's ground for "reality" or "truth."[8] The memories of "Spanish" racial purity were not "truth" but an illusion; not observable, but based on an "unbridled fantasy" of racial mastery.[9] Thus, there is a liberatory politics to McWilliams's deconstruction of fantasy heritage, especially in his reaffirmation of subaltern identities and submerged histories in California — a project that would later inspire nationalists of the Chicano Movement in their disavowal of (white) Spanish heritage and recovery of indigenous and mestizo racial identities for the formation of the nation.

I am interested in the concept of fantasy because I too want to appropriate it for twenty-first century cultural analysis and use it as a pretext for exploring my own ambivalence toward the "cultural opposition between illusion and reality."[10] I say "ambivalence" because although I reject the fundamental mistrust of fantasy and the imagination expressed by the investment in positivism on the part of modernist thinkers such as McWilliams, I understand the politics and ideology behind their suspicion. After all, "fantasy" in the service of the powerful (forces of domination) means one thing; in the service of the subjugated, quite another. McWilliams's penetrating study deals fundamentally with this problematic, detailing the ways in which fantasy heritage represented the phantasmagoric convergence of racial, economic, and cultural domination in the region.[11]

I also find the fantasy heritage concept to be useful for interrogating the construction of Chicana/o and Latino/a film history. One of the primary aims of Latino/a film historiography has been to deconstruct the exclusionary practices of mainstream (Eurocentric) film history. In the process, Latino historiography has unearthed a detailed account of Latina and Latino involvement in the Hollywood industry. Yet, to a certain degree, Latino revisionist historiography is also implicated in the construction of its own fantasy heritage. The meaning of "Latina bloodlines" in the title of this chapter takes me deeper into the problem at hand.

I deliberately chose to use the term "bloodlines" in my title in order to draw attention to the contradictions plaguing my initial desire to undertake a "genealogy," in Foucaldian terms. For Foucault, genealogy is a historical method that gives voice to marginal and submerged people in their resistance to the forces of power and domination. In the process of retrieving and resurrecting "subjugated knowledges," the practice of genealogy alerts us to alternative accounts of the resistances, struggles, and conflicts that in fact constitute history. Genealogy is a method reflected in the scholarly practices of feminist, multicultural, queer, and postcolonial historiographers and researchers.[12] Although I initially considered my project to be informed by this notion of genealogy as retrieval of "subjugated knowledges," in the course of my study, I came to realize that my understanding of the term was contaminated by a very literal and archaic notion of genealogy as bloodlines, or descent from a family pedigree. An example from my initial focus on Latinas in the movie industry will serve to illustrate my point.

I first read about Myrtle González and Beatriz Michelena in Antonio Ríos-Bustamante's essay, "Latino Participation in the Hollywood Film Industry." I was driven and inspired by his ebullient descriptions of early silent film stars. About Myrtle González, the first Mexican American film star, Ríos-Bustamante writes: "In marked contrast to the experience of later Latinas who used their own names, González portrayed vigorous outdoor heroines"; about the Latina diva from San Francisco, Beatriz Michelena, he tells us: "Motion Picture World featured her picture on its cover with the caption, 'Beatriz Michelena, Greatest and Most Beautiful Artist Now Appearing in Motion Pictures.'"[13] Prior to this reference by Ríos-Bustamante, I had never heard of Myrtle González or Beatriz Michelena. It was their erasure from mainstream film historiography that initially animated my own desire to track their imprint on the public sphere of culture.

The daughter of a native Californio family of grocers in Los Angeles, Myrtle González was a talented child soprano who sang in local church choirs and performed in theaters throughout the city. In 1911, González debuted in the film *Ghosts* and later starred in more than forty films for Universal and Vitagraph Studios, delivering a highly acclaimed performance in the film *The Chalice of Courage* (1915). However, González's stardom would be short-lived. After six years in motion pictures, she died of heart failure, attributed to a "severe fall suffered three years [earlier] while doing 'stunt' riding in a photoplay."[14] González was twenty-seven years old when she died. Married to Universal Studios director Allen Watt, she was survived by a son from a previous marriage. I was so surprised to learn that Myrtle González was the first bona fide Mexican American movie star and by the fact that she played against type. Yet she remained absent from mainstream film history.

The *San Francisco Chronicle* embraced the second star in my study, Beatriz Michelena (figure 7), as a "native, California prima donna." And her preeminent stature in the performing arts extended well beyond California. In 1914 she was featured on the cover of the premier theatrical newspaper of the time (1878–1921), *The Dramatic Mirror.* The daughter of Venezuelan-born Fernando Michelena, Beatriz inherited her father's musical talents, initiating her stardom as a soprano in opera and stage musical comedy in the early 1910s. In 1913, she met and married George Middleton, a member of the San Francisco elite whose wealth derived from interests in the railroad and the motor car industries. Middleton was also executive producer of the California Motion Picture Corporation, an independent studio based in San Francisco with studios in Marin County (years before the movie industry became concentrated in Hollywood).[15]

Michelena's career in cinema was launched with Middleton's production of Bret Harte's best-selling novel, *Salomy Jane* (1914). In the years she worked with the CMPC, she starred as lead in sixteen of their feature-length productions. Unlike many of the early screen stars, Michelena was able to exercise considerable control over the production process, shaping her career by making the "final decision in choice of stories and cast," as well as in the allocation of funds for sets, wardrobe, and locations, largely because of her marriage to Middleton.[16] After a dispute over back wages with the financially strapped owners, she eventually became the company's executive producer and co-owner when CMPC ownership was transferred to Michelena and her husband.

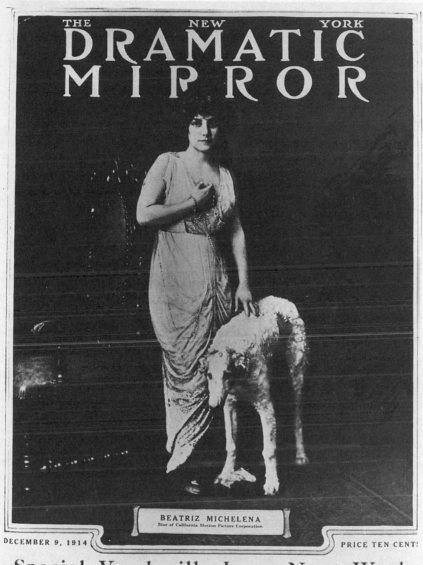

FIGURE 7. Beatriz Michelena. *The Golden Gate and the Silver Screen,* Collection of Geoffrey Bell. Courtesy of the Academy of Motion Picture Arts and Sciences.

What most appealed to me about Beatriz Michelena was her coupling of artistic talent with entrepreneurship. Here was the Latina equivalent of Mary Pickford: a screen and stage performer/star and businesswoman. In the late 1910s, Michelena contributed to the city's unsuccessful campaign to establish the San Francisco Bay Area as the movie production center, working closely with city officials and offering her studios in San Rafael free of charge.[17] Although her work on screen ended in 1920, Michelena's public stature as operatic star and "internationally known prima donna" continued to be the subject of media attention. In 1927, she introduced the operas *Carmen* and *Madame Butterfly* in Latin America, traveling with a company of thirty singers and dancers in a tour that the *San Francisco Chronicle* characterized as "the first invasion of those countries by an American operatic star in repertoire performances."[18]

If I left the story here, I would certainly be constructing a genealogy in terms of bloodlines, that is to say, unearthing the histories of Latina stars on the basis of their descent from the family of the Latin race. Just as significant, I would be furthering the making of yet another fantasy heritage. And here I would like to give the meaning of fantasy heritage a different inflection, one that goes beyond the modernist "cultural opposition between illusion and reality," to talk about fantasy heritage as the process of historical recovery that glosses over contradictions, struggles, and conflicts.

As we know, the recovery of new objects of knowledge is the first phase in the formation of such disciplines as women's/gender studies, Chicano/a and Afro-American studies, and queer studies. But twenty years after the formation of Chicana/o studies, it seems necessary to go beyond the celebration of "Latino participation in the Hollywood industry," for this kind of Chicano/Latino historiography is based on an essentialist notion of identity, one that considers ethnicity/race to be the guarantee and ultimately the origin of an oppositional politics. It is not enough to simply enumerate a litany of Chicano and Latino names and faces without specifying the nature, ideology, and politics of their very involvement in the imperially, sexually, and racially charged agenda of the movie industry. I object to a historiography centered on celebratory claims about Latinos in Hollywood because in the end it can lead to the invention of a new myth: a nationalist fantasy heritage.

I too would be constructing a "fantasy heritage" if I simply focused on the participation of Myrtle González and Beatriz Michelena in motion pictures without confronting the nature of their relationship to the industry. What did their presence on the silver screen symbolize? Did their

FIGURE 8. Colonialist romance: Myrtle González (far left) in
one of several films in which she crossed the color line. From the
collection of Paul Ballard.

latina-ness matter? Did it disturb the supremacist pseudohistory unfolding as the dominant primal myth of California? Did their bodies "symbolize the nexus of gender and race," as Hershfield writes about Dolores
del Rio?[19] Did González and Michelena tap into the nation's growing
anxieties around race? Or its shifting imagination of racialized sexuality?

It seems clear from the roles González and Michelena played that both
"were more easily able to move in and out of ethnic roles" because they
were light-skinned.[20] In fact, unlike most of the actors coded as nonwhite
(i.e., Latinos/as, Asians, and blacks), both women mostly portrayed
white characters, thus crossing the color line (figure 8). And, although

from today's perspective González and Michelena appear to us as racial-ized ("Latinas"/"Mexicanas"), the biographical sketching of their ances-try as "Spanish" meant that, in the early twentieth century, neither was coded as "nonwhite."[21] For example, González's obituary in the *Los Angeles Times* states the following: "A writer in a Tokio *[sic]* magazine once called her 'The Virgin White Lily of the Screen,' and that was the tribute she most prized of the hundreds she received during her career."[22] Which explains why, at the height of the eugenics movement, both women were able to evade restrictions around interracial marriage and procreation. Michelena married a wealthy white man; González was married twice to white men.

When we examine the films they starred in and the white characters that these "white" Latinas played, the limits of genealogy as bloodline become even more transparent.[23] The two films I screened at the Library of Congress starring Myrtle González were colonialist adventure films, with González portraying white women who cross the border of "civi-lization" into the unknown terrain of wilderness or "barbarie." For exam-ple, in *A Natural Man* (1915), González plays Rose, a modern young woman who, "tired of social hypocrisy" in the city, decides to visit her uncle's ranch in the country, only to be kidnapped by a young boy called the "wild child." The dichotomy between the modern and the primitive is also the theme in *The Showdown* (1917), where González portrays a mod-ern white woman named Lydia Benson, who as the film opens is reading the book, *Back to the Primitive*. Later, in one of those mysterious leaps in plot typical of early films, Lydia is marooned on a Pacific island with her dog and an escaped African slave.

Although the entire collection of the California Motion Picture Corporation's master prints and negatives was destroyed in a vault fire, two of Michelena's films survive. I managed to screen *Just Squaw* (1919) at the LOC and found its colonialist overtones to be even more pro-nounced than those in González's films. Michelena plays "Fawn," a love-stricken Indian described as "just a half-breed squaw" by another charac-ter. The object of Fawn's love is a "white stranger" whom she refuses to marry because it would violate social prohibitions around miscegenation: "No, you're white. I'm Indian," she tells him. In the end, Fawn's unspar-ing abnegation is duly rewarded with the discovery of her true identity as biologically white. As a child, the Indian woman who Fawn believed to be her mother had kidnapped Fawn from her parents. In addition to reproducing dominant social taboos around interracial marriage and blood quantum definitions of race, *Just Squaw* ends by reinscribing the ideology of white supremacy. The final scene, in which Fawn discovers that she's white, ends with a shot of other characters looking up at Fawn, then by a close-up of an angelic Fawn, smiling ecstatically. This framing of Fawn as "saint" or "virgin," enshrouded in a luminous whiteness, underscores the extent to which *Just Squaw* deliberately conjures up the association of whiteness with goodness and purity — the hallmark of white supremacist ideology.

My screenings of Latina representations at the LOC were, to say the least, disappointing. And I recount my distress surrounding the roles that these Latina stars portrayed in order to emphasize that the project of historical rediscovery is myopic if it fails to recognize the politics of representation that these Latina predecessors embodied.

In many ways, Latino/a film historiography has appropriately disrupted the Eurocentric bias of mainstream film history, unearthing the hidden presence of Latinos/as in the movie industry since the early days of cinema, as actors, directors, cinematographers, technicians, musicians, and so forth. As part of its corrective to dominant film history, the discourse of Latino studies has celebrated both Myrtle González and Beatriz Michelena for their pioneering roles, for playing leading and "diverse roles." Both women are praised for not conforming to the early-twentieth-century cult of femininity and domesticity through their portrayals of "vigorous outdoor heroines," adventurous women who excelled in the male-dominated activities of horseback riding and fighting.[24] Yet, as I have noted, the project of Latino/a historical recovery has not attended as vigorously to the ways in which Latina actors like González and Michelena were in fact complicitous with the racial ideology of the time, especially the dominant racist colonialism of early cinema. So what would an alternative Latina genealogy look like? I turn now to my story of the "Queen of the Bs."

She was known as the "Mexican Spitfire," but also as "Whoopee Lupee," "Hot Tamale," and "Tropical Hurricane." She is often dismissed for embodying the "negative" extreme of Mexican femininity: hot-blooded, volatile, sexually promiscuous — the "tragic prototype of the Latina Spitfire stereotype," according to Ríos-Bustamante.[25] Born María Guadalupe Villalobos in San Luis Potosí, Mexico, Lupe Vélez started performing in musical comedies in Mexico City during the 1920s. In 1926, at the age of seventeen, she left for California, joining three thousand Mexicans with dreams of making it in Hollywood. Initially playing minor parts in two-reel shorts, Vélez had her big break the following year, when she co-starred with Douglas Fairbanks in the silent feature *Gaucho*

(1927). During the span of her seventeen-year career, Lupe Vélez was one of a handful of actresses who excelled both on the screen and in Broadway musicals. By the time she died, at age thirty-five, Lupe Vélez had starred in forty-five feature films, working in Hollywood, London, and Mexico, though she is best known for her title roles in screwball comedy, the eight feature films known as the Mexican Spitfire series.

One way of studying Lupe Vélez would be to focus on her otherness — her racialized, gendered star persona within the Hollywood industry, which stands in relation to the dominant racial and gender ideology in the United States. Although I recognize this as an important task, my genealogy of Lupe Vélez takes a more circuitous route, one that examines the meaning of her embodied otherness (public persona and star text) as a metaphor for shifting, contradictory, and ambiguous social identities.

In her own time, Vélez's most rancorous critics often positioned her in that shifting social identity of Mexican-ness that today one would characterize as Chicana. At the time, critics in Mexico often measured Vélez against another exotic Mexican star in Hollywood of the period, the "sedate and lady-like" Dolores del Rio, who was "carefully crafted" by the industry as a "high class ethnic woman of impeccable morals."[26] They vilified Lupe Vélez as a "commoner" (populachera), "vulgar and unmannerly" (una chica incorrigiblemente vulgar) or, as one Mexican critic would write, Vélez had "traces we notice solely in lower class people, without culture, nor ideals, nor patriotism."[27]

These attitudes echo those of the Mexican elite toward the poor workers leaving Mexico for el norte. Like her Mexican compatriots working and living in the United States, Vélez was denounced as "agringada" and "apochada" (anglicized and assimilated), for "disowning her country" — in sum, for being a pocha/Chicana.[28] To a great extent, the construction by the Mexican national elite of Vélez's identity as pocha/Chicana reveals the degree to which her public persona evoked anxieties about the solidity and stability of Mexican national identity during the 1930s. Emerging from decades of social upheavals, postrevolutionary Mexico had embarked on a comprehensive social, political, and cultural project for unifying the nation and defining its "Mexicanidad," or national identity — a unity threatened by the ever-growing exodus of its citizens to the United States. Even though the Mexican diaspora — nearly one-tenth of Mexico's population migrated to the United States between 1910 and 1930, among them Lupe — disrupted Mexican nationalism's imaginary unity, there are also ways in which her otherness raised anxieties about the shifting and contradictory nature of Mexican femininity.[29]

Gabriel Ramírez characterizes her as a "flapper Azteca," an Aztec flapper of Mexico City's "roaring 1920s." In 1925, at age sixteen, Lupe Vélez bobbed her hair and donned the flapper style, becoming an instant hit with her debut performance of the Charleston at the Teatro Principal.[30] She was part of modernity's revolution in lifestyle in Mexico City, of the modern, "refreshing," "vigorous," new manners and morals that topped the "musty and frivolous European conservativism" dominant in early twentieth-century Mexico.[31] Influenced by jazz, the Charleston, and Hollywood movies, Lupe Vélez was very much a "modern, new woman" of Mexico City, expressing the "new visibility of the erotic in popular culture" through her performances, fashion, and lifestyle.[32] A liberated woman of the twenties, Vélez followed in the footsteps of her mother, who had been an opera singer and her most "enthusiastic" and "unconditional" champion.[33] And when her father prohibited the use of his family name for public performances, she adopted her mother's maiden name, "Vélez." Independent and undomesticated, she embodied the new sexual liberalism, the new erotic impulse that surged into the public realm during the 1920s, challenging the existing framework of strict gender roles and providing a new model for Mexican femininity.

At seventeen, Lupe Vélez left Mexico for the United States, where she entered the "youth-centered world" in full swing during the 1920s. She encountered the "new freedoms that post-suffrage women seemed to possess," as well as the new autonomy and mobility of U.S. youth.[34] Arriving in the winter of 1926, unemployed and with a few dollars in her pocket, she would later recall this early resolve: "I was determined to make money and defend myself, because the woman who wants to, doesn't need anyone to defend her."[35]

As Vélez's career flourished, she was adored by fans in the United States and Mexico alike. Mexican critics, in sharp contrast, were threatened by her subversive form of femininity and decried her negative influence on young Mexican women.[36] Her subversion of traditional notions of femininity — especially her newfound sexual freedom — probably also scandalized the parents of a new generation of Mexican American youth. After all, Lupe Vélez openly advocated sex beyond the confines of marriage. In a 1929 article, also translated into Spanish, the columnist Virginia Lane reports: "Lupe can love five men at the same time, with incredible ease, and love them all for five different reasons" — a statement sure to scandalize Catholic Mexican sensibilities.[37]

By 1930, there were "150,000 people of Mexican birth or heritage" residing in Los Angeles. And like adolescents elsewhere, Mexican

American teenagers "moved in a youth-centered world" and embraced "the revolution in manners and morals" sweeping the country.[38] In many ways, the social and cultural transformations that were ushered in by the new ethic of capitalist consumerism shook the foundations of Mexican "familial oligarchy," especially its "ideology of control."[39]

Indeed, Los Angeles, the home of Hollywood and Lupe Vélez, was ground zero of the losing battle to discipline and regulate new expressions of sexuality and economic independence among Mexican American youth. They "bobbed their hair like flappers of the screen."[40] "They moved out of their family home and into apartments. . . . They could go out with men unsupervised as was the practice among their Anglo peers."[41] They copied the "models made stylish by movie stars and actresses."[42] And, finally, as Vicki Ruiz observes about these young women of the 1930s: "Sparked by manufactured fantasies and clinging to youthful hopes, many Mexican women teenagers avidly read celebrity gossip columns, attended Saturday matinees, cruised Hollywood and Vine, and nurtured their visions of stardom."[43] The favorite actresses among thirty-seven Mexican teenagers living in a settlement house in 1929 included Greta Garbo, Dolores del Rio, Mary Pickford, Clara Bow, and Lupe Vélez.[44]

In Lupe Vélez, Mexican American young women found alternatives to a femininity circumscribed by marriage and masculine authority: "I've always been afraid of marriage," Vélez explained in 1934. "It seems to me like being imprisoned in an iron cage . . . I do not tolerate anyone telling me what I can and cannot do."[45] Vélez was also a model for female independence and autonomy: "Do you want to know Lupe, the real Lupe? I love freedom. I want to be free to sing and dance always and when I so desire."[46] And through her public persona and movie characters, Lupe Vélez portrayed strong women who were active agents in public spaces both as career women and as players in romance and courtship. In this manner, she provided young women with an alternative model of female behavior and identity. Although she more often symbolized the "new visibility of the erotic," especially the exotic blend of race and sex so stylish in the 1920s, in other ways Lupe Vélez's image worked to undermine the gendered framework of female identity tied exclusively to motherhood. "I have only one solution for whatever difficulties I encounter . . . work, work, work, and more work . . . My father and mother taught me and my two sisters to work since we were very young. My two sisters are singers and at the age of 15, I was already dancing professionally."[47] The photograph of Vélez holding a pair of turtles she named "Lupe" and "Gary" (for

FIGURE 9. Lupe Vélez holding a pair of turtles named "Lupe" and "Gary" (circa 1930). Courtesy of the Academy of Motion Picture Arts and Sciences.

Gary Cooper) is a prime example of her trendsetting nature and of the persona of the modern "new" woman which she cultivated. Vélez is credited with starting the Hollywood fad (circa 1930) of collecting shelled reptiles (figure 9).

This model of a modern "new woman" is not the dominant image of Mexican femininity lodged in cultural memory; it is not the image of Mexican female identity that circulated in public discourses, either in Mexico, where the dominant feminine ideal was calcified in self-sacrificing motherhood, or in the United States, with its colonialist investment in an image of premodern Mexican primitivism. In the embrace of sexual liberalism, financial independence, and personal meaning derived from something other than motherhood, Lupe Vélez subverted the prevailing gendered framework and rejected dominant tropes associated with Mexican femininity, especially the ideal of motherhood and passivity made visible in the rebozo-draped Mexicana of Hollywood films. This is not, I should note, the dominant narrative one hears about Lupe Vélez, who is more often maligned in Latino historiography for perpetuating a negative stereotype of Latina identity.[48]

What I find most curious (and unfortunate) about the legacy of Lupe Vélez as "the Mexican Spitfire" is the confusion that exists between the characters she portrayed and her public persona. Vélez's visibility within the star system was predicated on an identity that she herself cultivated, as a woman who was "uninhibited," "unpretentious" and "frank," "extravagant" and "unconventional" — a woman who broke with all social conventions. Often this visibility was interpreted differently within Hollywood circles, where she was known for being "impetuous," for her "irreverence" and "heavy-handed pranks," for "a very rich repertoire of bad words," for a "difficult and aggressive personality."

The confusion between Vélez's persona and her characters is nowhere more evident than in the way the term "Mexican Spitfire" is used in Latino historiography today. Initially associated with Lupe's comedic performance in cinema, the term is now interpreted as an insignia for all that masculinist discourse judges as "negative" about Vélez's public persona, as synonymous for the "sexually alluring and available . . . fallen [Latin] woman."[49] In the process, Vélez's talent as a performer — actor, comedian, and dancer, on stage and screen — is erased.

I owe my interest in Lupe Vélez in part to historian Tatcho Mindiola, who characterized Vélez as a "predecessor to Lucille Ball."[50] I now consider Lupe Vélez to be the Chicana Queen of the Bs. She is rarely considered as important as Katharine Hepburn or Irene Dunne, but she was one of the most accomplished and popular screwball comedians of the time.[51]

The 1940s was a contradictory period for Mexican Americans in Hollywood: the growing economic crisis in the industry was exacerbating the anti-immigrant xenophobia already under way in the country; then there was the backlash against the sexual liberalism of the 1920s, resulting in a return to gender conservatism, while the introduction of the industry's Production (sex and racial) Codes redefined the limits of the "cinematic melting pot," tying restrictions around interracial liaisons to "skin color."[52] In fact, a few years earlier, the dark-skinned Vélez had been explicitly singled out in the media's anti-immigrant campaigns in defense of "U.S.-born" workers during the Great Depression, as this commentator makes evident: "It is time for [Lupe Vélez] and her foreign accent to disappear so that our own American actresses can occupy the space that corresponds to them."[53]

Within this unsettling wartime context, the character Lupe Vélez portrayed in the Mexican Spitfire series seemed to violate all the norms. Carmelita Fuentes, the "spitfire" in the eight films directed by Leslie Goodwins for RKO Studios, was a "new woman" who, though married, maintained her career as a singer and dancer. In spite of Hollywood's unofficial policy imposing limits on the depiction of interracial marriage, Carmelita married a white advertising executive she met in Mexico and later moved with him to an upscale apartment in Manhattan — a characterization that inspired the Mexican critic Emilio García Riera to dub Carmelita as a "high-class" Chicana. As he explains: "For once, a Mexican woman is removed from the haciendas, churches, cantinas and cactuses, dressed in fashionable, cosmopolitan clothing, and situated in the most worldly of U.S. urban settings: New York."[54]

The first few films in the series were extremely successful, rekindling Vélez's popularity among U.S. audiences. *The Mexican Spitfire*, released in 1939, played for three weeks to sold-out crowds at the Rialto in New York. And in Mexico, *The Girl from Mexico* (1939) received high praise from some critics, who described it as a "great comedy," "an hour of nonstop laughter," and Lupe as a "great actress" and dancer.[55]

Undoubtedly, the plots of the Mexican Spitfire series were simpleminded and formulaic, exploiting, for comedic effect, the deliberate malapropisms and "foreign-ness" in her overblown accent, along with her racialized gender. Throughout her career, Vélez starred mostly in B movies; however, as Ruby Rich reminded me, the revival of B movies as the "true American cinema" during the 1970s makes her contributions as an actress of the forties even more significant today. And while in Latin American her status as a star reached mythic proportions, Vélez was marginalized within the Hollywood star system.[56] Yet, despite failing in her aspirations to play the dramatic roles that she believed would launch her into the realm of "true" stardom, Vélez was always highly regarded as a performer, receiving mostly favorable reviews throughout her career, especially for her comedic performances in film, Broadway musicals, and interestingly, her irreverent camp impersonations of female stars like Katharine Hepburn, Shirley Temple, Gloria Swanson, Dolores del Rio, and Marlene Dietrich.

At the Library of Congress I was able to screen Vélez's last U.S. film, *Redhead from Manhattan* (1943), a wartime musical combining the prosaic theme of patriotism with a favorable stance on immigrants from south of the border — a perspective undoubtedly influenced by the Good Neighbor Policy's marketing strategies in Latin America. In *Redhead from Manhattan* Vélez performs multiple roles, including Rita, an immigrant from Latin America who has recently arrived illegally, as a stowaway; Rita's cousin, Maria, a star in Broadway musicals who attempts to keep her marriage (and pregnancy) a secret from her manager; and Mandy Lou, a black maid. I was disappointed by Vélez's use of the degrading tradition of "blackface" for impersonating Mandy Lou, especially since Vélez had also been the object of anti-immigrant racism. I wondered how a Mexicana living in California during the height of anti-Mexican xenophobia could uncritically adopt the racist codes of blackface performance.

The plot revolves around Rita's dreams of becoming a star: "In New York I shall be a new discovery. I shall be a great star like Carmen Miranda" — a desire fulfilled when Rita is convinced by her cousin, Maria, to take her place on stage. To the tune of "Somewhere South of Here," Vélez displays her superb talents in camp performance, dancing in front of a chorus line, dressed excessively "ethnic" in tricolor rebozo halters, wearing an outrageous wide-rim hat topped with large antennaed bumblebees — an obvious parody of Carmen Miranda. As Rita, Vélez is able to occupy the place of Carmen Miranda momentarily, intentionally mobilizing a "hyper-latinidad" in her histrionic performance of Carmen Miranda, which in many respects parodies not only the Hollywood success of the "Brazilian bombshell" but also Vélez's own desire for stardom, at any price. *Redhead from Manhattan* was, after all, the final film she made in Hollywood before her death.

In exploring the meaning of Lupe Vélez's embodied otherness as startext, I came to realize that this "excess" — her penchant for over-the-top, histrionic impersonations and camp performances — has often been misinterpreted as literal embodiments of Latina otherness, in other words, a "stereotype," particularly by a later generation of Latino film historians. The politics of Latino and Chicano historiography has been unable (or unwilling) to appreciate the subversive humor of Vélez's performances. Vélez is often compared with the other great Mexicana star of the period, Dolores del Rio, who, although often idealized for being sedate and "aristocratic," seems trapped in her own seriousness. Vélez, by contrast, was deliberately transgressive, deploying her own image to comment on her position within the industry.

It is thus not surprising that Lupe Vélez has been reclaimed in the world of video art, for one of the basic elements of the genre is appropriation as well as the refashioning of a space of camp performance and excess. In the recent experimental video *The Assumption of Lupe Vélez* (1999), Rita González examines the "cult of Lupe Vélez" by juxtaposing scenes from two underground films of the 1960s, *Lupe* (directed by Andy Warhol, 1965) and *Lupe* (directed by Jose Rodríguez-Soltero, 1966), with footage from a performance by "La Lupe" (Bianco Arellano), a Latino drag queen in Echo Park (Los Angeles) who "customizes her/his glamour according to the cult of Vélez," according to González's publicity flyer.

González's video is a poetic memorial to Vélez's transgressive performances, one that opens up a space for the multiple meanings in the word "assumption" — as "adoption" and "appropriation," but also as the "Assumption (to heaven) of the Virgin Mary" — and in the process enshrines her significance in queer performance and avant-garde filmmaking. As Ramon Garcia explains: "The 'assumption' in the title of the piece refers to Lupe Vélez's iconographic status as 'saint' or 'martyr' in a queer hagiography in which movie stars and their drag queen impersonators occupy the Catholic narrative of saint's lives."[57]

The Assumption of Lupe Vélez is itself framed by experimental visual and (non)narrative techniques, yet within its experimental mode, González manages to convey a legibly nuanced message about the cultural impact of Vélez beyond the historical context in which the star lived. González meditates on the reconstruction of Vélez as "legend of saintly proportions, as Evita Perón or Selena for queer counter-cultural community," inspiring such avant-garde artists as Andy Warhol, Kenneth Anger, and Jose Rodríguez-Soltero.[58] Throughout the video González strategically summons the haunting presence of Lupe Vélez, mainly through visually blurred, surreal images, accompanied by the tormented voice of Mexican experimental artist Ximena Cuevas, who as Vélez comments on her own exploitation by Hollywood and reads excerpts from her own obituary (written by Heda Hopper).

It was "La Lupe's" camp performances in *The Assumption of Lupe Vélez* that led me on the search for other excesses in the public persona of Lupe Vélez, for transgressions beyond the sexual liberalism and female autonomy I mentioned earlier. I found evidence of what Yvonne Yarbro-Bejarano calls "queer quotes or traces," beginning with the fact that as a child, Vélez played with boys because girls considered her to be too rough.[59] "I used to dress in my brother, Emigdio's, pants and jackets," she told a reporter. "I also imitated the dance steps, walking style, gestures and attitudes of all the boys I played with."[60]

There are further "queer traces" of the adult Lupe Vélez in drag: a sighting of Lupe wearing a "sports jacket and a cap" in New York city; a commentary on the oil-stained pants she often wore while repairing cars.[61] And then there was Vélez's passion for boxing: "She never missed boxing matches, attending almost every Friday, when she would be spotted in front row seats at the American Legion Stadium, wearing a red wig and standing on her seat, yelling outrageous instructions to the boxers."[62] I often wonder if it is this androgyny in Lupe Vélez's gender identity that scandalized her critics, or perhaps it was the combination of transgressions that made her so unacceptable.

In closing, I would like to return to the question of fantasy. Vélez committed suicide two days after throwing a big bash in honor of her saint's day, "Our Lady of Guadalupe," on December 12, 1944. Four months pregnant, she died of an overdose of Seconal. It does not surprise me that even in death Lupe Vélez was the source of controversy (her death having been the subject of discrepant accounts) or that a proliferation of other fantasies, including my own, would be animated by this controversy. In his biography of Vélez, Gabriel Ramírez writes: "Her death, a marvel of theatricality and of poor taste, was fitting of Hollywood. And perhaps, even of Lupe Vélez."[63]

As González's video reminds us, the major culprit behind the sensational controversies surrounding Vélez's death is Kenneth Anger's "underground classic," *Hollywood Babylon*. In his gossip-riddled "exposé" of Hollywood scandals, the chapter entitled "Chop Suicide" describes the sordid details about Vélez's death that he claims newspapers refused to publish:

When Juanita, the chambermaid, had opened the bedroom door at nine, the morning after the suicide, no Lupe was in sight. The bed was empty. The aroma of scented candles, the fragrance of tuberoses almost, but not quite masked a stench recalling that left by Skid-Row derelicts. Juanita traced the vomit trail from the bed, followed the spotty track over to the orchid-filed bathroom. There she found her mistress, Señorita Velez, head jammed down in the toilet bowl, drowned.

The huge dose of Seconal had not been fatal in the expected fashion. It had mixed retch-erously with the Spitfire's Mexi-Spice Last Supper. The gut action, her stomach churning, had revived the dazed Lupe. Violently sick, an ultimate fastidiousness drove her to stagger towards the sanitary sanctum of the *salle de bain* where she slipped on the tiles and plunged head first into her Egyptian Chartreuse Onyx Hush-Flush Model Deluxe.[64]

Initially I found Anger's account of Vélez's death to be mean-spirited and degrading; it constructed her as a figure of abjection. However, reading Matthew Tinkcom's study of the discursive production and context of *Hollywood Babylon* forced me to rethink my initial impulse. Reclaiming the "camp sensibilities" in Anger's writings on Hollywood, Tinkcom characterizes *Hollywood Babylon* as a form of "queer fan textual production," one that employs "the discursive strategies of queer male camp," including "dissemblance, subterfuge and ironic play."[65] From the perspective of queer camp sensibilities, Anger's account of Vélez's death is less demeaning or degrading as much as it is irreverent and ironic, deriving from his liberal use of tabloid imagery and gossip. Like his other over-the-top stories of Hollywood celebrities in the book, Anger's version of Vélez's suicide represents a counterhistory to the idealized publicity which animated Hollywood's production of stardom and fandom. According to Tinkcom, a literal reading of the book ignores both Anger's "antagonistic stance towards Hollywood" and his critique of scandal and tabloid culture as well as of "Hollywood's own impulse to profit from gossip-driven knowledge."[66]

Anger's irreverent satire would find echoes in Warhol's *Lupe,* which features Edie Sedgwick as Lupe Vélez. One of Warhol's first experimental films in multiple projection, *Lupe* re-enacts "the last evening in the life of Lupe Vélez."[67] Playing on both Warhol and Anger, González's video opens with a disturbing toilet-drowning scene. This grotesque framing of Lupe's suicide as excess has fueled distortions and confusions about the details surrounding Lupe Vélez's death.

A few things are known, and none substantiate the sensational accounts that were spun from the account given by Anger. For one, Juanita was not the name of her "chambermaid," as Anger would refer to the woman who found Lupe Vélez. It was, rather, Beulah Kinder, Vélez's secretary and companion of ten years (and whom Vélez referred to as "mammy") who first discovered her body, lying on "a soft-feathered cover, between silk sheets, wearing her favorite blue, shimmering silk pajamas, with her blond hair carefully arranged over a pink pillow." "'I thought she was asleep. She looked so peaceful,' Kinder adds, 'But when I touched her head, it was cold, so I called the police.'"[68]

Then there are the reasons behind her suicide, given by Vélez herself, in two notes she left on a nightstand by her bed. The first is to Harald Raymond, an aspiring actor she had been involved with during the preceding few months:

To Harald,
    May God forgive you and forgive me, too but I prefer to take my life away and our baby's before I bring him with shame or killin him.
Lupe

On the back of the same note she wrote:

How could you, Harald, fake such a great love for me and our baby when all the time you didn't want us? I see no other way out for me so goodbye and good luck to you.
Love Lupe

I am skeptical. For the reason even Vélez herself provides is too transparent and patently obvious, too one-faceted, lacking complexity and, from my perspective just as important, going against the grain of the feminist genealogy I have just constructed. Not that I am looking for a conspiracy, or for Mafia perpetrators as in the "suicide" of Marilyn Monroe. But, it does seem so uncharacteristic that Lupe Vélez—a survivor of spousal battery at the hands of ex-husband Johnny Weissmuller, the ninth Tarzan—would fall victim to unrequited love or would be unable to resolve the contradictions in her Catholic upbringing.

I find comfort in the words of Jorge Labra, published in the obituary he wrote for the *Diario del Sureste:*

Why did Lupe commit suicide? According to the letter she left, because she was having a baby without a father. She wanted to escape the shame and scandal. Then, why would she write it? She could have very well died, taking this secret to her tomb. On the other hand, who would believe that Little Lupe would fear a scandal? It is difficult to believe that a woman who marries, divorces, and lives through various *romances,* as they call them there, would be so easily tormented by the same ups and downs of a "quinceañera" [fifteen-year-old girl] who has slipped lamentably, and decides to hide her offense with death.[69]

Labra explains her suicide in moralistic terms ("She was a young woman living during frivolous times . . . far away from the moral principles designed to guide young women . . . at the mercy of her passions . . ."). Yet his comments prompt me to look elsewhere. Perhaps a structural explanation makes more sense: Lupe as victim of modernity, a woman ahead of her times, or belonging to another time, a woman overwhelmed at the crossroads by contradictions, unable to resolve the conflicts between sexual liberalism and gender equality, on the one hand, and Mexican Catholicism, familial oligarchy, and gender backlash in this country, on the other.

I look elsewhere, combing the pages of her biography, searching for other meanings to the "Mexican Spitfire": she was "uncontrollably impatient."[70] Then there is the "uncomfortable behavior in which sudden bursts of euphoria and depression emerged constantly."[71] As early as 1932, Frank Cordon of the *Saturday Evening Post* reported that "Lupe could not stay still for more than ten seconds. Sitting on her legs in a chair, she wrapped herself like a Mexican pretzel and while she talked her mouth, hands, eyes and shoulders moved rapidly."[72]

There's more. While filming in Mexico during the last year of her life, she exhibited symptoms of "disequilibrium." "Her angry outbursts became intolerable. . . . she progressively became more depressed and exalted; her mood swings left her out of control."[73] Celebrating her saint's day with "a big party" on December 12, she invited "many Mexicans in the industry, employed and unemployed, wealthy and poor" to her house on North Rodeo Drive, where "many saw her nervous, confused, and visibly disconcerted."[74]

And then I remember Kay Redfield Jamison's research on moods and madness, her memoir of manic depression, *An Unquiet Mind,* in which she details moods which remind me of Lupe Vélez's: an electrifying bolt of energy, overflowing with laughter, exuberance, and fluctuating tides of emotion. And the photograph I discovered at the Academy of Motion Picture Arts and Sciences in Los Angeles lent credence to my hypothesis. Although the phantasmic multiple image of Vélez is an effect of technical manipulation, I believe its photographer, Ernest A. Bachrach, serendipitously (or perhaps knowingly) captured her oscillating temperament. I recognize that I am veering toward speculative psychobiography, even bordering on pseudoscience, in my attempt to diagnose Lupe Vélez with manic-depressive illness. Yet, like Kay Redfield Jamison, Vélez "lived a life particularly intense in moods" (figure 10).[75]

In an earlier book on the subject, *Touched with Fire,* Jamison explores the controversial claim of the relation between "artistic temperament and manic depressive illness." In the introduction, she writes:

The fiery aspects of thought and feeling that initially compel the artistic voyage — fiery energy, high mood, and quick intelligence; a sense of the visionary and the grand; a restless and feverish temperament — commonly carry with them the capacity for vastly darker moods, grimmer energies, and, occasionally, bouts of "madness." The opposite moods and energies, often interlaced, can appear to the world as mercurial, intemperate, volatile, brooding, troubled, or stormy. In short, they form the common view of the artistic temperament, and. . . . they also form the basis of the manic-depressive temperament.[76]

FIGURE 10. Haunted by an artistic temperament: This "composite shot on one negative," entered in the Hollywood studios' still photography show of 1941 by RKO Radio Pictures, eerily captures the overlapping moods of Lupe Vélez. Photograph by Ernest A. Bachrach, RKO Studios. Courtesy of the Academy of Motion Picture Arts and Sciences.

The Assumption of Lupe Vélez closes with Mexican ranchera singer Chavela Vargas's interpretation of the melancholic tune "No soy de aquí; ni soy de allá" rolling over the credits. Herself an international figure of lesbian excess, Vargas seems to be guiding us toward an understanding of Lupe Vélez's death. "No soy de aquí; ni soy de allá." Lupe was neither from here nor from there; she embodied an otherness that was too excessive for México and Hollywood. Unlike Dolores del Rio, who returned to Mexico after Orson Wells jilted her, the jilted and pregnant Lupe Vélez could not go back. In the mournful lyrics by Chavela Vargas I find a clue to Lupe's final predicament: in the end, she had nowhere to go.

There are scientific arguments "associating the artistic and manic depressive temperaments," Jamison tells us, scientific studies documenting "the high rate of mood disorders and suicide" in the lives of "eminent poets, artists, and composers."[77] I offer biographical evidence for the possibility of "overlapping natures of artistic and manic depressive temperaments" in the life/body of Lupe Vélez.[78] Perhaps the meaning of "Mexican Spitfire," of the Mexicana who spit fire (as the literal translation of her nickname would read), has less to do with sexuality (sexual promiscuity) or cultural temperament (hot-bloodedness) and more to do with moods and emotions. Perhaps to have been a "Spitfire" means more: an artistic temperament that is "touched with fire."

CHAPTER SEVEN

Haunted by Miscegenation

One year after the war between Mexico and the United States has ended, the native Californios (California Mexicans) notice a shift in public perception. The year is 1849. Tens of thousands invade California, not from the southern hemisphere but from the eastern part of the continent. They are lured into the region by the discovery of gold in Sutter's Coloma Mill. It is soon after the white, Anglo immigrants outnumber the Californios that the surprising shift occurs:

When rumor circulated that "foreigners" had no right to work the pacers and would be pushed out of the mining area . . . the Californios began to recognize that invasion had brought an inversion of both discursive and power relations. No longer dominant, the Californios had now become the dominated population and also the "foreigners," foreigners in their own native land . . . as Juan Seguin would write in another context.[1]

The Californios, of course, were not exactly "native" as we understand the word today. They too had displaced an earlier population — the truly native indigenous population — a hundred years before the nineteenth-century Anglo conquest. In many ways, the displacement of the California Mexicans by these new colonizers could be read as "karmic" were it not for the white supremacist and genocidal undertones fueling this curious inversion of power relations. Whites repeatedly described the

Californios as a "degraded race" of "mixed blood" with "scarcely a visible grade in the scale of intelligence, above the barbarous tribes by whom they are surrounded."[2] Unlike Anglo immigrants, the native Californios were racially mixed: indigenous, European, African.

As Rosaura Sánchez indicates above, it took just one year after the U.S.–Mexico War of 1848 for the inversion of history to occur. It took one year for Anglo immigrants to reinvent themselves as "native" by recasting the inhabitants of the former Mexican territory as "foreign" — thereby disavowing the prior visibility of Mexicans. In executing the inversion, these white colonizers would deploy a repertoire of racist representational strategies and practices, including the stereotypes of degeneracy, banditry, inhumanity — negative stereotypes used to "achieve racial/cultural domination of colonized populations."[3] As a central strategy in colonial discourse, stereotypes of Mexican depravity would be repeated endlessly for the rest of the nineteenth and early twentieth centuries, as the United States attempted to define the origins of the nation-state and articulate its own national identity. The denigrating images would justify mob lynching of Mexicans and mass deportation campaigns; they would be fixed in the popular imagination, made visible in cultural discourses through a process of repetition. Some of the most enduring examples of this process are found today in early films of the silent cinema era.

In the following pages I wish to explore this contradiction by focusing on the "Mexicanist presence" in the narratives of silent moviemakers.[4] As the first racialized group to be granted citizenship in the era when white male embodiment reigned supreme, why is it that, to this date, Mexican Americans, along with Asian Americans, are, in the words of Lora Romero, "often thought of as an alien presence rather than part of 'American' history?"[5] Why have Mexicans been unable to shed their inscription as "foreigners"? What are the stories whiteness has had to tell itself in order to reproduce and consolidate national identity? And how has Mexicana visibility in the Southwest disrupted the articulation of a national identity based exclusively on whiteness? Films provide us with vivid glimpses into how the nation imagines itself in the early twentieth century. As part of cultural memory they reflect the formulation of a U.S. national identity predicated not just on racial subordination of the other, but also on the disavowal of the Mexicanist presence.[6]

This chapter probes the interweaving of racial formation processes and cinema in the tortuous history of nation building. I will analyze how a group of films contributes to a cultural memory of disavowal by focusing on instances where Mexicana visibility figures prominently in questions of national identity. My interest in the ways in which women mark the boundaries of racial, ethnic, and national groupings led me to examine images of Mexicana subjects in early cinema as a way of determining their role in the nation-building project. Through the course of my examination I found that films of the Western genre set in the "frontier," especially those dealing with Mexicana subjects, best capture the nation's anxieties about the Mexicanist presence — anxieties mirrored in the ambivalent representation of women. For unlike the near-total abjection of Mexican males found in the roughly two thousand silent films about Mexicans made during the first decades of the twentieth century, the repertoire of Mexicana representation was more complex and much broader in scope, ranging from portrayals of Mexicanas as objects of derision to objects of desire and finally as embodiments of the moral limits of white womanhood.

In light of this fascination/repulsion, I hope to untangle the ambivalent and contradictory representation of Mexicana subjects in the cinematic imagination, focusing on the few surviving films available for public viewing in archives throughout the country.[7] As we move toward a deeper understanding of how the process of historical inversion (the reinvention of whites as natives by recasting Mexicans as foreign) is entangled in social anxieties and fears, we must first look at one extreme in cultural representation: films which fixed and repeated abject images of Mexicanas in U.S. cultural memory.

Sixty years after the war, Biograph Pictures released *Red Girl* (1908), a film staging an origins story for the nation-state. One of several films D. W. Griffith made featuring Mexican characters, *Red Girl* is set during the California Gold Rush and, as is the case with his other early films containing Mexican characters, its acting style is histrionic, with wildly exaggerated and flamboyant character moves. The film opens in a Western saloon, where Kate Miller, the girl gold miner, displays a bag full of gold nuggets she has just retrieved from the gold mines. Kate is followed to her hotel room by a woman visibly coded as Mexican who, after gambling away her own money, decides to steal the nuggets. The Mexican woman enters the room to take the bag while Kate Miller sleeps. A struggle ensues, Kate Miller fires her pistol but misses, and the Mexican woman gets away with the bag of gold. Fleeing into the woods with Kate Miller in chase, the Mexican woman befriends Red Girl, a Native American woman camping along the river with her "half-breed" husband. Red Girl hides the Mexican woman, who in turn seduces the half-breed husband and convinces him to tie up Red Girl and leave her by the river while they escape. Red Girl manages to untie herself and joins Kate Miller's posse. In the end, the fugitives are caught in the river; the "Mexican jezebel" (as she is referred to in the film intertitles) is arrested and, even though the husband repents, an indignant Red Girl rejects him.

The film ends by reasserting the earlier alliance established between the "Red" and the "White" women against the "Mexican woman" — an alliance described as pastoral by the Biograph *Bulletin* of 1908: "We leave her [Red Girl] and Kate standing on the cliff, enfolded in each other's arms, bathed in the golden rays of a setting sun — indeed a most beautiful scene" (and a scene, we might add, with lesbian overtones).[8]

To some degree, the plot of *Red Girl* is resolved in nonmasculinist terms, through female homosocial bonding. Its heroic characters are women, and masculinity remains at the margins, with men neither coming to women's rescue nor "saving the day." Surprisingly, women's heroism and bonding provide the resolution to the film's dramatic tension, and its homosocial subtext disrupts heteronormativity, or the ways in which the nation and nationhood depend on heterosexual coupling and reproduction. Yet, despite this ostensibly subversive ending, *Red Girl* portrays women in patriarchal terms, as the "symbolic figuration of the nation."[9]

Each of the three female characters symbolizes racially distinct nations: the white (modern) nation, embodied in Kate Miller, who is not just the main character but the only character with a regular name (as opposed to a color name) and who is thus the legitimate agent of the plot; the "foreign" nation, embodied in the "Mexican jezebel," the story's villain, whose mantilla functions as the veil of otherness; and the premodern, Indian nation, embodied in Red Girl, who lives in nature (as opposed to civilization) and whose name marks her as racially other. Read against the historical backdrop of nineteenth-century conflict between the Californios and Anglo immigrants, *Red Girl* replays the scenario of historical inversion, rewriting an origin story of white national identity based on the myth of Anglo nativeness and Mexican foreignness.

We have seen how the Anglo newcomers kept the Californios from working in the mines, recodifying them as "foreign." A similar process occurred with the dispossession of California land. According to Cheryl Harris, whites consolidated their claims to land by rejecting native Americans' rights to *first possession:* "Although the Indians were the first occupants and possessors of the land of the New World," Harris explains, "their racial and cultural otherness allowed this fact to be reinterpreted and ultimately erased as a basis for asserting rights in land."[10] In California, whites deployed this logic against Mexicans, using race as well as culture as the basis for asserting rights to property (land and gold mines) and for interpreting who was native and who was other or foreign. Thus Anglo-Saxons based their claims to the gold mines — and even who could labor in them — on whiteness, on property rights derived from race.

In *Red Girl* (a film whose very title makes a racial designation), "gold nuggets" figure as the symbols of property, the "miner girl's" legitimate possession and products of her labor. Her claims to the gold nuggets are based on property rights protected by law. The film's narrative discourse excludes the Mexican woman from any legitimate claims to property by virtue of her otherness. She is foreign, she is nonwhite, and she is a criminal. As a gambler, she is implicated in nonproductive labor, but, even worse, she steals the rightful property of others (the gold nuggets and Red Girl's husband). The combination of engaging in nonproductive labor and theft places her beyond the margins of the social order.

Here we have an instance of the process of repetition and fixity: the recycling of an earlier narrative of Mexican banditry, degeneracy, and inhumanity in order to further the historical inversion. From her position as an outsider, the Mexican woman introduces disorder into the worlds of both the white nation (the world of culture) and the native nation (the world of nature). Her role in the plot is purely instrumental, serving to consolidate the white nation's authority on the frontier as well as its claims to property in the West. And here the alliance between Kate Miller and Red Girl (who gains entrance into civilization and history through this alliance) is crucial in that it unifies "the first occupants and possessors of the land of the New World" (the Indians) with those who now exercise enforceable property rights (white Anglos) against the Mexicans, the group whose racial and cultural otherness (their designated foreignness) erased their claims not only to property in California but, just as significantly, to national identity. The alliance thus reinforces the notion of whiteness as "the quintessential property of personhood." Writing in another context Harris explains: "Whiteness as property is derived from the deep historical roots of systemic white supremacy that has given rise to definitions of group identity predicated on the racial subordination of the other."[11]

To be sure, the Mexican inhabitants of the former Mexican territories disturbed the nation's investment in whiteness as the basis for citizenship and, more significantly, national identity. Since the early days of the republic, citizenship was intertwined with white racial identity, as Ian Haney López explains: "In 1790, only a few months after ratification of the Constitution, Congress limited naturalization to 'any alien being a free white person who shall have resided within the limits and under the jurisdiction of the United States for a term of two years."[12] White supremacist notions of citizenship, however, were complicated by the Treaty of Guadalupe-Hidalgo, which ended the war between Mexico and the United States, because it granted citizenship to Mexicans even though from whites' point of view or "common perception" Mexicans did not appear to be racially "white." Indeed, according to "common knowledge," they were of "mixed race."

The mixed-race designation of Mexicans had been a vexed issue in public debates around annexation of the former Mexican territories. The popular press sensationalized the topic by noting, as the *Democratic Review* did in 1846, that of the estimated 7 million Mexicans, "we must set down six million as composed of Indians or half breeds."[13] Indeed, expansion and conquest were justified precisely on the basis that Mexico was "a nation of mestizos not . . . predisposed to democracy" who were thus unfit to occupy California.[14] And race was a key element in the debate over annexation of the former Mexican territories: "The Whig party opposition to the War feared the extension of slavery, but they also feared the amalgamation of an inferior race into the nation." Or, as another view published in the *Southern Quarterly Review* in 1847 put it: "The Mexicans were a mongrel race, and annexation would benefit only them, not the United States."[15]

"From the founding of the nation," Dorothy Roberts writes, "the meaning of American citizenship rested on the denial of citizenship to nonwhites living within its borders."[16] Mexicans were granted citizenship at a time when naturalization was linked to white racial identity, so it threatened the nation's imaginary, especially its "valorization of whiteness as treasured property," as an attribute belonging only to the Anglo-Saxon race.[17] During this crucial period of the nation-building process, at the height of the dominance of theories of race as a biological fact, the status of Mexicans was ambivalent at best, for whites perceived Mexicans simultaneously as "citizens" and "aliens"; "naturalized" by law yet "foreign" in popular discourse; excluded from definitions of U.S. national identity by virtue of their cultural and racial otherness, yet ruled to be "white" by the courts.[18] The formidable contradiction between Mexicans' juridical status as white and the popular perception of them as nonwhites lies at the root of the historical inversion with which I began this chapter. And, if anxieties and fears structure the process of historical inversion, nowhere is this more evident than in films dealing with the subject of "miscegenation." For as the "biological reproducers" of the "mixed-race" nation, Mexicanas threatened to disturb the racial homogeneity of the nation's identity in other ways as well.

A forcefully dramatized performance of gender is found in another early Griffith film that exploits the theme of Mexican otherness, *Mexican Sweethearts* (1909) — one of a handful of silent films on Mexicans that, along with *Red Girl,* can be screened at the Library of Congress in Washington, D.C. Despite its short length (three minutes), *Mexican Sweethearts* is fraught with meaning, typifying the filmmaker's fascination with racial and cultural others, his investment in white supremacy, and his obsession with the titillating subject of miscegenation. A review of the film published in 1909 describes *Mexican Sweethearts* favorably, as "one of the most beautiful pieces of high class acting ever attempted," without mentioning its unsophisticated camera techniques or simple plot structure. One of the common practices of the time, evident in *Mexican Sweethearts,* is the use of white actors to perform as Mexicans. In highly dramatized performances of racial otherness, white actors reinvented Mexican cultural practices and racial difference for mainstream audiences of early cinema. It is ironic that a movie critic of the time would attempt to hide the process of racialization evident in racial cross-dressing, describing the lead actress of *Mexican Sweethearts* as a "native Spaniard" when in fact the credits list her as Lottie Pickford, the sister of Mary Pickford — both well known Anglo-Canadian stars of the silent cinema.[19]

As the film's full title, *Mexican Sweethearts: The Impetuous Nature of Latin Love,* makes evident, Griffith's production of Mexican otherness is, from the inception, framed within the discourse of Anglo-Saxon morality. The title alone indicts the nonnormative sexuality of the "Latin race" as much as the simple plot stages the dangers inherent in interracial sexual encounters. The lead character is a flirtatious "Señorita" (Mexicana) who works as a waitress in a restaurant/bar. Wearing the exotic vestments of Griffith's idea of a gypsy woman (flowing skirt, bandanna around her head, large hoop earrings), the Señorita seductively flirts with a white U.S. soldier. At the moment when she professes her love to the white soldier, the Señorita's flamboyant, hot-blooded Mexican lover enters the bar, and in an outburst of violent rage attempts to kill the soldier until she intervenes. Narrative resolution is even more melodramatic, rendered in displays of histrionic (nonnaturalistic) acting styles (wildly exaggerated hand and facial gestures) as the Mexican lovers reconcile, embracing and smoking cigarettes together.

In the span of three minutes, Griffith's race film reinvents Mexican otherness as features of exotic costuming, flamboyant gestures, and immoral behavior. As in *Red Girl*, the Mexicana character of *Mexican Sweethearts* plays a key role in the filmmaker's representational strategy, especially since her behavior is the most transgressive. As the female embodiment of nationhood, she signals the degeneracy of the Mexican race, and by virtue of her nonnormativity she stands as the other to the idealized white femininity of the early twentieth century. The film in fact dramatizes the eugenicist "discomfort with sexuality," involving "the tendency . . . to identify as depravity most sexual expression that fell outside the bounds of prevailing middle-class standards."[20] The bar, with its suggestion of bordello, is a classic site of transgression of middle-class norms: it is the locus of smoking, drinking beer, gambling, and indulging in illicit sexual relations. The Mexicana in *Mexican Sweethearts* not only smokes in this very public of places, but also asserts herself sexually with the white soldier, thus crossing several taboos. However, it is in the thwarted romance between the Señorita and the soldier where the filmmaker's white supremacist ideology is most clearly revealed, including his stance against mixed-race unions and moral judgments about the dangers of romantic entanglements with the raced and gendered other.

Films like *Mexican Sweethearts* did not exist in a social or cultural vacuum but were intimately connected to — if not intentionally influenced by ongoing processes of — racial formation during the period these films were made. In dramatizing the impossibility of interracial sexual play, a film like *Mexican Sweethearts*, for example, is haunted by the social taboo around "miscegenation."

To some extent, during the conquest of the former Mexican territories, the Anglo-Saxon characterization of Mexicans as a "mongrel race" complicated and even shifted the nation's obsession with racial purity away from the "black race." Historians of the emancipation period have traced white supremacist discourse of intolerance around "miscegenation" in the South to white fears of racial contamination by the recently freed blacks. In fact, it was after the abolition of slavery that the earlier social acceptance of mixed-raced relationships declined: "The fear of mixing led southern states to pass new laws to prevent interracial marriage during the 1860s and the term miscegenation first appeared in these laws."[21] A curious word taken from the lexicon of nineteenth-century sexual discourse, it "embodies a fear not merely of interracial sexuality, but of its supposed result, the decline of the population," which accounts for the institutionalization of segregation by white southerners: their fear "that social mixing would lead to sexual mixing."[22] But just as significant, the emerging racist discourse against miscegenation was further exacerbated during the white invasion of the Southwest, where Anglos encountered an entire race of "mixed breeds." Paredes notes, "Racialists regarded mixed-breeds as impulsive, unstable and prone to insanity. The Mexicans, as the most conspicuous products of mass miscegenation, inevitably were assigned these qualities."[23]

Paredes's observations underscore the fact that decades before emancipation, there circulated a prior discourse on interracial intolerance centered not just around "mulattos" but on "mestizos," and expressed in the Anglo-Saxon disdain for the multiracial composition of the California pueblos and rancherías. In early-nineteenth-century "travelogues," Anglo colonizers deployed racial and colonialist epithets to describe the population they encountered and the effects that their racial "amalgamation" produced: "a wild turbulent humanity characterized by ignorance and fanaticism."[24] Thomas Jefferson Farnham, an Anglo immigrant from Illinois influenced by race theories of the mid-nineteenth century, wrote the following:

No one acquainted with the indolent mixed race of California, will ever believe that they will populate, much less, for any length of time, govern the country. The law of Nature, which curses the mulatto here with a constitution less robust than that of either race from which he sprang, lays a similar penalty upon the mingling of the Indian and white races in California and Mexico. . . . They must fade away.[25]

It is in the Southwest, therefore, where whites' social (and sexual) anxieties coalesced around the Mexican race, the people Anglos considered to be the "doomed progeny" of miscegenation: "As one southerner explained, 'if we have intermarriage, we shall degenerate; we shall become a race of mulattos; we shall be another Mexico; we shall be ruled out of the family of white nations. Sir, it is a matter of life and death with the Southern people to keep their blood pure."[26]

The devalorization of Mexicans as "mixed-race" others, their depreciation to a species low on the social hierarchy, derives in part from the then-current pseudoscientific theories of race and racial ranking, themselves molded by an earlier discourse of theology. Indeed, nineteenth-century "race science," in particular the science of human variation and difference, or biosocial science, set out to prove the scientific basis of religious ideology about the races.[27] A legion of experts like ethnologists, phrenologists, naturalists, surgeons, and physicians — known today as the "race scientists" — invented "new technologies of measurement: the calipers, cephalometers and crainometers," to confirm their racist, pseudoscientific hypothesis on racial variation.[28]

Scientific theorizing of this kind led to the circulation of two major theories on racial ranking: monogeism and polygenism — both recycled from Christian theology, in particular the biblical story of Adam and Eve.[29] Monogeism was based on the "orthodox Christian view of the unity of man — of one race descended in less than six thousand years from Adam and Eve" — and was considered the "softer argument" of scientific racism because it affirmed a single lineage for all human beings.[30] The exponents of monogenism justified human variation and difference in racial ranking by drawing on the "theory of degeneracy": the idea that each race represented differing degrees of degeneration from the perfect utopia in the Garden of Eden. In the words of one race scientist: "Races have declined to different degrees, whites least, blacks most."[31]

Yet scientific theorizing about the races in the United States led to the development of an equally abhorrent theory: polygenism, a doctrine propagating the belief of multiple lineages, or distinct human races originating from multiple Adams.[32] Its exponents "spoke of races as distinct species, incapable of crossing to produce viable 'hybrids.'"[33] Within this context, laws against miscegenation received "scientific" credibility from race (pseudo) scientists like the naturalist Louis Agassiz, who considered "interbreeding" across racial groups to be "unnatural and repugnant": "Conceive for a moment the difference it would make in future ages, for the prospect of a republican institution and our civilization generally, if instead of the manly population descended from cognate nations, the United States should hereafter be inhabited by the effeminate progeny of mixed races, half Indian, half Negro, sprinkled with white blood."[34]

The description of "hybrids" in metaphors and analogies of femininity was a common rhetorical strategy for naturalizing social differences in scientific discourse. During the nineteenth century, the biosocial sciences deployed the analogy linking race to gender to such a degree that race scientists "use[d] racial difference to explain gender difference and vice versa."[35] In fact, race scientists like Agassiz used this analogy to legitimate the lower position of women and nonwhite races in the social hierarchy; thus their "scientific" theories served to "perpetuate the racial and gender status quo."[36]

This discursive construction of Mexicans as the "effeminate progeny of mixed races, half Indian, half Negro, sprinkled with white blood" was certainly part of the colonial process of dispossessing Mexicans of their land rights in the Southwest. Yet supremacist obsession with Mexicans as feminized "hybrids," as "degraded" and "polluted," as the "doomed progeny of miscegenation," expresses deeper psychic anxieties and fears. To be sure, the "mongrel breed, adulterated by extensive intermarriage with an inferior Indian race" stood in the way of white colonial expansion to the West.[37] However, the obsessive discursive repetition of racial and gender othering reveals a deeper compulsion, a more profound disturbance in the racist imaginary. On what grounds would a militarily superior colonizing force fear a numerically inferior colonized population of "half-breeds," a race whites considered lower on the scale of racial ranking, a group Anglos feminized and racialized as a "mixed race of degenerates?" Perhaps the key is found in the meaning of miscegenation in the national imaginary, in the profound social alteration it signifies. For if miscegenation embodies the fear of population decline, Mexican visibility epitomized, materially and literally, the extinction of a race whose privilege is based on whiteness.

One way to broach this vexed question of white supremacist racial fears and anxieties is through Michel Foucault's writings on biopower. In *The History of Sexuality* Foucault argues against the notion that modernity is characterized by "repression," or "a principle of the limitations of pleasures of others by what have traditionally been called the 'ruling classes.'"[38] Instead, during the last three centuries there has been an expansion of discourses on sex designed to extend the life, the social body of the ruling classes. In order to insure their own "survival" or social reproduction, the ruling classes have historically developed what Foucault calls technologies of sex and techniques for maximizing life precisely "because of what the cultivation of its own body could represent politically, economically, and historically for the present and future of the bourgeoisie." The discourse on sexuality spread through the domains of pedagogy, medicine, economics, and public policy:

The works published in great numbers at the end of the eighteenth century, on body hygiene, the art of longevity, ways of having healthy children and of keeping them alive as long as possible, and methods for improving the human lineage, bear witness to the fact: they thus attest to the correlation of this concern with the body and sex to a type of "racism."[39]

Thus the exorbitant spread of a discourse on sexuality, its actualization, and the growth of various technologies related to sexuality are connected to the "self affirmation of one class" over others, and to a "type of racism" or a "racism of expansion." The expansion Foucault speaks of,

however, is not solely economic, political, and territorial, but fundamentally biological: a ruling class fixated on its progeny, on expanding "its
well being and survival."[40]

These observations about the reciprocity between a concern with the
body/sex and a type of racism are useful for understanding the proliferation of the discourse on race in the Americas. Here too the ruling class
(white colonizers), in this case the white Anglo-Saxon ruling class, was
obsessed with the survival of its species/race. Foucault restricts his study
to the European context, but Laura Ann Stoler teases out the occulted
history of empire in his writings, underscoring that "colonial regimes
anticipated the policing of sexuality in modern Europe."[41]

The deployment of sexuality gets clarified during colonizing processes,
for "the racial configurations of the imperial world" were in fact constitutive of the "cultivation of the nineteenth-century bourgeois self."[42]
Stoler disentangles the ways in which a raced sexuality was "part and par-
cel" of the modern state: "It was in the late nineteenth century that technologies of sex were most fully mobilized around issues of race with the
pseudo-scientific theory of degeneracy at their core . . . the 'vast theoretical and legislative edifice' that was the theory of degeneracy secured the
relationship between racism and sexuality."[43]

And here the place of the Southwest in consolidating the discourse on
miscegenation begins to be clarified: the white ruling class institutionalized segregation because it feared "social mixing would lead to sexual mixing"; Anglo-Saxons legislated antimiscegenation laws because they feared
becoming "a race of mulattos . . . another Mexico." Obsessed as they were
with the extinction of their race, white Anglo-Saxons produced a discourse of racism that functioned as a "means of introducing . . . a fundamental division between those who must live and those who must die."[44]
As we know from the history of the origins of the nation, racism in the
Americas begot genocide, enslavement, conquest, and internment. From
the perspective of biological racism, the colonial encounter with "mixed-
race" Mexicans forced white Anglo-Saxons to confront their own mor-
tality as a "species." For it was the mirroring effects of that encounter, the
fact that multiracial Mexicans foreshadowed the end of whiteness, that
produced such a virulent response.

If racism is constitutive of the power of the modern normalizing state,
it also occasioned territorial expansion and the ideology of Manifest
Destiny, the baffling notion that "no race but our [white] own can either
cultivate or rule the Western Hemisphere."[45] Although U.S. national identity is rooted in racial subordination — on the legal distinction between

white, free subjects (property owners) and black slaves (property) — a much earlier articulation of the nation takes shape around a different form of racial opposition: the binary of Culture (with whites as its subjects) and Nature (with Indians as its embodiment).

This prior national formation repeats itself a century later with the reiteration of national identity through Manifest Destiny and the conquest of the former Mexican territories. It is the encounter with Mexicans that would ultimately consolidate a discourse of white superiority as the basis for national identity, one that posited citizenship and immigration in terms of the racial differences: civilization (whites as insiders to the nation) and wilderness (Mexicans as outsiders). Thus, if "whites-only" were destined to rule the Western Hemisphere, if citizenship could only be constituted through whiteness, then annexing a nation of "mixed-race" inhabitants, granting citizenship to multiracial Mexicans, complicated the bloodlines of the modern nation.

Silent films played a crucial role in congealing as well as spreading a colonialist discourse marked by persuasively staged performances of gendered sexuality nuanced by race, nationality, and ethnicity. Part of the ideological work of many early films concentrated on reinventing the myth of racial homogeneity, and as a result these cultural objects sublimated whites' fear of extinction onto a discourse of white racial superiority and mixed-race inferiority. Often, modes of pseudoscientific racism, especially the doctrines of monogenism and polygenism, legitimated white supremacist ideology in cultural representation. The disdain for "interbreeding" inherent in the polygenist doctrine informed cultural representations such as *Mexican Sweethearts* as well as of other films of the period that portrayed the impossibility and dangers of interracial romance.[46]

Mexicanas, as the "biological reproducers" of the "mixed race," disturbed the racial homogeneity of the nation's identity more than any other subject. By containing "mixed-race" women on the margins of narrative discourse, antimiscegenation films fixed and repeated an abject image of Mexicanas in the cultural imaginary, reaffirming their racial difference from whiteness, their exclusion from a national identity based on racial homogeneity. Certainly one feature of the ambivalent relation of whiteness to Mexicana visibility is reflected in films inspired by the popular doctrine of polygenism and pseudoscientific theories warning of the dangers of miscegenation.

But the ambivalence erupting from the anxieties that structured the process of historical inversion is also indicative of another logic at work, and this is certainly the case in representations of Mexicanas, especially given the large number of films portraying miscegenation in positive light. While only a couple of these films survive in the film archives, I found evidence of their existence in trade publications. My review of written synopses indicated that films favoring interracial liaisons did not contain simple, straightforward plots of white male/Mexicana sex play. Instead, the film narratives implied a much broader articulation of racial/sexual politics within the discourse of the nation. And while I discovered films dealing with interracial romance far outnumbering portrayals of its impossibility, they nonetheless operated within a racist, masculinist logic.

Of the approximately thirty pro-miscegenation films described in published film synopses, the bulk fall into one of two categories: (1) rescue fantasy, where the white male protagonist saves the Mexican female from the excesses of her culture (embodied in either a possessive father or a degenerate lover); and (2) romantic conquest of a Mexicana, involving the white male triumphant over one or more Mexican males.[47] With the exception of four films within these categories, cinematic portrayals of interracial sex play reaffirmed white racial superiority and the masculinist rescue fantasy, as dramatized in the film *Licking the Greasers* (1914).

Previously entitled *Shorty's Trip to Mexico*, *Licking the Greasers* features the then-popular actor Shorty Hamilton as a white cowboy on the borderlands who joins Pedro and his gang in the running of guns across the border. Despite Shorty's complicity in illegal gunrunning, his role is decriminalized within the narrative because his ulterior motive is a noble one. Shorty is driven by a love for his "sweetheart" Anita in Mexico, as the dissolve into Shorty's memories of his love make evident. But it is Shorty's role as white savior that ultimately absolves him of culpability.

While Shorty, Pedro, and the Mexican gang prepare their cargo, the action shifts to another context, across the border into Mexico, where the mayhem of the Mexican Revolution is in full force. The despotic General Caramba leads the revolution and a band of equally loathsome soldiers in a pillaging campaign against innocent victims like Anita and her father. Although Shorty is responsible for negotiating the gun deal with General Caramba, he instead decides to visit Anita's home, where he discovers that both Anita and her father are being held hostage by the general's drunken soldiers. Fortunately the Mexican troops are as incompetent as they are inebriated. Shorty single-handedly rescues Anita and, stealing the car from his Mexican partners, heads for the U.S. border with Anita and her father, with General Caramba's troops and Pedro and his gang in pursuit. The story ends as Shorty, Anita, and her father cross the border into the United States, where Shorty declares to Anita: "And your future name and address is to be Mrs. Shorty USA."

Licking the Greasers, like many other films of the period, used the figure of the feminine to represent the conquest of Mexicans as a decisive moment in the nation-building project. As *Licking the Greasers* makes evident, even a film favoring miscegenation was ruled by a colonialist logic in which whiteness proved superior to Mexican-ness or "mixed-race-ness": Shorty out-guns, out-smarts, and out-runs hundreds of Mexican men. These films would not render a love story between a white male and a Mexican female without framing it in Manichean terms, in the narrative contrast between the races. In *Licking the Greasers,* the racial superiority of whites depends on portrayals of Mexican inferiority (their criminality, brutality, and degeneracy), thereby legitimating the colonialist project: the victory (Manifest Destiny) of white masculinity over Mexicans in the conquest of the Mexican female body (land/the U.S. Southwest). Embedded in the film's masculinist rescue fantasy is an allegory of conquest and colonization, with Anita as symbol of Mexican land, joining Shorty (the symbol of Uncle Sam/U.S. state) in marriage (uniting the female/land with the white male/nation-state). The subtext of conquest figures prominently in other cultural representations featuring a white male rescuing the Mexicana from the excesses of her culture, especially in films set in nineteenth-century California, during the time of the most violent racial conflicts between Anglos and California Mexicans over land and mining rights.[48]

If there is a fascination with interracial sexual play present in the *Licking the Greasers,* Mexicana femininity undergoes a metamorphosis: racialized sexuality is no longer emphasized, nor are degeneracy, criminality, and immorality, as in *Mexican Sweethearts.* The image of Anita in *Licking the Greasers* is a prime example of a "domesticated" Mexicana who is cast into the mold of white Victorian femininity, as demure as she is defenseless. Without this process of deracialization, the theme of inter-racial (Anglo-Mexican) marriage dramatized in early silent films would have, in all likelihood, compromised a national identity organized around the grammar of racial purity and homogeneity.

Even those films portraying interracial sexual relations as socially acceptable recycled the dominant racial and sexual regimes of the time. For example, the allure of bonds between white males and brown females echoes the eugenics logic of racial improvement — the idea that "white male impregnation" of inferior races led to their betterment.[49] These films also convey a power structure that Yuval-Davis and Anthias call the "alliance-based system," whereby the colonial power authorizes marriage between men from the ruling class and women from subaltern groups. Within the sexual contract, men from the dominant racial or colonial group are granted access to colonized women, and colonized men are prohibited from intermarriage with women from the ruling classes, who functions as "reproducers of boundaries."[50]

In the context of the Southwest, the "alliance-based system" dates to a colonial regime of the nineteenth century that fomented interracial marriages between Anglos and Mexicanas. The dynamic that Stoler writes about in the Dutch case is the same: "The 'deployment of alliance,' to use Foucault's term, allowed Dutch men access to privilege and profits through a calculated series of marriage links to Asian and creole women."[51]

In California, the "system of alliance" would undermine the power of the California elite, for it authorized Anglo men's access to large land holdings precisely through "a calculated series of marriage links" to daughters of the Mexican elite. It also allowed for the creative manipulation of Mexicana images: their deracialization, which involved the "Europanization of California mestizas and mulattas," who were now proclaimed to be "industrious, moral and chaste." In the words of Antonia Castañeda: "The image of Californianas as 'good' women emerged from these marriages and economic alliances on the eve of the Mexican American War."[52] Half a century later, at the height of racist scientific theories and social taboos around miscegenation, moviemakers drew from the cultural memory of "genteel Spanish aristocrats with virtue and morals intact" to construct new and renewed, less threatening representations of Mexicana sexuality.[53] In any case, films extolling the virtues of Mexicanas played a minor role in the racial imaginary of white filmmakers, who were much more concerned with Mexican "degeneracy" than with their "desirability," as this movie review published in 1913 makes evident: "There are no meaner men on earth than many who are directly interested in the manufacture and sale of patent medicine. They are so crooked at heart and so criminal of intent that they commit more murders than all the gunman [sic], Mexicans, paranoiacs [sic] and infanticides put together" (my emphasis).[54]

It is clear that filmmakers drew from a wide repertoire of available social discourses, interweaving colonialist and pseudoscientific discourse of the nineteenth century with emerging political, social, and pseudoscientific paradigms of the new century. The association of Mexicans with violence derives from the convergence of colonialist ideology with twentieth-century political debates about the Mexican Revolution of 1910 and journalistic coverage of the war in Mexico; views about Mexicans as pathogens in the body politic stems from social anxieties about venereal disease on the borderlands; and constructions of Mexican criminality originate in the notion, propagated by the pseudoscience of eugenics, that "temperament and behavior" are genetically linked to race.[55]

In fixing the image of Mexicans in these terms, cultural producers contributed to the ongoing process of racial formation during the early twentieth century. The fascination/repulsion with interracial sexual play and relations in cinematic representations was one feature of the process. In addition to animating the boundaries of race and representation, Mexicana imagery served to regulate the fault lines of white femininity.

Imagine an Anglo-Saxon adventurer roaming through the rancherías of New Mexico, Texas, Arizona, and California during the first half of the nineteenth century. His views of womanhood are steeped in Anglo-Saxon, Victorian ideology, including notions about women's innate sexual purity and moral virtue, chastity, passionlessness, submissiveness, piety, and above all, restraint in sexual manners, comportment, and fashion. The women he encounters on the northern Mexican territories are a far cry from his ideal of feminine domesticity. There, on the borderlands, white male colonizers came into contact with a less differentiated gender/sex system and spatial divisions, especially in terms of gender roles and public/private spheres; what they encountered differed from the norms engrained in "the civilized morality" of the Anglo-Saxon middle class.

Historical records confirm the widespread production of sexual and racial imagery on the part of white colonizers who were shocked by the differences they saw. In the former Mexican territories, whites discovered a Mexican sexual system, hybridized by Spanish Moor and indigenous native practices, that was much less repressive around the body. Mexicanas living in the northern Mexican region — the soon-to-be "Southwest" — openly expressed sexuality, sexual desire, and sexual pleasure — courting in public, dancing and drinking at fandangos and street celebrations, and smoking and gambling alongside Mexican men. White colonizers did not appreciate the "fact that Spanish-Mexicans ritualized celebration and socializing and that gambling — along with church-organized parties, pageants and affairs — allowed an outlet for this activity."[56]

The physical openness of Mexicanas even extended into the domain of other bodily practices such as health and hygiene, including the "suckling of infants in public" and bathing "nude within viewing distance of men."[57] White colonizers associated cultural differences in dress style to moral inferiority and a lack of female chastity, evident in how they described Mexicanas as wearing "very short skirts" and dressing "without the benefit of underwear, petticoats, bodices or long sleeves."[58] A lawyer visiting California from Illinois made the following observations regarding their "indelicate form": "A pity it is that they have not stay and corset makers' signs among them, for they allow their waists to grow as God designed they should, like Venus de Medici, that ill-bred statue that had no kind mother to lash its vitals into delicate form."[59]

White colonizers perceived differences in sexual customs and bodily practices to be signs of the racial inferiority that confirmed the pathology they attributed to Mexicans and that justified the conquest. As D'Emilio and Freeman note,

Ever since the seventeenth century, European immigrants to America had merged racial and sexual ideology in order to differentiate themselves from Indians and blacks, to strengthen the mechanisms of social control over slaves, and to justify the appropriation of Indian and Mexican lands through the destruction of native peoples and their culture. In the nineteenth century, sexuality continued to serve as a powerful means by which white Americans maintained dominance over people of other races.[60]

Yet dominance over other races was only part of the equation. In the dualistic framework of white racist patriarchy, any form of sexual or bodily expression that did not conform to the ruling ideals of femininity came to be associated with a pathological model of sexuality. Just as by the eighteenth century blacks "had become the icon for deviant sexuality in general," so during the nineteenth, especially in Gold Rush literature, "Mexican woman" was synonymous with "prostitute" — the icon for nonnormative sexuality. As "the embodiment of sexuality and of all that is associated with sexuality, disease as well as passion," the Mexicana qua prostitute marked the outer limits of white femininity.[61]

In light of the social transformations of the late nineteenth century, the presence of nonnormative or "deviant" bodily and sexual practices in cultural memory was subversive, undermining patriarchal authority over white womanhood. Already by the turn of the century sexual behaviors and values had started to shift among the white middle class, due in large part to structural changes in society, including the growth of industrial and consumer capitalism and urbanization. It was the entry of middle-class women into the labor market, together with their participation in the spheres of capitalist consumption and commodified leisure, that ultimately worked to undermine the dominant sexual order of the nineteenth century.

Young white women started to exert their presence in the public sphere, as subjects of leisure and entertainment, venturing outside the home, interacting face-to-face with men "on downtown sidewalks and streetcars, in offices, department stores, restaurants, factories, and in parks at lunch hour, in dance halls, amusement parks, pleasure streamers and nickel movie houses."[62] It is within the context of white women's visibility in the public sphere that the import of Mexicana bodies is most relevant.

Decades after the Mexicanas of the Southwest, white women began to openly express their sensuality and eroticism, abandoning the restraints on corporal pleasures imposed by "civilized morality." Similar to Mexicanas of the previous century, modern white women embraced passion and alternative pleasures of the body, leisure, and liberating forms of expression. In fact the white women of the new century no longer lashed their vitals or wore petticoats. They now courted, danced, and amused themselves in public so much that these newly emergent practices of the body, new sexual values, behaviors, and expressions appeared to mimic those practiced by Mexicanas half a century earlier. The emergent public expressions of pleasure, desire, and erotics did not escape the attention of middle-class reformers, who, unable to distinguish between women who went to dance halls for amusement and prostitutes, began to wage a campaign against amusement parks, dancing halls, motion picture houses, and prostitution.[63]

They were aided in their efforts by zealous motion picture producers, who readily revived the trope of racialized sexuality. The fact that women of color like Mexicanas figure as the embodiment of "deviant sexuality" and mark the outer limits of white femininity is evident from the sexual/racial imagery associated with their silent film portrayals. Images of Mexicana immorality created by early film producers contributed to the belief in white superiority as much as these representations served to circumscribe the moral parameters of white female sexuality. In fact, open expressions of erotics associated with Mexicana femininity posed such a formidable threat to the dominant racial/sexual regime that the only way to contain alternative sexuality was through a process of racialization that repeated and fixed the image of Mexicanas in the cultural imaginary as nonnormative or racially and sexually deviant.

The year that Griffith made *Mexican Sweethearts,* 1909, "marks the emergence in American cinema of the middle class vision of sexual morality," according to Janet Staiger, "a period of intense struggle within the middle class to define an appropriate version of and explanation for Woman and women's sexuality."[64] Examining the system for regulating sexual and gender content of early cinema, Staiger documents how white middle-class reformers viewed movies instrumentally, as tools for instructing U.S. audiences on appropriate sexual values and behaviors. The movement to reform cinema worked through the National Board of Censorship — a voluntary, self-regulatory group comprised of exhibitors, producers, and civic organizations — to insure film stories would be pre-scriptive, directing behavior in appropriate ways. "Reviews during the period 1907–1912 illustrate this regulatory assumption about the function of narrative. Narratives were tools for constructing social consensus and controlling deviance."[65]

In many ways, silent films from the early twentieth century demon-strate the widespread social concern with regulating white women's sex-uality, identities, and desires, along with the specific narrative techniques for a cinema designed with that objective in mind. Just as the National Board of Censorship privileged stories that focused on "individuated characters and personal agency as reasons for events" and that were guided by moralizing imperatives through which "virtue" triumphed over "vice," so too were the films about modern women expected to adhere to a certain level of propriety. According to Staiger, "Inappropriate desire — of sexuality or of consumer products — could harm social stability," and therefore films dealing with the desires of new women were expected to "regulate that desire to the right degree and right object."[66]

Unlike Victorian images of "true womanhood" rooted in domesticity, chastity, purity, and submissiveness, the images of women depicted in early cinema were "not condemned for existing or functioning in the pub-lic sphere, but they [were] encouraged to be dutiful, respectful, properly passionate and thoughtful."[67] White women were encouraged to follow the "proper" direction through the "moral lesson" afforded by contrast-ing representations of "improper" or deviant femininities, mostly ren-dered through images of women from other races and classes. Like the "Bad Woman" that Staiger tells us "exists to provide a lesson in narratives about her alternative," the presence of Mexicana characters in the plot serves to modulate white female desire for and indulgence in alternative sexual and bodily practices.

Through the depiction of sexual delinquency and rebellion of two Mexicana characters in *Red Girl* and *Mexican Sweethearts,* Griffith reworks eugenicist ideology's discomfort with alternative sexualities. Other films of the silent era confirm the existence of "bad" Mexicana characters as plot devices, to serve as moral lessons for both white characters in the film and white female spectators of the film.[68] Yet the strategy of visual counterpoint proved the most effective for establishing the moral parameters of white femininity.

Cecil B. DeMille's *Girl of the Golden West* (1915) also contrasts white and Mexicana femininity. Set in a California mining town during the nineteenth century, the film tells the tale of male redemption through the interracial romance between the white "Gal" who runs a saloon she has inherited from her father and "Ramereez," the head of a band of Mexican bandits who is passing for white. The pair meet and fall in love by the river, where Ramereez claims to be Rick Johnston from Sacramento. Throughout the narrative, the dual identities of the male lead are rendered visually, through the imaging contrast between the white female, Gal, and the Mexicana, Nina. Before the racialized, violent, passionate, vengeful, and jealous Nina, who not only smokes but also ultimately betrays him, Ramereez plays the degenerate (Mexican) bandit; yet he is a law-abiding citizen/gentleman (i.e., white) around the hardworking, pious, proper, and morally restrained Gal. In this regard, the Mexicana character is simply a plot device used to circumscribe the moral parameters of both masculinity and femininity. White womanhood is the primary agent of transformation, enabling the male subject's metamorphosis from the racialized Ramereez to the good, white guy. In the end, Ramereez abandons his "evil" ways, leaving Nina for Gal and a life as Rick Johnson.

To some degree, *Martyrs of the Alamo,* directed by Christy Cabanne under the tutelage of Griffith, is even more effective in staking out the moral boundaries for white femininity. As a historical film, *Martyrs of the Alamo* adheres to the prerequisite standards of period costuming, so my concern focuses less on racial contrasts in dress/fashion than on differences in bodily practices, sexual values, and sexual behaviors. The narrative develops in parallel structure, alternating between sharply contrasted spaces: white women are shot mostly indoors; Mexicanas, outdoors. I noted in chapter three the film mechanisms used to stage white femininity under assault, as indicated by the opening intertitle: "Under the Dictator's rule, the honor and life of American womanhood was held in contempt." The following scene emphasizes the point dramatically by depicting a white woman horrified at the sight of a Mexican soldier who violates her honor when he touches the quintessential bodily symbol of sexual purity and moral virtue: her blonde locks. The contrast with racialized femininity is immediately established in the next scene of

Mexicanas dancing outdoors with the same soldiers, who will assault white womanhood throughout the story.

As the film unfolds, the link between Mexican cultural practices such as dancing and a model of nonnormativity intensifies. The president of Mexico, General Santana (described by an intertitle as an "inveterate drug fiend . . . also famous for his shameful orgies") sits in a drunken stupor, next to four Mexicana women who also appear drugged as they observe a fifth Mexicana dancing. Wearing culturally specific clothing (vests, skirts, mantillas) in dark colors, the Mexicanas are hypersexualized in the film as General Santana's prostitutes, as females who entertain (work) "while Mexicans indulged in their afternoon siesta," according to the preceding intertitle. Without a doubt, these intensely erotic displays of Mexicanas dancing for General Santana (imaged here as the culprit of one of his "shameful orgies") conjured up images of "border-town prostitutes" among moviegoers who had heard from eugenicists about the Mexican women spreading venereal disease and causing racial degeneration on the U.S.-Mexico border.[69]

The discursive constructions of Mexicana nonnormativity and conflation of Mexicana and prostitute can be traced to the same masculinist logic that is unable to distinguish "women who went to dance halls for amusement" from prostitutes. It is a racist, masculinist logic of white eugenicists who would "identify as depravity most sexual expressions that fell outside the bounds of prevailing middle-class standards."[70] Nonnormative bodily expressions, an emphasis on body erotics, and the appearance of alternative sexual practices, gestures, and behaviors came to be understood as signs of sexual pathology and to be linked to racial degeneracy. And for a ruling order suffering from a "repressed discomfort with sexuality," Mexicanas qua prostitutes came to symbolize the outer limits of sexuality.[71]

Open expressions of sexuality on the part of Mexicanas in the Southwest remained as subversive and even ominous residues in cultural memory. For in setting "negative" examples for white women to emulate, the very visibility of Mexicanas in the public sphere came to be seen as threatening the social control and management of white womanhood. Out of the racial/sexual fears of the ruling order came a destructive urge to devalorize and dehumanize the alternative erotics that Mexicana bodies represented. The racial and sexual othering of Mexicanas in cinematic space was part of a system of representation obsessed with regulating white women's sexuality, identities, and desires in the early twentieth century.

CHAPTER EIGHT

Ghosts of a Mexican Past

This chapter is dedicated to the memory of Tío Daniel Garza Jr.,
Ponciano Mendoza, Cipriano Villarreal, and Federico Treviño —
early Tejano pioneers in the movie industry. And to Gramma
Angelita Garza for remembering their stories.

*My grandmother looks at me through abalone-rim spectacles:
"Me gustaban mucho las vistas, con Mary Pickford, y tambien
con Rudolph Valentino, pero nunca las de Tom Mix porque en
ellas los mexicanos siempre aparecían como greasers."*

This book evolved over decades, beginning in a time when I first connected to the old story of Mexican Corpus Christi through my Gramma
Angelita's memories. On this day in 1971, my maternal grandmother has
taken time off from tending the store to indulge me in an interview for a
history assignment. As part of a "time capsule" project, my history class
was charged with chronicling the life story of the family's eldest member.
I recall that the transcripts of the interviews we conducted were to be col-
located in a time capsule together with other identifiable memorabilia of
our time and scheduled for opening a century later, in 2071. I don't
remember ever actually seeing the time capsule, though its image is forever implanted in my mind as a small cigar-shaped spacecraft, invulner-
able even to a nuclear attack, like the cockroaches we were told would
outlive us. Gramma Angelita was a perfect subject for the project. She had
not forgotten her Mexican past, a past that reached deep into the heart of

South Texas. She conjured up the ghosts of Mexican Corpus with each pondered step she took through her fragmentary memories.

She remembers the year 1914, standing patiently for hours, under the marquis of the Amusu Theater, wearing a wine-colored skirt and matching vest. It was during the *canícula* (dog days), when the summer's scalding heat clenches the earth, that Gramma Angelita and her best friend Cuquita lined up at the ticket window of the Amusu in downtown Corpus Christi. For weeks, she had anticipated the grand opening of the theater and was prepared to wait in line from twelve noon to 10:30 P.M. with several thousand eager moviegoers who rode in from surrounding towns. It was Ponciano Mendoza's enticing descriptions of the theater's "luxuriousness" and "conveniences" which had stirred up so much barrio furor about the Amusu, labeling it the most "modern" photo playhouse in Texas, distinguished from most others by its "excellence in pictures." Mr. Mendoza should know; he was a local projectionist.

The seven-hundred-seat theater was modern in many respects. Patrons entered through a ten-foot-high lobby refurbished in marble and glass plates and brightly polished tile floors, then went through a smaller lobby with laboratories poised at each end, and finally into the grand auditorium, its walls adorned in French gray, ivory, and maroon with an added touch of gold stenciling, resembling the finest movie palaces in the country. To dissuade potential pickpockets, the building's architects opted for indirect lighting, which remained dimly lit during the performances.[1]

Gramma Angelita explains how she formed a more or less vivid image of the theater based on Ponciano's descriptions, culled from his daily visits to the construction site. On opening day, Angelita could not keep the cooling system out of her mind as she fanned herself on that humid August afternoon, for the newly installed air conditioner, described back then as a "system of temperature control," promised to make the Amusu into a truly ultra-modern marvel of the border region.

The supply of fresh air into the Amusu Theater would be continuous, brought into the building by a stack extending well above the auditorium, with changes in the entire air supply every quarter hour. Vent flues located in the opposite side of the building would insure the removal of foul air. During the cold months of Corpus, roughly December and January, the air supply would be warmed by steam in the basement and circulated into the auditorium through a ceiling line at the rate of 4,500 cubic feet per minute. In hot weather, from April through October, radiation pipes filled with cold water were designed to cool the air before delivering it into the auditorium for the patrons' comfort.

After a long wait in the suffocating heat, Angelita and Cuquita finally approached the ticket booth to purchase their tickets for the premiere matinee of *A Romance of Normandy* and *A Circle of Love,* and their orchestral accompaniment. Both teenage girls were then ushered in through the rear entrance of the building and directed to the hundred-seat section for "colored" patrons.

The bulky reel-to-reel recorder I borrowed from my father to record Gramma Angelita's interview served me well in documenting several hours of her recollections about Corpus's Mexican past — details unrecorded and unpublished in any official history about the city. There is little written about Tejanas and Tejanos or about the booming Mexican part of Corpus. We are mentioned in generic terms: an amalgamated mass of hands, as "cheap laborers," without names or discernible faces, working in the agriculture and cattle industries. Tejanas and Tejanos — those who built the downtown skyscrapers, the railroads and connecting roadways for transporting cotton and oil; the city's construction crews, its carpenters, electricians, and bricklayers; the shoeshine boys, sales clerks in downtown department stores, butchers, seamstresses in haute couture, magazine and newspaper vendors, owners of grocery stores and bicycle shops; the telephone operators, those who painted billboards and those who swept the city streets; the tailors, the theater owners, the barrileros who hauled fresh water; the Texas Mexicans who consumed mass entertainment and other products of consumer capitalism — all absent from official historical pronouncements about the forefathers of this "Sparkling City by the Sea." The lost memories of the Mexicans *de este lado* (from this side of the border) haunted Gramma Angelita, seeming to devour her until she told stories of that earlier time.

Thirty years later as I document Mexican visibility I too am haunted by ghosts of Corpus's old Mexican barrios, the human actors in a history I never lived. I ask Angelita about Mexican entertainment in the old days ("¿Cómo se divertían los mexicanos?"); her reply includes *las vistas* (the movies), along with *baños en la playa* (beach bathing) and family *pachangas* (gatherings). Of course, it makes sense that in the parallel world of Mexicans — hidden from public (white) sight but not from their public scrutiny — the movies would be an unforgettable part of everyday life. Despite being ignored by the white people of Corpus, Mexicans were agents and participants of modernity. Thanks to a few diligent history scholars, there are now several publications documenting the history of Mexican and Latina/o stars and movie directors. Yet we know very little about the off-screen, behind-the-scenes presence of Mexicans, about those who brought the movies to barrios in Texas, New Mexico, California. Who were the exhibitors of las vistas? The owners of small movie houses and nickelodeons? The projectionists and even more, their audiences?

We know a great deal about immigrant moviegoers in the northeastern United States, but little about the Texas Mexicans, the Arizona Mexicans, the California Mexicans, both native and immigrant audiences of Mexican descent who embraced U.S. movies with enthusiasm. How did they experience *las vistas mudas* (moving pictures)? When did they attend? What were the material conditions of those early movie houses and the storefront nickelodeons? How were audiences segregated? Who were the Mexican and Latina theater owners? What meaning did the movies have in the everyday lives of Mexicans in the United States?

The writing of this book is inseparable from the efforts and insights of ancestors like Gramma Angelita who memorized the stories of Corpus's Mexican past, knowing quite well that they would not find themselves in the textbooks or museum displays of the city's founding fathers or into the media's perpetual reinvention of the city's glorious past. My Gramma Angelita was intuitive in that way, and clear about racial politics in South Texas. Which is why she planted the seed of curiosity in me at a young age, mindful that one day I would track the footprints of Mexican foremothers and fathers in Texas. As I struggle to rescue my Gramma Angelita's ghosts, her memories converge with my own (figure 11).

Angelita was fifteen years old when the Amusu Theater opened its doors. She was the only daughter of six children born to Manuela Cavazos and Daniel Garza. The Garzas left the border region of Brownsville/Matamoros a few years after the turn of the century, twelve years after *el primo*, Catarino Garza, launched a failed Texas-based invasion into Mexico in 1892 to dethrone Mexican dictator Porfirio Díaz. It wasn't the violence of the Mexican Revolution, but the violence perpetrated by Texas Rangers and U.S. military troops against Mexicans on the border which forced the Garzas to migrate to *el norte*. Like many other Tejano/a familias, the Garzas felt that the savage rampages by the *rinches* (Texas Rangers) had made the border an unsafe place for raising children.

Besides, at the turn of the century, poor landless Mexicans like the Garzas had few job options in South Texas. Some labored for the old cattle ranches as peons within a paternalistic, semifeudal system; others worked for wages as cowboys, cotton and fruit pickers, or railroad work-

FIGURE 11. My grandmother, Angelita Garza Orea, in an interior shot of "Garza's #2," one of thirteen grocery stores she owned with her four brothers during the 1920s in Mexican Corpus Christi. The photo was taken by her then boyfriend, my grandfather, Alfonso Orea Vélez. Personal collection.

ers.[2] Daniel Garza pursued a different path, as a fisherman. In this choice he followed his father, who had sold freshly caught fish from the warm waters of the Texas/Tamaulipas Gulf coast.

Knowing this was still the homeland, *este lado*, far yet near from *el otro lado*, as Mexico was called, Manuela and Daniel left the borderlands, packed their six children, came and settled near that other border, the Nueces River. After living in a horse-drawn wagon in an encampment on the outskirts of town for one year, near a section known today as "Six Points," the Garzas moved into a one-bedroom shot-gun house five blocks west of the Convent of the Incarnate Word.

While Daniel Garza fished off the Gulf Coast, the ever-resourceful Manuela did a much better job of schooling her children than the Corpus teachers would have. They prepared Mexicans for a life of menial labor. A tall, stout woman with a strong aquiline nose and skin the color of *dulce de leche,* Manuela braided her hair twice a day, after waking and before going to sleep. She possessed the independent spirit of border women from the ranchos, those skillful *fronterizas* who shunned *trabajo de raya* (wage labor), preferring *sus labores* (self-employment). Passing her disdain for trabajo de raya on to her children, Mamá Mere, as she would be called by her grandchildren and great-grandchildren, taught the young Garzas the vendor's trade. At first she supervised them as they carried buckets of fish while scurrying door to door selling their father's daily catch. By the time my great-grandfather Daniel died five years later, Angelita and the five young Garza boys were past the apprentice stage, ready to be launched by Mamá Mere on their own, as bona fide vendors on the streets of the business district.

Angelita remembers the day when they arrived in Corpus in July of 1904, driving straight into the Peoples Street pier over the railroad tracks by way of the Bluff, where the wealthy residents of the seaport town lived. Angelita had never seen such grand and stately homes anywhere on the border. Overlooking the bay, the mansions, shaded by mesquites and salt cedars, were kept separate from the sidewalk and electrical poles by white picket fences running continuously down Upper Broadway. A few blocks from the Bluff, Angelita saw the town's business district, crowded with ebullient passersby and shoppers walking or riding in horse-drawn buggies down streets with Spanish names like Chaparral and Mesquite. Once they crossed Water Street, Angelita noticed the bay front glistening with the activity of weekend bathers enjoying the gentle surf and cool Gulf Coast breeze as couples rowed in small boats under the opaque Corpus afternoon sky. Near the Central Wharf, where a modest boat was loading local tourists for its excursion around the bay, the Garzas jumped into the warm salty Gulf water, which, Angelita would later recall, compensated for those weeks of traveling during the Hadean heat of the summer. Las vistas came to Texas soon after the Garzas first swam in the waters of the Gulf of Mexico.

By 1907, according to film historians, there were nine electric theaters operating in Austin, and in the fall of the same year Dallas opened its first picture house.[3] Perhaps because Corpus was developing as a summer tourist spot, moving pictures had arrived in this small seaport town two years earlier. The Grand Theater opened its doors in 1905 and was one of a handful of theaters in the country featuring "Synchroscope Moving Pictures"—a costly method of synchronizing sounds with images by means of a phonograph record that played along simultaneously with the movie.[4] The owner of the Grand, William Hamil, advertised the unique attraction in 1907: "See and Hear the marvelous Synchroscope pictures that talk and sing."[5]

By 1906, a mixed bill of vaudeville shows with movies at the end of each performance was standard fare in at least three Corpus theaters, including the Grand on Mesquite, the Pavilion on the city's big bay front pier attraction (owned by a corporation whose officers included four women), and the Crystal Theater in the downtown district on Chaparral.[6] And in 1906, the Seaside Electric Theater opened as the city's first movies-only show palace.

As a child Angelita's favorite entertainment was las vistas. Once a week the Garzas walked downtown in a straight line, children strolling in pairs, with Manuela and Daniel at the rear of the procession, to the Seaside Theater across the street from the Seaside Hotel. On Sundays after Mass they headed for the heart of the uptown shopping district to the nick-elodeon near the Fenix Cafe on Leopard Street. Arriving half an hour before the first matinee, they paid the five-cent entrance fee, entered the converted storefront movie house, and joined dozens of other mostly Tejana/o patrons, sitting on wooden crates or standing in the jam-packed room for the fifteen-minute shows. The room was filled with laughter and the chatter of women, men and children talking back to the funny images of those moving stories of a man falling from a second-story building, another looking through a window while a woman undressed, a third being chased by a mob of women, the disappearing acts of clowns who pulled rabbits out of hats. Each movie lasted a couple of minutes.

The titles escape Angelita's memory, but she probably watched early movies with names like *Pull Down Curtain, Susie, Princess Nicotine,* and *Visit to the Spiritualist.* She took great pleasure in munching peanuts and in the enchantment of the dancing fairies. The hypnotic effect of those early moving pictures with images of people no larger than three feet, projected on that white wall in front of her by the Edison machine, invaded her own dream-movies well into her crone years.

Tío Charlie, son of Daniel Garza, the eldest brother of Angelita, remembered another Mexican projectionist, Cipriano Villarreal, who also mesmerized the Garza children with colorful stories.[7] Like the Garzas, Cipriano traced his lineage to a time when Texas was Mexico. He claimed to be the direct descendent of el Capitán Enrique de Villarreal, a ranchero who ten years after Mexico's independence from Spain in 1821 had been granted the territory known as Rincón del Oso, which included today's Corpus Christi.

Cipriano's mother lived next door to the Garzas and once or twice a year, usually at Easter and Christmas, he came to visit, staying for a month at a time, amusing the neighborhood kids on Antelope Street with extravagant tales about his life on the rancho and his travels to other states. Angelita once told me that Cipriano worked as a cowboy, herding cows and horses for the large cattle ranches as far north as Waco, Texas. She remembers stories of his adventures north to Chicago and as far east as New York, and how he filled the children's minds with fantastic reports of riding wild bucks, rounding up cattle near the breath of a giant tornado, lassoing horses in three feet of snow, and wandering from city to city in search of moving pictures he had not seen before. Perhaps Cipriano first developed his addiction for movies much earlier, in Waco, around 1896, at the Kinetoscope Parlor — Living Pictures, where he first saw and fell in love with Carmencita.

I am no longer surprised to hear how the Mexicans (or Spanish) who first settled the area were so intertwined with modernity. The love of Cipriano's life, the Spanish dancer Carmencita, was known as the "first queen of the movies." She had already become a "national sensation" in New York City, prior to the turn of the century, dancing first on live stage and later for the kinetograph — the Edison camera that recorded pictures in motion.[8] Before collective viewings became possible by large projection machines, movie viewing was restricted to one person at a time on the Edison peep-show machine, also known as the kinetoscope. One fateful day in Waco, Cipriano inserted a coin into the slot of a small, single-viewer contraption that started the picture of the Latin dancing queen rolling, and in that diabolical North Texas heat, Carmencita's sensual movements hypnotized and forever transformed him into an avid consumer of modern amusements.

Tío Charlie says that Cipriano roamed the northern states for four years, visiting cities where movies showed continuously from ten in the morning to ten at night. He might have wandered into penny arcades and kinetoscope parlors, dime museums and storefront nickelodeons, often catching two shows an hour, but always searching for Carmencita. His love deepened whenever he encountered the "original queen of the movies," seeing her several times again in various parts of the country as she danced endlessly for single viewers — those countless wandering customers, lonely men and curious women — the true amusement buyers created by storefront theaters that in the mid-1890s became the first venues for picture shows. Then as the country entered the twentieth century, Carmencita disappeared abruptly from sight, foreshadowing the fate of countless "Latina" actresses throughout the new century. Although her image evaporated, she left Cipriano with a deep longing that he often placated with reports of her apparition in places as far away as Colombia and

Venezuela: Carmencita, the Spanish dancer, "the first queen of the movies," inciting the passions of Latin America's men and women for years to come.

Around the time Cipriano abandoned his pilgrimages to the northern states, Angelita remembers the magic of movies starting to dot the lives of Tejanos and Tejanas, who were first introduced to modern amusements through *la carpa* (tent theater). A traveling show of dancers and magicians, comedians, and musicians, la carpa provided Spanish-language entertainment to Mexicans working in the ranchos, to cotton pickers during the ten-week harvest season, to barrio residents in urban centers like Corpus. Movies brought in by showmen of itinerant carpas were sandwiched into risqué burlesque numbers, fandangos, and comedy acts, cultivating a loyal clientele among South Texas Mexicans for picture houses, especially the cheaper venues, known as nickelodeons. The nickelodeon — a name coined by a Philadelphia exhibitor from "nickel" (for five cents) and "odeon" (the Greek term for theater) — spread rapidly as exhibition outlets; there were thousands operating throughout the United States by 1910.[9]

Few Tejanos would remember the names of these little shops and converted storefronts littering the busy business district of Corpus. What they would recall were the crowded, dark, and dingy spaces, poorly ventilated, with the stench of tobacco mixed with mildew, the smell of body odor, cheap perfumes, powders, and liniments, the grating Mexican music ringing from phonographs. These pioneer movie houses evaporated as quickly as they had appeared on the streets of this seaport town, but many upscale theaters remained in operation until the great storm devastated Corpus on September 14, 1919.[10]

Angelita's memory is ancient, native memory, literally inscribed on her body. "Mira," she would often say while raising the sleeve of her blouse, "ni un solo pelo, como los indios." Not a single hair, like the Indians. I imagine her ancestors to be the alleged six-foot human-flesh eaters, known as the Karankawas, who roamed the coastal plains with the Comanches, Apaches, and Tonkawas before white men conquered the region. Or perhaps she is a direct descendent of the mestizo progeny of Indians and the Spanish conquistadors of the Gulf Coast, men like Alonzo Alvarez de Pineda, who sailed into the bay on the Feast of Corpus Christi in 1519 and baptized the area with this name. Angelita's people were here before the second conquest of Texas by Anglo-Americanos, before Colonel H. L. Kinney allegedly founded the town in

1839. She traces her genealogy to Indian times, to a time when Texas is Mexico, to a time before history is recorded in English. She once told me how she was worried that they were erasing Mexicans: "Nos están borrando poco a poco." And she was right. Like every official account of Corpus's past, the history of early movie houses is white history, written in English.

In Corpus Christi, the growth of movie houses catering to whites coincided with the advent of the star system and the popularity of Westerns in 1909 and 1910. Programming was geared toward English-speaking audiences, particularly to the white middle class, who could afford to pay the ten-, twenty-, and even thirty-cent entrance fees for a mixed program of vaudeville and movies. As in other parts of the country, middle-class audiences "embraced the movies before the advent of features."[11]

Prior to the release of features containing five or more reels, like *Quo Vadis,* which premiered in 1913 for an entrance fee of $1, the typical storytelling film was one thousand feet of reel in length and ran for fourteen minutes. For twenty cents, Corpus's white middle class would catch a two-hour show at the Crystal Theater: live performances by Irish comedians and clog dancers, followed by the storytelling films — *Girl Sweet, Road to Love,* and *Wheel of Justice.* Miss St. Claire sang regularly at the Grand before the nightly movie showings.

These large-capacity movie houses were able to attract middle-class, English-speaking audiences because the theaters were larger, cleaner, and better ventilated than the lower end picture houses, where the programming was not of the highest quality, with breaks and scratches on the celluloid reels producing blurred images. The higher end venues guaranteed better quality movies and thus could afford to charge pricey entrance fees. Besides, upscale movie houses changed programming twice and even three times a week, renting from exchanges or distributors movies that had not shown in other theaters around town. On one night, a well-to-do moviegoer could watch a combination of shorts and storytelling films like *Hanson's Folly, The Aviation Meet in Los Angeles,* and *Baby's First Tooth* at the Seaside; on a second night attend the Crystal's showing of Biograph's *Saved from Conviction,* along with *Eavesdropper, Suicide Club, His Masterpiece,* and *A Man with Three Wives;* and on a third night catch the Olympic by the Sea's movie-drama presentation, *Cupid against the Dollar,* for the price of twenty or thirty cents per visit, depending on the time of day.[12]

Since Angelita and her five brothers sold Spanish and English newspapers and magazines along the burgeoning downtown strip, with people coming and going throughout the day and into the early evening, they must have witnessed the transformation of the Grand into the Ideal Theater in 1913, and the addition of more movie houses like the Palm Garden Theater and the Lyric. I believe they were even present when the first single-viewer movie house, the Penny Arcade, opened its doors that same year.

The Seaside Theater was the first exclusive motion picture playhouse in Corpus, featuring continuous showings from 6:30 P.M. daily, with Wednesday and Saturday matinees. As the legal battles intensified between the consortium of production companies banded under the Motion Picture Patents Company and independent production companies, the Seaside Theater opened its doors in 1912.[13] Seeking to establish its distance from the independents, who were being threatened with closure by Edison lawyers for using "outlaw" projectors and movies, the Seaside Theater ran the following ad for its opening night: "Shows only licensed photoplays."

In addition to its daily change in movies, the Seaside hired musicians such as the "four-piece lady orchestra" to accompany its movie showings. It was also the first theater to advertise pictures with stars. On opening night the theater featured the Edison comedy *Three of a Kind,* two Essanay movies, *An Indian's Sacrifice* (a love story set on the reservation) and a Western, *The Stage Driver's Daughter,* with G. M. Anderson starring as Bronco Billy.[14] A vaudeville actor of Jewish origin, Anderson was born in Arkansas as Max Aaronson, and his character, Bronco Billy, became famous internationally. Filming in outdoor sets in Oakland, California, in replicas of the "authentic Old West," Anderson directed many of his Bronco Billy films and originated what became known as the "double system" — an effect created by shots and editing in which "the more daring stunts were executed by a skilled cowboy or trained athlete" in long shot, while the star appeared in the close-ups.[15]

Angelita celebrated her eleventh birthday one week before her father passed away, and she stopped attending school after the fifth grade. After my great-grandfather Daniel died, the Garza children worked most of the day, leaving them with little time, much less money, to sustain their weekly moviegoing habits. "Cuando se abrió el Teatro Juárez en la calle Leopardo," Angelita tells me, "empezamos a ir al cine mucho más seguido." The Garzas were now in their teens, working as vendors in different sections of the business district. Early every morning, Tío Dan, the eldest, walked uptown and unlocked the small wooden stand that the

Garzas rented in front of the C. C. Bicycle Shop and waited for the daily delivery of newspapers and magazines from throughout Texas and Mexico. Tío Dan and Gramma Angelita ran the makeshift stand while the younger Garzas divided up the magazines, weeklies, and dailies for street and delivery sales. They would meet every evening to tabulate their sales and hand over their money to Mamá Mere, who took care of the operation's accounting, paying rental and licensing fees and distributor's accounts. Gramma remembers that as she closed the newsstand each evening, her brother would go over to the C. C. Bicycle Shop so he could learn to repair bicycles under the direction its owner, Federico Treviño. He too had grown up as an orphan and for that reason took Tío Dan under his wing.

My granduncle, Tío Dan, was known in the Mexican part of town as a "jack-of-all-trades." Always a die-hard merchant, ambitious and hard-working, as cagey as he was curious. Throughout the years, Tío Dan left no stone of opportunity unturned, mastering as many trades as his years on earth would let him. Tío Dan made one exception to Mamá Mere's rule about trabajo de raya. He would work for others if there was trade knowledge to be gained. That's how he learned to be a tailor, a bicycle maker, an owner of a chain of grocery stores, a publisher, a projectionist, and so forth. The Garzas were clannish in part because of Tío Dan, who took the Mexican adulation for "la familia" to an extreme. Family loyalty was the first rule; guarding family secrets the second. Years later I witnessed Tío Dan's familia orientation in action when, rather than buy from a much cheaper grocery supermarket, my Gramma Angelita often insisted that I drive her around town as she made the rounds, buying groceries from each of her brothers, who still owned small corner tienditas, even as ancianos. To this day no one will talk about Tío Dan's womanizing or his failed business ventures, or about his controlling nature, though rumors circulated about the reasons for his extreme clannishness.

I heard about the time his grade school classmates nicknamed him "el chuequito" because he was born deformed, with a crooked neck, given to him by a brusque partera (midwife) who had such a difficult time guiding Tío Dan into the world that she yanked his malleable little head to one side as he was exiting Mamá Mere's birth canal. Pained at the sight of her son walking around with a slanted neck, Mamá Mere tried every known cure. A harbinger of the secret sciences, she knew how to cure with ancient indigenous and African Moorish remedies, giving Tío Dan te de Malabar to dilate the blood vessels, rubbing camphor oil, pomada de vivora de cascabel, unguento de los doce milagros, and linimento de los siete met-

ales (a special mixture of metals such as copper, iron, gold, silver, mercury, ore, and nickel) on his neck each night. She even tried tying his head to a board while Tío Dan slept at night, but every morning his neck would return to its original position, barely floating on his right shoulder. A Western medicine doctor in Brownsville suggested operating for the condition he termed "neck nerve compression," but Mamá Mere opted to take Tío Dan to the healer of Los Olmos, Don Pedrito Jaramillo, who prayed over Tío Dan while giving him special healing water to drink. Even Don Pedrito's miracles would not reverse my tío's fate, so the crooked neck stayed with him the rest of his life, perhaps I suspect, even causing his suspicion of others.

The Chicana librarian is startled by my request. "There are no books in the library about Mexican American businesses," she whispers to me. In April of 1996 I am searching Corpus's public library for book, newspaper, or magazine accounts of the old Mexican merchant class, my ancestors, and for any archival evidence of Mexican theaters, nickelodeons, or movie houses in the early twentieth century, at the very least for written acknowledgment of their existence. She brings me an overflowing manila folder labeled "Corpus Christi Theaters," containing newspaper articles dating from the teens to the present. It is here that I find Frank Wagner's unpublished article on the history of early movie houses in Corpus. As I return the folder the librarian, she whispers once again, "If you really want to find any record of Mexican American businesses, you can look through old phone books."

I would not find any evidence of the Teatro Juárez, which Angelita remembers as a majestic two-story building on Leopard Street, built in 1910 or 1911. Neither in Wagner's compilation of movie theaters nor in the phone books. "The hurricane of 1919 destroyed all the newspaper files and city records," Frank Wagner explains over the phone when I call him to discuss his article. Could this be why the parallel world that Corpus Mexicans inhabited in the old days disappeared from official memory?

The growth of entertainment houses throughout the region coincided with the rise in xenophobia, as South Texas entered the second decade of the twentieth century with more lynchings and growing segregation at schools, restaurants, bathing beaches, and picture shows. Texas Mexicans had not been passive victims of Anglo discrimination and prejudice. They organized politically in 1911 at a meeting in Laredo, Texas, known as the Congreso Mexicanista, where leaders of the Texas Mexican community called for an end to "educational discrimination, lynchings, and urged Texas Mexicans not to sell their lands." Race relations reached a boiling point in 1915 when *los sediciosos* issued the Plan de San Diego, which encouraged the unity of Mexicans, Asians, Indians, and blacks against the white race, and urged Texas Mexicans to reclaim the lands taken by Anglos. After los sediciosos staged raids into the United States from Mexico, the Texas Rangers unleashed a reign of terror in South Texas, lynching three thousand Texas Mexicans and transforming the border region into a war zone from 1915 to 1917. President Teddy Roosevelt eventually ordered U.S. troops into the region to prevent the invasion of so-called Mexican bandits who, to the knowledge of everyone in South Texas, were actually Texas Mexicans.[16]

The united uprising that los sediciosos had envisioned never materialized. Texas Mexicans were too terrified by the U.S. military's show of force and by the indiscriminate and unprosecuted lynchings carried out by Texas Rangers. But the spirit of rebellion of los sediciosos lingered on in corridos and conversations at social gatherings, political meetings, street corners, barrio stores, and repair shops — like the evening when Federico, Cipriano, and Tío Dan talked about *"el desprecio a nuestra raza"* (the disdain toward our race/people) in the downtown movie houses.

There were the little things that annoyed Cipriano and kept Corpus Mexicans from patronizing the major movie theaters. In the years Cipriano worked at one of these movie houses, not once did its owners hire Mexican musicians to accompany the picture shows or Mexican vaudeville acts to perform during the reel changes. Efforts to attract a "mixed house" were generally geared toward white ethnic groups like the Irish; the "Mexican race" was not welcome. Although theater owners slanted their photoplays to their white English-speaking clientele, they did not necessarily shun movies with "Mexican" content. And this is what offended some in the Texas Mexican community even more.

Gramma Angelita recalls the "greaser" movies showing at the downtown theaters, the photoplays ridiculing Mexicans, depicting *"a nuestra raza como bandidos y asesinos"* (our race as bandits and assassins). Tejanos were outraged about the "greaser" films in other places as well, especially along the border. Many Tejano theater owners along the border refused to exhibit offensive movies about Mexicans. Newspaper publishers editorialized against movies that represented *"a los mexicanos como seres amorales y repugnantes, como miembros miserables de un pueblo despreciable y bárbaro"* (Mexicans as amoral and repugnant, as members of a despicable and barbarian people); and countless Tejanas and Tejanos walked out of movie houses that exhibited "*las películas denigrantes para los mexicanos*" (movies that Mexicans considered to be degrading).[17] Gramma Angelita remembers that around the time los sediciosos were circulating the Plan de San Diego, Tío Dan talked about Federico's plan to open up a second movie theater for Spanish-speaking patrons, similar to the now-defunct Teatro Juárez.

Federico envisioned a modest venue, improvising in the design and furnishings of the movie house. He rented an empty lot on Waco Street, off the major Mexican shopping district, set up a canvas enclosure like those used by las carpas, arranged discarded wooden crates in place of the more costly portable *butacas* (theater chairs), and hired local Tejano musicians to play guitar during the showing to avoid the expense of a mechanical piano. Acquaintances in the movie industry helped him obtain a large Vitascope Special projector and rent movies from an agent based in Matamoros.

"Así empezó Dan a operar la máquina de películas" (That was how Dan learned to operate the movie machine), Angelita tells me. "Había muy poca gente que sabía como operarla" (There were few people back then who knew how to operate one). In exchange for unlimited access to the weekend movie pictures, Treviño had one of the Garzas selling tickets, Angelita collecting them at the door, and the other Garzas distributing flyers that advertised "*las vistas en la carpa Treviño.*" She remembers Tío Dan learning how to operate the projector from Cipriano and Ponciano and then working for Treviño on a part-time basis. I later learned that Tío Dan would not be the youngest Tejano trained by Ponciano Mendoza. Two years after the opening of Treviño's carpa, a young boy named Félix Longoria walked into the Amusu Theater to watch a matinee after school. A few minutes before the scheduled movie began showing, Ponciano dashed out of the enclosed projection booth, clutching his heart, and collapsed near the young Felix. Although Ponciano survived the heart attack, on that evening he was unable to work. However, the show continued with Félix helping the manager run the Selig Polyscope projector. Once Ponciano recovered, he taught Félix everything he knew about movie projection.[18]

No one had anticipated the overwhelming response to Treviño's movie house for Spanish-speaking patrons. In one month, news of "*las vistas en la carpa de Corpus*" had spread throughout the outlying areas, bringing Texas Mexicans into town from neighboring ranchos and cotton fields near Robstown, Mathis, Alice, Kingsville, and Edroy. Only around seventy-five to a hundred wooden crates could fit comfortably inside the canvas enclosure; Angelita remembers the canvas tent filled beyond its capacity, often with twice the number of ticket holders than seats. Patrons squeezed in wherever they could, sitting two to a crate, with parents piling as many as three children on their lap while other customers stood in the rear next to Tío Dan and his movie machine. When movie-goers began to line up for hours, Federico decided to add additional evening shows.

Problems with the tent enclosure started about six months into Treviño's first year of business. First came the interlopers, who would slip in through the side of the tent without paying, angering others who had purchased tickets yet could not be accommodated for the showing. Then there were rumors about the Anglos living near the uptown district who had filed complaints about the "loud, noisy phonograph" playing late into the night and the Spanish music played by the Tejano trios. Given the cli-mate of racial tensions in South Texas at the time, it seems more plausi-ble that Anglo residents were actually terrified at the sight of so many Mexicans lining up outside the carpa at night.

Unable to prevent eager Tejano moviegoers from sneaking into the tent, much less accommodate the Anglo property owners in the district, Federico purchased a vacant building a block from where la carpa was located, naming the building "Teatro Hidalgo" in honor of the father of Mexico's independence, el Padre Miguel Hidalgo y Costilla. A month after he disassembled the canvas enclosure on Artesian Street, Treviño opened the doors of his Teatro Hidalgo for business.

I supplement Gramma's fragmentary remembrance with sources who write about movie history in other contexts: I imagine Treviño hiring local construction workers to remodel the vacant warehouse and install a raised platform for the projection booth, which would be located at the rear of the building. Like the other downtown movie theaters, Treviño's had to conform to the city's building codes, especially in terms of lining the projection booth with asbestos, which was supposed to keep flames from spreading into the movie house in the event that the highly com-bustible nitrate film caught on fire.[19]

Men like Tío Dan, Ponciano Mendoza, and Cipriano Villarreal took special pride in the movie performances, especially in their own per-formances as projectionists, measured in part by the steady and coordi-nated movement of the hand crank on the part of the machine operator, who controlled the persistent flow of the celluloid strip passing through the lamp and creating the illusion of physical movement. Although Tío Dan found it difficult to keep las vistas flowing in a rhythmic pattern when he worked in the crowded space of la carpa, at the Teatro Hidalgo things were much different.

Carpenters built a ticket booth next to the main entrance, a laboratory on the side of the building, and a spacious, one-floor viewing room, furnished with the butacas that Ponciano had probably purchased from a Dallas-based firm. To accommodate the *espectáculos* — the live Mexican performances of comedy acts, dance numbers, singers, and musicians, as well as the new phonograph that sometimes played synchronized music and dialogue in Spanish — a small stage was built to one side of the screen. Teatro Hidalgo featured continuous shows daily, beginning at 6:00 P.M. and closing at 10:00 P.M., with Saturday and Tuesday matinees and a complete change in pictures and music twice a week. Patrons paid ten cents for one hour's worth of entertainment, usually three reels of film and two live Mexican acts. Besides obtaining movies with narrative panels written in Spanish from Mexico, I wonder if Federico also rented from the film exchanges based in New York, New Jersey, and California, which started distributing U.S.-made movies to Spanish-speaking audiences throughout the Southwest.

Gramma Angelita recalls that a year after the grand opening of el Teatro Hidalgo, Tío Dan was stricken with pneumonia and lay in bed for two weeks. He had been a sickly child, catching colds every winter. Although his propensity for illness had subsided as he got older, during the days he worked at the Teatro Hidalgo, Tío Dan was stricken with colds much more often and not just in the winter, but also on days when the air was humid and the sun warmed the waters of the Gulf Coast. Before his bout with pneumonia, Dan was infected with a case of tonsillitis so severe that his throat and the nose membranes swelled, leaving him unable to speak for weeks. As he lay in bed shivering, Mamá Mere alleviated the symptoms with baths of camphor and eucalyptus, which she forced him to inhale twice a day, but Tío Dan eventually developed pneumonia.

While Gramma did not associate Tío Dan's deteriorating health with his work as a projectionist, I have learned otherwise from my later readings of the hazards related to working in those early projection booths, written by historians of early cinema. Charles Musser tells us: "The projection booth became a furnace from the immense heat generated by the arc light and rheostat. City and state legislatures frequently passed fire laws requiring booths made of steel, with very limited openings for ventilation. Temperatures of 113 Fahrenheit were typical. . . . the carbon dust from the arc lamps used for projection also filled the booth and with it the operator's lungs."[20]

Musser, quoting Willis Elliot Reynolds, who wrote an editorial in a 1908 issue of *Modern Picture World,* describes how the asbestos-lined projection booths, mandated by fire marshals and insurance underwriters, exacerbated many health problems:

"It may not matter for months; perhaps a year, but in time the tiny particles of dust will produce irritation of the mucous membrane. It is therefore highly injurious to the lungs, throat and membrane of the nose," warned Reynolds. "From this irritation may result pneumonia, pleurisy, tonsillitis and chronic catarrh of the nose. It also produces weakness of the brain, excites the nervous system and impoverishes the blood."[21]

Tío Dan's life as a projectionist lasted for nearly four years, until the great hurricane destroyed most of the city's movie houses in 1919, including the Teatro Hidalgo. Although Treviño reopened his movie house the following year under the new name of Teatro Latino, Angelita recalls that Tío Dan moved on to the business of selling groceries, forever leaving behind those cans of celluloid, shadow personalities on the screen, that had already left such an imprint on the lives of Texas Mexicans.

There is a final piece in my recollection of Gramma Angelita's memories worth telling for its significance in the construction of social identities: the "greasers" Gramma Angelita remembers from Westerns with white stars like Tom Mix and Billy Anderson. She detested the word "greaser" as much as the movies in which Tom Mix, former ranch foreman, town marshal, performer in Wild West shows, and director of Selig Westerns, starred as the hero/cowboy. Mix was actually a favorite among audiences in Mexico, who were charmed by his participation in the Mexican Revolution and his alleged association with the revolutionaries Pancho Villa and Francisco Madero. Mexican audiences were also amused by the cowboy/actor's taste for outlandish costumes, which were inspired by the wardrobe of actual Mexican vaqueros.[22] For Mexican audiences on the U.S. side, like my Gramma Angelita, the star and "real-life" persona of Tom Mix signified something entirely different.

The Tom Mix Westerns reminded some in the Texas Mexican community of the ongoing battle between the races under way in South Texas during the early twentieth century. His fictional roles as "good guy" cowboy pitted against "menacing greasers" paralleled the nonfictional power struggles between Anglos and Mexicans on the borderlands. Mix's militarism — culled from his days fighting in the Spanish-American War and as one of Teddy Roosevelt's "Rough Riders" — peppered his cowboy persona, reminding Gramma Angelita of the "rinches" who defended the border from the "greasers."

I knew from Gramma Angelita that whites used the racial epithet "greaser" because "they see us as dirty." At least that is how she explained my first encounter with the word. In the seventh grade, an Anglo classmate had called me "greaser" with such pleasure that, had I missed the hatred spuming from his light blue eyes, I would never have imagined its abusive, contemptuous, and deprecatory nature. Like the equally pernicious slurs "nigger" and "redskin," "greaser" is "skin-deep," to quote Ann du Cille, a reference to the body. I can remember feeling shame after Gramma Angelita explained how the term "greaser" aligned us with "dirt."

There are many version about how "greaser" came to displace "Mexican" in white vernacular culture. Arnoldo de León traces its beginnings to the nineteenth century, when Anglo colonizers first referenced "similarities between Mexicans' color and that of grease." De León goes on to speculate that "greaser" might have been used for Native Americans as well "since the Indians' olive color was thought to be a result of their practice of anointing their skins with oils and greases."[23]

Through the years, I have heard other theories about how the term originated, some of them outrageous, like the one claiming we are called "greasers" because of our culinary delight in lard-fried foods (a very unlikely theory given the countless other ethnic/racial groups, including Anglos, who also revel in deep-fried cuisine); or the other theory tracing "greaser" to Mexican males' extravagant use of pomade to fashion slicked-back hairstyles. A more plausible version is rooted in colonialist discourse, in the "contact zones," a term coined by Mary Louise Pratt, to describe "the space of colonial encounters, the space in which peoples geographically and historically separated come into contact with each other and establish ongoing relations, usually involving conditions of coercion, radical inequality and intractible conflict."[24] One of these contact zones took place in 1836, between Californios and Anglo traders, somewhere north of San Diego, while the war over Texas was being waged and California still belonged to Mexico.

In *A Southwestern Vocabulary,* Cornelius Smith traces "greaser" to a colonial encounter documented in Richard Henry Dana's *Two Years before the Mast,* a travelogue widely read throughout the United States and England. Besides chronicling life on California's rancherías, Dana's writings detail the exploits of Anglo hide and tallow traders traveling through California. "Greaser" originated during one of these exploits, when an Anglo captain of the trade vessel the *Pilgrim* hired California Mexican stevedores to load "fresh uncured hides" onto his ship. The work involved tossing the hides "over a sheer cliff onto the rocky beach below," rowing the hides in small boats, then loading them onto the larger ship: "Working under the boiling sun . . . the Mexican bearers became as greasy as candle-tallow, and were called 'greasers' by the [Anglo] sailors of the Pilgrim."[25]

They called them "greasers" because they "became as greasy as candle tallow," as greasy as the white, solid fat from cattle and sheep used for making candles. Now, how do we get from Dana's account of a seemingly innocuous, even playful (just sailors having some fun) origin for the term, to its racist use? There must be more to Dana's interpretation of the event. Did Anglo sailors taunt the California Mexicans while calling them "greasers?" Or perhaps hatred spumed from the sapphire-colored eyes of white men who yelled "greasers?" How did the California Mexicans respond? And how did the term become so acceptable in public discourse? Were the dime novels of the Wild West responsible for its propagation? Or was it the later silent films about "greasers" that legitimated its use in Anglo vernacular culture? Sure, the birth of "greaser" in the space of colonial encounters, in the contact zone, accounts in large measure for its veering into the domain of xenophobia. But what matters more than its origin is the social use of "greaser," its symbolic capital. "Greaser" is more than a code word and euphemism for Mexican: it points to the ways in which the skin, at least in this country, is the ultimate signifier of abjection. For how else does one get from "as greasy as candle tallow" to my Gramma Angelita's understanding about "greaser's" connection to dirt?

My definition of dirt is also a modern one, related to ideas of hygiene and aesthetics. It is this modern usage of the term, especially its association with hygiene and aesthetics, that for de León explains the racism behind white perceptions of Mexicans, or what I would call the white gaze: "To whites, dark colors connoted filth and therefore Mexicans were a dirty, putrid people, existing in squalor. Thus observers made statements about Mexicans having habits 'as filthy as their persons' or living in the 'most shocking state of filth.'"[26] In displacing "Mexican" with "greaser," whites got caught in a reasoning loop, a false syllogism of sorts. "Greaser" first meant "greasy" and later "dirty" within a racist logic that equates dark skin with racial inferiority, dirt with darkness, Mexican with dirt. If all

Mexicans are greasy and all Mexicans are dirty, then "greasers" are also "dirty."

Within this racial conundrum, "greaser" shares with its synonym, "dirt," an association with modern notions of hygiene and aesthetics. Yet it is the premodern idea of "dirt" as disorder that reveals the power dynamics behind the term "greaser." "What is considered disruptive or transgressive of boundaries," Elizabeth Grosz writes, "is represented as dirt. . . . Dirt is what disrupts order, and order is conceived of as an arbitrary arrangement of elements in relative stability or harmony."[27] Grosz bases her observations on anthropologist Mary Douglas's insight about the relativity of the concept: "There is no such thing as absolute dirt: it exists in the eyes of the beholder."[28] According to Douglas, Western ideas of dirt, dirt avoidance, and pollution behavior are based on the nineteenth-century discovery of the "bacterial transmission of disease" and "knowledge of pathogenetic organisms." Yet underneath these contemporary understanding, lies "the old definition of dirt as matter out of place."[29] Greasers as Mexicans, as dirt, as matter out of place. I am reminded of my Gramma Angelita's colonial encounter with Texas Anglos on the streets of Corpus Christi, of my own over half a century later.

The boy who confronted me in junior high must have heard the term from his father, who heard it from his own father, who, in turn, probably sat with his father in one of those Corpus Christi movie palaces, munching peanuts, having some fun while watching the opening of Biograph's *Licking the Greasers,* believing everything the story had to say about Mexicans. I imagine father and son walking out of the Seaside Electric Theater, running into my Gramma Angelita, who sold newspapers on the streets of downtown Corpus Christi and, while having some more fun they would probably yell, "Look, there goes a little 'greaser' girl . . ."

Epilogue

"We are a people that has seen the ground beneath our feet renamed several times over the last five hundred years."[1] From the perverse images of meXicanas circulating in the cultural landscape, one would never know the historical truth behind John Phillip Santos's words. There in the "unrecorded parallel history" of meXicanas is evidence of an "absence/presence" that haunts the national imaginary. One cannot underestimate the import of their abjection in the realm of culture, for through the disavowal of the former Mexican inhabitants of the Southwest, through their eviction, the nation defined itself.

On the eve of the twenty-first century an editorial in the *San Francisco Chronicle* celebrated California's sesquicentennial (150 years of statehood) and the Gold Rush, which transformed the state from a "wild frontier on the edge of the continent to El Dorado, a land of unlimited wealth and unrestricted promise."[2] What constitutes a "wild frontier" from one perspective is "home" from another's. Once again, I tell myself, the primal myth of the "nation" is bogged down in repression and disavowal, in a "promise" that occults its history in conquest and dispossession. The California of my dream is not stroked by "gilded visions of easy riches and adventure," like the editor's, but by the return of the repressed.

To this day, questions around how a nation defines itself, who is "native" or "foreign," and even the obligatory stories for constructing national identity, continue to beleaguer cultural politics in the United States. Racial and sexual othering in cultural representations — like the discourse of sexuality — serve the critical function of "identifying marginal members of the body politic" in order to stake out the "moral parameters of the . . . nation."[3] For years, culture has played a pioneering role in the ongoing battle to define the nation on the basis of racial homogeneity, tagging racial, gendered, sexual subjects as outsiders and excluded citizens of the nation. As the fault lines of the nation make clearly evident, the myth of racial, gender, and sexual homogeneity could never be sustained without the process of repeating and fixing impressions of these "others" in the cultural imagination.

It is in the silence of all other referents besides the symbolic, in the unspoken and unacknowledged, that the nation's ambivalence toward its Mexican "others" is best captured — an ambivalence mirrored in the paradoxical fascination/repulsion with meXicanas in cultural representation. The murders and disappearances of women on the borderlands are the culmination of more than a century of abjection in discourses of the nation.

Among the transformative possibilities available to California immigrants since the nineteenth century are either becoming a "native" Californian or remaining "foreign." The first is a process available to white immigrants; the second an essence projected onto nonwhites in the process of racial formation. The "native" belongs to the nation; the "foreign" is a transplant, forever marginal to the body politic. In my California dream about the return of the repressed, the Mexican diaspora returns home and meXicanas claim their space in culture and the body politic of the nation, not as progenitors of another the nation, but as paisanas, heirs, distant relations to the nineteenth-century "mixed-race" inhabitants of California, Texas, New Mexico . . .

Notes

Preface

1. The meaning of "Sankofa" is taken from the website sankofa.com. I also thank Dana Takagi for recognizing the theoretical importance of the book's chronological inversion and for bringing to my attention the Mauri cosmological saying, "The past is in front." She explained, "To see the future one must have one's back to it, and rather be oriented to the past."

2. I am drawing from Ramon Garcia's excellent reading of the subversive practices of Chicana countercinema: "New Iconographies: Film Culture in Chicano Cultural Production," in *Decolonial Voices,* ed. Arturo J. Aldama and Naomi Quiñonez (Bloomington: Indiana University Press, 2002), 74.

Chapter One

A shorter version of this chapter was published in *Emergences* 10, no. 1 (May 2000), as "Voices without Echo: The Global Gendered Apartheid."

1. The epigraph is from Jean Franco, *The Decline and Fall of the Lettered State* (Cambridge and London: Harvard University Press, 2002), 234. Ciudad Juárez is the fourth-largest city in Mexico. During the 1990s, the city was host to five hundred export processing factories (maquiladoras) employing three hundred thousand workers. The maquila industry dates back to Mexico's Border Industrialization Program of 1965, when the country created an export processing zone along the Mexico–United States border; the industry was given a boost in 1993 with NAFTA (North American Free Trade Agreement).

2. The term "feminicide" is theorized by Dianna Russell and Jill Radford in *Feminicide: The Politics of Woman Killing* (New York: Twayne, 1999). Julia Estela Monárrez draws from their work and defines feminicide as "the misogynist mur-

der of women for being women." See her excellent "La cultura del feminicidio en Ciudad Juárez, 1993–1999," *Frontera Norte* 12, no. 23 (January–June 2000): 87–117 (quote, 89).

3. In November 2001, seven months after the group's report was released, the bodies of eight slain women were discovered in an area of the city known as the *"zona dorada."* See Ruben Villalpando, "Hallan en Juárez los cuerpos de tres mujeres asesinadas," *La Jornada* (Mexico City), 7 November 2001, 34; Ruben Villalpando and Miroslava Breach, "Hallan 5 cadáveres más de jovencitas en Juárez," *La Jornada* (Mexico City), 8 November 2001, 27. See Mitch Deacon, "Juarez Groups Demand Justice as Murders Continue," *The News Staff*, 15 November 2001, and Kent Paterson, "New Killings of Border Women Condemned." Both available online at www.us-mex.org.

4. This report was presented to Marta Altolaguirre, the special rapporteur for women's rights for the Interamerican Human Rights Commission. See Araly Castañon, "Exige ONG salvaguardar integridad de mujeres," *El Diario* (Ciudad Juárez), 8 March 2002. Available online at www.diario.com.mx, accessed March 8, 2002.

5. Factual information contained in this section has been culled from various sources, including the research of Mexican journalists working independently from the state, who have based their findings on the examination of the files of 137 victims murdered between January 1993 and December 1998. The results have been published in Rohry Benítez et al., *El silencio que la voz de todas quiebra* (Chihuahua, Mexico: Ediciones del Azar, 1999). See also Monárrez, "La cultura del feminicidio," and Víctor Ronquillo, *Las muertas de Juárez* (Mexico City: Editorial Planeta, 1999).

6. The majority of the victims were dark and thin, with long black hair. Of 137 victims, 5 percent were light-skinned, 41 percent dark. Information is not available for the other 54 percent. Many of the murdered women had been gagged, raped, strangled, and mutilated, with nipples and breasts cut off and buttocks lacerated like cattle, or they had been penetrated with objects. The number of murders tabulated as sexual killings is disputed because city authorities don't count it as rape if an object was used in penetration. For example, a woman found with a blanket in her anus was not recorded in police investigations as having been raped. See Benítez et al., *El silencio*, 13–18.

7. Monárrez, "La cultura del feminicidio," 94.

8. Franco, *The Decline and Fall*, 16.

9. Ibid, 234.

10. I am building upon my previous characterization of the state's interpretive framework as the "discourse of morality," which I have since modified to draw attention to the state's shifting framework of interpretation. See Fregoso, "Voices without Echo: The Global Gendered Apartheid," *Emergences* 10, no. 1 (May 2000): 137–56.

11. I am indebted to George Lipsitz for bringing to my attention the literature on nonheteronormative sexuality, especially Roderick Ferguson, "The Nightmares of the Heteronormative," *Cultural Values* 4, no. 4 (October 2000):

419–44, and Nayan Shah, *Contagious Divides: Epidemics and Race in San Francisco's Chinatown* (Berkeley: University of California Press, 2001). See also Benítez et al., *El silencio,* 27, 110.

12. Benítez et al., *El silencio,* 61. My translation. The original reads: "Muchas de las mujeres asesinadas trabajaban entre semana de obreras y en los fines de semana como prostitutas para hacerse de mayores recursos."

13. Ibid., 36. My translation: "Visitaba un centro en el que se dan cita homosexuales y lesbianas"; "Gustaba salir con diferentes hombres y era asidua asistente a salones de baile."

14. Ibid., 128. My translation: "¿Qué, no tienen otra cosa que inventar? De todos los casos han dicho lo mismo: Que la manera de vestir, su supuesta doble vida."

15. Quoted in Anne Marie Mackler, "Another Expert Explains Murders of Women," *Frontera Norte Sur* website, http://frontera.nmsu.edu, accessed September 1998.

16. This point was made by the chief of police of Ciudad Juárez at the Burials on the Border conference.

17. Other documents have "disaggregated" the murders, such as "Informe de homicidios en perjuicio de mujeres en Ciudad Juárez, Chihuahua, 1993–1998"; however, this was the first time the state used numbers in a media campaign against activists. See Elizabeth Velasco C., "Milenio Femenista anuncia que pedirá a la CIDH pesquisa sobre las 258 asesinadas en Juárez," *La Jornada* (Mexico City), 10 December 2001, 11.

18. The state's new numbers were reported in the following articles: Ruben Villalpando and Miroslava Breach, "'Pasional,' la mayoría de crímenes contra mujeres en Juárez: Procurador," *La Jornada* (Mexico City), 13 March 2002, 47; Kris Axtman, "Border Mystery: 274 Murders in Nine Years," *Christian Science Monitor,* 2 May 2002, 3.

19. Ruben Villalpando and Miroslava Breach, "Arribó a Ciudad Juárez el éxodo por la vida," *La Jornada* (Mexico City), 14 March 2002, 47.

20. This seems mostly to be the case among reporters from the United States. See for instance Evelyn Nieves, "To Work and Die in Juarez," *Mother Jones,* June 2002, 50–55.

21. Gustavo Castillo Garcia, "Ordenó Fox a PGR investigar a fondo los asesinatos de mujeres en Ciudad Juárez, *La Jornada* (Mexico City), 13 December 2001, 17.

22. My use of the term "globalism" draws from the work of Michael Burawoy, who calls the tendency to explain the local in terms of the global "the fallacy of globalism — namely that one can characterize changes of the whole without examining changes of the parts or, to put the fallacy the other way around, that the secrets of the part can be found in the whole." See "Grounding Globalization," in *Global Ethnography: Forces, Connections, and Imaginations in a Postmodern World,* ed. Michael Burawoy et al. (Berkeley: University of California Press, 2001), 343.

23. In my article "Voices without Echo" I provide a detailed analysis of antiglobalization discourse as it appears in journalistic writing on feminicide.

24. Debbie Nathan, "Death Comes to the Maquilas: A Border Story," *The Nation,* January 1997, 22.

25. Researchers in the region, such as sociologist Victor M. Quintana, are now talking about the "end of the maquila" era. Since 2001, thousands of factory workers have lost their jobs as five hundred foreign-owned maquiladoras have shifted their operations to China. In the state of Chihuahua alone, more than one hundred thousand workers have lost their jobs. See Saul Landau, "A Report on NAFTA and the State of Health of Maquilas," *Progreso Weekly* (Miami), 22 July 2002 (www.progreso.com).

26. Quoted in Saskia Sassen, *Losing Control? Sovereignty in an Age of Globalization* (New York: Columbia University Press, 1996), III. See the films *The Global Assembly Line* (1986); *Love, Women, and Flowers* (1988). See also María Patricia Fernández-Kelly, *For We Are Sold, I and My People: Women and Industry in Mexico's Frontier* (Albany: State University of New York Press, 1983).

27. Nathan "Death Comes to the Maquilas," 18.

28. Noam Chomsky, "Preface: Notes on NAFTA: The Masters of Mankind," in *Juárez: The Laboratory of our Future,* ed. Charles Bowden (New York: Aperture, 1998), 13–20.

29. And while the incorporation of women into wage employment has been growing in export-processing zones throughout the Third World, to some extent the situation on Mexico's border cities differs. The traditionally female workforce of the maquiladora industry peaked in the 1960s. Due in large measure to Mexico's economic crisis of 1982, border cities like Ciudad Juárez experienced a drop in female participation in the maquiladora labor force, from 68 to 53 percent in the years between 1981 and 1989, with the hire of men rising in matching proportions. Transnational corporations on the border export zone took advantage of the cheap male labor force produced by high unemployment and inflation during the Mexican recession of the 1980s, creating the phenomenon researchers are calling "the remasculinization of maquila labor" in Ciudad Juárez. Another factor, according to Maria de la O Martínez, is that maquila technology and organizational structures have become increasingly complex, leading to the perceived need for more highly trained technicians — typically, men. De la O Martínez argues that today "women are marginalized by the hierarchical structures now in place in the maquiladora industry." De la O Martínez, "Maquiladora, mujer, y cambios productivos: Estudio de caso en la industria maquiladora de Ciudad Juárez," in *Mujeres, migración, y maquila en la frontera norte,* ed. Soledad González Montes et al. (Mexico City: El Colegio de México, Programa Interdisciplinario de Estudios de la Mujer, 1995), 261.

30. See Chomsky, "Preface," 13–20.

31. See for example Landau, "A Report on NAFTA."

32. That the murders have been "maquiladora killings" has also been a common assumption in news programs on ABC, CBS, Fox, and UNIVISION,

including *20/20, 60 Minutes, Fox News,* and UNIVISION's *Ocurrió así* and *Primer impacto.*

33. The occupations of the murder victims are listed in Benítez et al., *El silencio,* 11-22.

34. Monárrez, "La cultura del feminicidio," 110.

35. See Zygmunt Bauman, *Globalization: The Human Consequence* (New York: Columbia University Press, 1998), 59.

36. See David Harvey, *Spaces of Hope* (Berkeley: University of California Press, 2000), 65. Also see Bauman, *Globalization,* 69: "One of the most seminal consequences of the new global freedom of movement is that it becomes increasingly difficult, perhaps altogether impossible, to reforge social issues into effective collective action."

37. In her article, Nathan characterizes the women workers as "maquila girls," a description that perpetuates their "infantilization." As Laura Hyun Yi Kang writes about Asian women in another context, this characterization "reinforces the myth of their intellectual inferiority and docility." She adds: "The desubjectivization of Asian women workers is also affected through the discursive emphasis upon their youth. While it is true that many of these Asian female workers can be as young as fourteen — or in some cases even younger — many women are in their twenties and beyond." See Laura Hyun Yi Kang, "Si(gh)ting Asian/American Women as Transnational Labor," *Positions: East Asia Cultures Critique* 5, no. 2 (Fall 1997): 403-37. Quote from Nathan, "Death Comes to the Maquilas," 20. In regard to the purported hypersexuality, Nathan writes: "Downtown Juarez is clotted with bars whose clientele are mostly assembly-line workers. The week-end cover charge and beer are cheap at establishments such as Alive, Noa Noa, and La Tuna Country. U.S. rock, disco, and Mexican music throb from giant speakers by their dance floor, and intermission is punctuated with 'Most Daring Bra' and 'Wet String Bikini' contests for the women customers, as well as performances by handsome young male striptease dancers." Nathan, "Work, Sex, and Danger in Ciudad Juárez," *NACLA,* 33, no. 3 (November–December 1999): 27.

38. Nathan, "Death Comes to the Maquilas," 20.

39. Nathan, "Work, Sex, and Danger in Ciudad Juárez," 26.

40. Leslie Salzinger, "From High Heels to Swathed Bodies: Gendered Meanings under Production in Mexico's Export Processing Industry," *Feminist Studies* 23, no. 3 (Fall 1997): 570.

41. Ibid., 568.

42. Ibid., 567.

43. Ibid., 562.

44. Quoted in Melissa Wright, "Maquiladora Mestizas and a Feminist Border Politics: Revisiting Anzaldúa," *Hypatia* 13, no. 3 (Summer 1998): 120. One of Wright's interviewees is Steve, a plant manager who "explained that there were uniform regulations for the Mexican women in administration because 'you should have seen what they used to wear. It looked like one of those cantinas

down on Juarez avenue [the red light district]. It made some of the guys uncomfortable" (119).

45. Ibid., 130, n. 9.

46. Ibid., 119–20.

47. Nathan, "Work, Sex, and Danger in Ciudad Juárez," 30.

48. Ibid.

49. Ibid., 26.

50. Ella Shohat, "Multicultural Feminism in a Transnational Age," in *Talking Visions,* ed. Ella Shohat (New York: MIT Press, 1998), 9.

51. Vasuki Nesiah, "Toward a Feminist Intersectionality: A Critique of U.S. Feminist Legal Scholarship," in *Global Critical Race Feminism,* edited by Adrien Katherine Wing (New York: New York University Press, 2000), 48.

52. Quoted in Franco, *The Decline and Fall of the Lettered State,* 244.

53. Charles Bowden, "I Wanna Dance with the Strawberry Girl," *Talk,* September 1999, 114.

54. Ibid.

55. Ibid., 118.

56. Charles Bowden, *Juárez: The Laboratory of Our Future* (New York: Aperture, 1998), 103.

57. Ibid., 67.

58. Ibid., 105.

59. Walter Benjamin, "The Work of Art in the Age of Mechanical Reproduction," in *Illuminations,* ed. Hannah Arendt, trans. Harry Zohn (New York: Schocken, 1969), 223.

60. Bowden, *Juárez: The Laboratory of Our Future,* 105.

61. See Charles Bowden, "While You Were Sleeping: In Juárez, Mexico, Photographers Expose the Violent Realities of Free Trade," *Harper's,* December 1996, 44–52.

62. Michael Taussig, *Defacement* (Stanford University Press, 1999), 25. Special thanks to Alejandro Lugo for bringing this text to my attention.

63. Taussig, *Defacement,* 1. As Taussig adds: "What's more, it's not only as if disfiguring the copy acts on what it is a copy of, but that, associated with this, the defaced copy emits a charge which seems — how else can we say this? — to enter the body of the observer and to extend and to physically overflow, and therewith create an effusion of proliferating defacements."

64. Michael Taussig, *Shamanism, Colonialism, and the Wild Man* (Chicago and London: University of Chicago Press, 1987), 10.

65. Bowden, *Juárez,* 105.

66. Michael Peter Smith, *Transnational Urbanism* (Malden, Mass.: Blackwell, 2001), 98.

67. See for example Bauman, *Globalization.*

68. Smith, *Transnational Urbanism,* 148.

69. The same holds true of the discourse which attributes the violence on the Mexican border to narco-trafficking, as in the discovery of mass graves in Ciudad Juárez in late November 1999. See Lowell Bergman and Tim Golden,

"Investigators Dig for Mass Graves at Mexico Border," *New York Times,* 30 November 1999, 1+; Ester Schrader and James F. Smith, "2 Mass Graves in Mexico May Hold Hundreds," *Los Angeles Times,* 30 November 1999, 1+.

70. See Ruben Villalpando, "Surgen en Chihuahua casos similares a los de las jovenes en Juárez," *La Jornada* (Mexico City), 6 April 2002, 35.

71. Susie Jacobs, Ruth Jacobson, and Jennifer Marchbank, "Introduction: States of Conflict," in *States of Conflict,* ed. Susie Jacobs, Ruth Jacobson, and Jennifer Marchbank (London and New York: Zed Books, 2000), 7.

72. I emphasize the word "outdated" because the legal system in Mexico is based on a family model that no longer exists (i.e., male breadwinner/head of household and female caretaker); the legal system fails to account for the growing number of female-headed households, working mothers, single and divorced households, and so forth. See José Galán, "Tres millones de hogares mexicanos son dirigidos por mujeres: Experta," *La Jornada* (Mexico City), 12 April 2001, 28.

73. United Nations, *Domestic Violence against Women in Latin America and the Caribbean,* Series on Women and Development (Santiago, Chile: Social Development Division, 1990), 22.

74. Angeles Cruz, "Letra muerta, ley contra violencia interfamiliar," *La Jornada* (Mexico City), 26 May 2002, 43; Naomi Neft and Ann D. Levine, *Where Women Stand: An International Report of the Status of Women in 140 Countries* (New York: Random House, 1997), 154.

75. See Gabriela Rodríguez, "Señoritas asesinadas en Juárez," *La Jornada* (Mexico City), 13 December 2001, 22. In addition to CEDAW, adopted for signature in 1979, there are other international instruments dealing with extending women's citizenship rights, such as the UN Declaration on the Elimination of Violence against Women (1993) and the Belem do Pará Convention for the Prevention, Punishment and Eradication of Violence against Women of the Organization of American states (1994).

76. See Fiona Macaulay's discussion of Latin American penal codes in "Tackling Violence against Women in Brazil: Converting International Principles into Effective Local Policy," in *States of Conflict,* ed. Susie Jacobs, Ruth Jacobson, and Jennifer Marchbank (New York: Zed Books, 2000), 149.

77. According to Macaulay, this is the case in the penal codes of all Latin American countries except for Cuba and Nicaragua.

78. Ruth Steifert, "War and Rape: A Preliminary Analysis," in *Mass Rape: The War against Women in Bosnia-Herzegovina,* ed. Alexandra Stiglmeyer (Lincoln: University of Nebraska Press, 1994), 68.

79. I am indebted to George Lipsitz for this important insight.

80. Jacobs et al., "Introduction," 8.

81. Macaulay, "Tackling Violence against Women in Brazil," 147.

82. Taussig, *Shamanism,* 128.

83. Walter Benjamin, "Theses on the Philosophy of History," in *Illuminations,* ed. Hannah Arendt, trans. Harry Zohn (New York: Schocken, 1969), 257.

84. Again, I thank George Lipsitz for pointing me in this direction.

85. Giorgio Agamben, "Form-of-Life," in *Means without End,* trans. Vincenzo Binetti and Cesare Casarino (Minneapolis: University of Minnesota Press, 2000), 4. According to the translator: "In the Italian translation of Benjamin's passage, 'state of emergency' is translated as 'state of exception,'" 142.

86. Taussig, *Shamanism,* 4.

87. Ibid., 8.

88. Heaven Crawley, "Engendering the State in Refugee Women's Claims for Asylum," in *States of Conflict,* ed. Susie Jacobs, Ruth Jacobson, and Jennifer Marchbank (New York: Zed Books, 2000), 88.

89. The use of rape as a weapon of war is quoted from the UN report on the human rights of women; see Human Rights Watch, Women's Rights Project, *The Human Rights Global Watch Report on Women's Human Rights* (New York: Human Rights Watch, 1995), 3.

90. Sharon K. Hom, "Female Infanticide in China," in *Global Critical Race Feminism,* ed. Adrien Katherine Wing (New York: New York University Press, 2000), especially 257, n. 5.

91. A poem read at the Burials on the Border gathering.

92. Until Guillermina González announced the "disintegration" of Voces sin Eco in July 2001, its members had gathered every weekend to paint more crosses as a symbol of their struggle for social justice. For an excellent analysis of the political resistance of mothers of the disappeared young women in Juárez, see Cynthia Bejarano, "Las Super Madres de Latino América: Transforming Motherhood and Houseskirts by Challenging Violence in Juárez, Mexico, Argentina, and El Salvador," *Frontiers: A Journal of Women's Studies* 23, no. 1 (2002).

93. Images of the murdered women were published in Mexican tabloids, newspapers, and television, as well as appearing in a traveling exhibit sponsored by Aperture Press in conjunction with the publication of Charles Bowden's *Juárez: The Laboratory of Our Future.*

94. In some cases, family members have unwittingly bought into the patriarchal ideology that justifies murder on the basis of nonnormative behavior. This sentiment can be seen in family members' defensive insistence that their murdered relatives were respectable — innocent, honorable young women who did not lead a "doble vida" or go to bars, discos, or strip joints. At the Burials on the Border gathering, a family member of one of the victims stood up holding a photograph and told us: "Esta es mi cuñada. No trabajaba en la maquila. No era prostituta. No más fue víctima inocente." (This is my sister-in-law, one of the victims. She was not a maquila worker. She was not a prostitute. She was just an innocent victim.) And Guillermina González — founder of Voces sin Echo, originator of the cross campaign, and sister of murder victim María Sagrario — addressed the audience as follows: "No son prostitutas. No son estadísticas. Pero sí tienen historia." (They are not prostitutes. They are not statistics. But they do have a history.).

95. Ana María Alonzo notes that Chihuahuans today boast of their collective whiteness. In the north of Mexico, "whiteness became central to the creation of

a regional sense of community and personhood. This invented tradition of origins is very much alive today and is regularly evoked in the construction of a distinct norteño identity, opposed to that of the Mexicans in the Center, who are subjectively apprehended as 'less white'" (68). Later she comments on the centrality of whiteness in "the definition of feminine beauty" (98). Alonzo, *Thread of Blood: Colonialism, Revolution, and Gender on Mexico's Northern Frontier* (Tucson: University of Arizona, 1995).

96. Interview of Mrs. González in the documentary *Maquila: A Tale of Two Mexicos* (2000).

97. Macaulay, "Tackling Violence against Women in Brazil," 144-62.

98. Nesiah, "Toward a Feminist Intersectionality," 45.

99. Celina Romany, "Themes for a Conversation on Race and Gender in International Human Rights Law," in *Global Critical Race Feminism,* ed. Adrien Katherine Wing (New York: New York University Press, 2000), 60.

100. See Gabriela Romero Sánchez, "Presentan iniciativa de reforma para castigar explotación sexual contra menores de edad," *La Jornada* (Mexico City), 2 May 2001, 48; Miguel Concha, "Contra la violencia familiar," *La Jornada* (Mexico City), 7 April 2001, 19.

101. Benítez et al., *El silencio,* 144.

102. President Vicente Fox continues government inaction even as he pays lip service to women's groups by speaking on behalf of gender equality and against gender violence. During International Women's Day, at the official ceremony for the appointment of Patricia Espinoza Torres (a feminist, ex-PAN deputy) as head of the Instituto Nacional de la Mujer, Fox broached the issue of gender and human rights: "En las ciudades, las mujeres sufren aún discriminación; en el campo, su situación es muchas veces violatoria de los derechos humanos y clama por una pronta y clara justicia." (In the cities, women still suffer discrimination; in the rural areas, the violation of their human rights is greater and it demands a clear and swift justice.) See Angeles Cruz and Roberto Garduño, "Fox: La mujer, nuevo actor político 'indispensable'; promete igualdad," *La Jornada* (Mexico City), 9 March 2001, 41.

103. For example: "Almost all of them because they are the domestics, the workers, the ones with dark skin, from the working-class neighborhoods, the poor ones, therefore, the exclusive targets of this sexist and classist genocide." My translation. The original reads: "Casi todas porque son las muchachas, las trabajadoras, las de color moreno, las de las colonias populares, las pobres, pues, el blanco exclusivo de este genocidio sexista y clasista." Victor M. Quintana, "Los feminicidios de Ciudad Juárez," *La Jornada* (Mexico City), 23 November 2001, 23; see also "Ciudad Juárez: Parar los homicidios," *La Jornada* (Mexico City), 13 December 2001, 13.

104. Nearly forty students in the course "Transnational Cinema and Feminism" (LALS 176) wrote critical essays on *Señorita extraviada.*

105. Jean Franco, *Critical Passions,* ed. Mary Louise Pratt and Kathleen Newman (Durham and London: Duke University Press, 1999), 31.

106. Taussig, *Defacement,* 224.

Chapter Two

1. Marianismo is an ideology derived from the cult of the Virgin Mary and functions to discipline and regulate Latina femininity by positing "women's spiritual superiority" and hence their "capacity to endure all suffering." Rosa Maria Gil and Carmen Inoa Vásquez, *The Maria Paradox: How Latinas Can Merge Old World Traditions with New World Self-Esteem* (New York: G. P. Putnam's Sons, 1996), 174.

2. Ibid., 222.

3. José Limón, *American Encounters: Greater Mexico, the United States, and the Erotics of Culture* (Boston: Beacon, 1998).

4. Ibid., 136.

5. Ibid., 145–46.

6. Ibid., 165–66.

7. Sandra Cisneros, *"Woman Hollering Creek" and Other Stories* (New York: Vintage, 1991), 52.

8. Limón, *American Encounters,* 146. My emphasis.

9. Cisneros, *"Woman Hollering Creek,"* 47.

10. Limón, *American Encounters,* 166. My emphasis.

11. Kimberlé Williams Crenshaw, "Mapping the Margins: Intersectionality, Identity Politics, and Violence against Women of Color," in *Critical Race Theory: The Key Writings That Formed the Movement,* ed. Kimberlé Williams Crenshaw et al. (New York: The New Press, 1995), 362. On the debates around Kingston, see Lisa Lowe, *Immigrant Acts* (Durham and London: Duke University Press, 1996), especially chapter three.

12. Crenshaw, "Mapping the Margins," 362.

13. United Nations, *Domestic Violence against Women in Latin America and the Caribbean,* Series on Women and Development (Santiago, Chile: United Nations, 1992), 11.

14. Valerie Smith, "Telling Family Secrets: Narrative and Ideology in *Suzanne Suzanne* by Camille Billops an James V. Hatch," in *Multiple Voices in Feminist Film Criticism,* ed. Linda Dittman, Diane Carson, and Janice R. Walsh (Minneapolis: University of Minnesota Press, 1994), 380.

15. Crenshaw, "Mapping the Margins," 362.

16. See Yvette Flores-Ortiz, "La Mujer y la Violencia: A Culturally Based Model for Understanding the Treatment of Domestic Violence in Chicana/Latina Communities," in *Chicana Critical Issues,* ed. Mujeres Activas en Letras y Cambio Social (Berkeley: Third Woman Press, 1993), 169–82; Gloria Bonilla-Santiago, "Latina Battered Women: Barriers to Service Delivery and Cultural Considerations," in *Helping Battered Women: New Perspectives and Remedies,* ed. Albert R. Roberts (Oxford: Oxford University Press, 1996), 229–34; Naomi Neft and Anna D. Levine, *Where Women Stand: An International Report on the Status of Women in 140 Countries* (New York: Random House, 1997).

17. Bonilla-Santiago, "Latina Battered Women," 229.

18. Cisneros, *"Woman Hollering Creek,"* 47.

19. Saba Bahar, "Women's Rights Are Human Rights," in *Global Feminism since 1945*, ed. Bonnie G. Smith (London and New York: Routledge, 2000), 267.

20. Ibid.

21. See Celina Romany, "Themes for a Conversation on Race and Gender in International Human Rights Law," in *Global Critical Race Feminism,* ed. Adrien Katherine Wing (New York: New York University Press, 2000), 59–60.

22. Human Rights Watch, Women's Rights Project, *The Human Rights Global Watch Report on Women's Human Rights* (New York: Human Rights Watch, 1995), 2.

23. Susie Jacobs, Ruth Jacobson, and Jennifer Marchbank, "Introduction: States of Conflict," in *States of Conflict,* ed. Susie Jacobs, Ruth Jacobson, and Jennifer Marchbank (New York: Zed Books, 2000), 16.

24. Ruth Steifert, "War and Rape: A Preliminary Analysis," in *Mass Rape: The War against Women in Bosnia-Herzegovina,* ed. Alexandra Stiglmeyer (Lincoln: University of Nebraska Press, 1994), 68.

25. Powell quoted in Ruth Rosen, "Women's Rights Go Global" (Op-Ed), *San Francisco Chronicle*, 3 December 2001, A19.

26. See Kevin Bales, *Disposable People* (Berkeley: University of California Press, 1999).

27. For further discussion, see Inderpal Grewal, "On the New Global Feminism and the Family of Nations," in *Talking Visions,* ed. Ella Shohat (Cambridge and London: MIT Press, 1998): 501–30.

28. Liz Kelly, "Wars against Women: Sexual Violence, Sexual Politics, and the Militarized State," in *States of Conflict,* ed. Susie Jacobs, Ruth Jacobson, and Jennifer Marchbank (New York: Zed Books, 2000), 46.

29. Ibid.

30. Patricia Arias, "La migración femenina en dos modelos de desarrollo: 1940–1970 y 1980–1992," in *Relaciones de genero y transformación agraria: Estudios sobre el campo mexicano,* ed. Soledad González Montes (Mexico City: El Colegio de México, 1995), 227–28.

31. Ibid.

32. Lourdes Arguelles and Anne M. Rivero, "Gender/Sexual Orientation Violence and Transnational Migration: Conversations with Some Latinas We Think We Know," *Urban Anthropology and Studies of Cultural Systems and World Economic Development,* 22, nos. 3–4 (1993): 271.

33. Laura Velasco Ortiz, "Migración femenina y estrategias de sobrevivencia de la unidad doméstica: Un caso de estudio de mujeres mixtecas en Tijuana," in *Mujeres, migración, y maquila en la frontera norte,* ed. Soledad González Montes et al. (Mexico City: El Colegio de México, 1994), 61. My translation.

34. Arguelles and Rivero, "Gender/Sexual Orientation Violence," 260–63.

35. Ibid., 260.

36. Holly Willis, "Uncommon History: An Interview with Barbara Hammer," *Film Quarterly* 47, no. 4 (Summer 1994): 11.

37. In the film, three different actresses play Paulina: Mariám Manzano

Durán (Paulina at age eight), Erika Isabel de la Cruz Ramírez (Paulina at age thirteen), and Mathyselene Heredia Castillo (Paulina as a young adult).

38. Sylvie Thouard, "Performances of *The Devil Never Sleeps/El diablo nunca duerme*," in *Lourdes Portillo: "The Devil Never Sleeps" and Other Films*, ed. Rosa Linda Fregoso (Austin: University of Texas Press, 2001), 119–43.

39. Steifert, "War and Rape," 55.

40. Adrien Katherine Wing, "A Critical Race Feminist Conceptualization of Violence," in *Global Critical Race Feminism*, ed. Adrien Katherine Wing (New York: New York University Press, 2000), 333.

41. Kelly Oliver, *Subjectivity without Subjects* (Lanham, Md.: Rowan and Littlefield, 1998), 174.

42. Ibid.

43. Vasuki Nesiah, "Toward a Feminist Intersectionality: A Critique of U.S. Feminist Legal Scholarship," in *Global Critical Race Feminism*, ed. Adrien Katherine Wing (New York: New York University Press, 2000), 48.

44. Romany, "Themes," 54.

45. Lisa Lowe, "Toward a Critical Modernity," *Anglistica* 4, no. 1 (2000): 87. As Oré-Aguilar explains in relation to the situation of poor and indigenous women in Latin American, gender violence "is more likely to occur to these groups of women due to their socioeconomic status, their educational levels, their age, or their ethnic background." See Gaby Oré-Aguilar, "Sexual Harassment and Human Rights in Latin America," in *Global Critical Race Feminism*, ed. Adrien Katherine Wing (New York: New York University Press, 2000), 368.

46. Lowe, "Toward a Critical Modernity," 83.

Chapter Three

Parts of this chapter were previously published in "Recycling Colonialist Fantasies on the Texas Borderlands," in the anthology *Home, Exile, Homeland: Film, Media, and the Politics of Place*, ed. Hamid Naficy (New York and London: Routledge, 1998), 169–92.

1. Toni Morrison, *Playing in the Dark: Whiteness and the Literary Imagination* (Cambridge: Harvard University Press, 1992), 42.

2. For example, *The Border* (1982); *Touch of Evil* (1958).

3. For further discussion of the racial melodrama in *Lone Star*, see Julianne Burton, "Oedipus Tex/Oedipus Mex: History, Mystery, and the Paternal Gaze in John Sayles's *Lone Star*," in *Multiculturalism, Transnationalism, and Film*, ed. Ella Shohat and Robert Stam (New Brunswick: Rutgers University Press, forthcoming).

4. Daniel Bernardi, "The Voices of Whiteness: D. W. Griffith's Biograph Films (1908–1913)," in *The Birth of Whiteness: Race and the Emergence of U.S. Cinema*, ed. Daniel Bernardi (New Brunswick: Rutgers University Press, 1996), 104.

5. Herman Gray, "Anxiety, Desire, and Conflict in the American Racial

Imagination," in *Media Scandals,* ed. James Lull and Stephen Hiverman (Malden, Mass.: Blackwell , 1997), 87–88.

6. Rafael Trujillo, *Olvídate del Alamo* (Mexico City: La Prensa, 1965).

7. In a book-length study, Norma Iglesias defines border cinema in terms of the following criteria: (1) the plot or a significant portion of the plot develops on the Mexico-U.S.A. border region; (2) the plot deals with a character from the borderlands region, irrespective of the setting; (3) the film refers to the Mexican-origin population living in the United States; (4) the film is shot on location in the borderlands, irrespective of the plot; (5) the story makes reference to the borderlands or to problems of national identity. See Norma Iglesias-Prieto, *Entre yerba, polvo, y plomo: Lo fronterizo visto por el cine mexicano* (Tijuana: El Colegio de la Frontera-norte, 1991), 17.

8. The U.S. film industry has likely made (if one counts all of the one-reel silent films) thousands of films dealing with the U.S.-Mexico border. While they are too numerous to list, among the better known examples of the border genre films are *Licking the Greasers* (1914), *Girl of the Rio* (1932), *Bordertown* (1935), *Border Incident* (1949) *Touch of Evil* (1958), *The Wild Bunch* (1969), *The Border* (1982), *Born in East L.A.* (1987).

9. According to Iglesias, between 1979 and 1989, 147 films were produced by the Mexican film industry.

10. Joan West and Dennis West, "Borders and Boundaries: An Interview with John Sayles," *Cineaste,* 22, no. 3 (1996): 14.

11. This information is contained in the press packet distributed by Castle Rock Entertainment.

12. Julianne Burton, "Oedipus Tex/Oedipus Mex."

13. An observation first brought to my attention by my colleague Sarah Projansky in the Department of Women and Gender Studies, UC-Davis.

14. John Sayles quoted in West and West, "Borders and Boundaries," 15.

15. Ibid.

16. José Limón, *American Encounters: Greater Mexico, the United States, and the Erotics of Culture* (Boston: Beacon, 1998), 155.

17. Much like Clarence Thomas "colored" the Supreme Court but left its conservatism intact.

18. See for example the conclusion to Emma Pérez, *The Decolonial Imaginary: Writing Chicanas into History* (Bloomington and Indianapolis: Indiana University Press, 1999). I have benefited much from discussions of the film with Aída Hurtado, Emma Pérez, Ramón Saldívar, and Alvina Quintana.

19. Limón, *American Encounters,* 154. I find this a curious conflation — or rather, a separation, of the realms of politics and the discursive. It is virtually impossible to conceive of a politics that is not informed by iconography given the predominance of visual culture (i.e., image, spectacle, iconography) in constituting social reality.

20. Ibid., 161.

21. I am referring to the dragging death of James Byrd Jr., a black man who

was chained to a pickup truck by three white supremacists in Jasper, Texas, on June 7, 1998.

22. Limón, *American Encounters,* 158.

23. Ibid., 159.

24. See Judith Mayne, "Cinema and Spectatorship," in *Star Gazing: Hollywood Cinema and Female Spectatorship,* ed. Jackie Stacey (New York: Routledge, 1994); E. Ann Kaplan, "Dialogue: Ann Kaplan Replies to Linda Williams's 'Something Else besides a Mother: Stella Dallas and the Maternal Melodrama,'" *Cinema Journal* 24, no. 2 (Fall 1984): 40–73.

25. E. Ann Kaplan, "Feminist Film Criticism: Current Issues and Problems," *Studies in Literary Imagination* 19, no. 1 (1992a): 13.

26. Limón, *American Encounters,* 152.

27. See Ella Shohat, "Gender and Culture of Empire: Toward a Feminist Ethnography of the Cinema," *Quarterly Review of Film and Video* 13, nos. 1–3 (1991–1992): 45–79.

28. Norma Alarcón, "Anzaldúa's Frontera: Inscribing Genetics," in *Displacement, Diaspora, and Geographies of Identity,* ed. Smadar Lavie and Ted Swedenburg (Durham: Duke University Press, 1995), 42.

29. Elizabeth Brown-Guillory, "Introduction," in *Women of Color: Mother-Daughter Relationships in Twentieth-Century Literature,* ed. Elizabeth Brown-Guillory (Austin: University of Texas Press, 1996), 2.

30. Alarcón, "Anzaldúa's Frontera," 43.

31. Kristeva quoted in E. Ann Kaplan, *Motherhood and Representation* (London and New York: Routledge, 1992b), 41.

32. Kaplan, *Motherhood and Representation,* 48.

33. Ibid.

34. Lucy Fischer, *Cinematernity: Film Motherhood, Genre* (Princeton: Princeton University Press, 1996), 30.

35. Ibid., 184.

36. Kaplan, *Motherhood and Representation,* 3.

37. Adrienne Rich, *Of Woman Born: Motherhood as Experience and Institution* (New York: Norton, 1976), 250–51.

38. I thank Ramon Rivera-Servera, a participant in the Latino Graduate Training Seminar at the Smithsonian Institution, who made these comments during my talk on the film.

Chapter Four

1. Carmen Huaco-Nuzum, "Mi Familia/My Family," *Aztlan* 23, no. 1 (Spring 1998): 142.

2. Stephanie Coontz, *The Way We Really Are* (New York: Basic Books, 1997), 1.

3. Quote from Judith Stacey, *In the Name of the Family* (Boston: Beacon,

1996), 48. For more on the "neo-family values movement" see Judith Stacey, "Family Values Forever," *The Nation*, 9 July 2001, 26–30.

4. For a detailed analysis of the representation of gender in *My Family,* see Lisa A. Flores and Michelle A. Holling, "Las Familias and las Latinas: Mediated Representations of Gender Roles," in *Mediated Women: Representations in Popular Culture,* ed. Marian Meyers (Cresskill, N.J.: Hampton Press, 2000), 339–53.

5. Stacey, *In the Name of the Family,* 48.

6. See Sonia Saldívar-Hull, *Feminism on the Border: Chicana Gender Politics and Literature* (Berkeley: University of California Press, 2000).

7. Anne McClintock, "No Longer in a Future Heaven: Gender, Race, and Nationalism," in *Dangerous Liaisons: Gender, Nation, and Postcolonial Perspectives,* ed. Ann McClintock, Aamir Mufti, and Ella Shohat (Minneapolis: University of Minnesota Press, 1997), 90.

8. Cherríe Moraga, *Loving in the War Years: Lo Que Nunca Pasó por Sus Labios* (Boston: South End Press, 1983), 131.

9. Maxine Baca Zinn, "Political Familism: Toward Sex Role Equality in Chicano Families," *Aztlan* 6, no. 1 (Spring 1975): 13–26.

10. See Baca Zinn, "Political Familism"; Aida Hurtado, "The Politics of Sexuality in the Gender Subordination of Chicanas," in *Living Chicana Theory,* ed. Carla Trujillo (Berkeley: Third Woman Press, 1998), 383–428.

11. Baca Zinn, "Political Familism," 15.

12. González quoted in ibid., 17.

13. Patricia Zavella, "The Problematic Relationship of Feminism and Chicana Studies," *Women's Studies* 17 (1989): 27.

14. Saldívar-Hull, *Feminism on the Border,* 141.

15. Lorena Oropeza, "His Story and Beyond: Cesar Chavez, Vietnam, and the Chicana/o Movement" (paper presented at the annual meeting of the American Studies Association, Washington, D.C., 1997). See also Angie Chabram-Dernersesian, "And, Yes . . . The Earth Did Part: On the Splitting of Chicana Subjectivity," in *Building with Our Hands,* ed. Adela de la Torre and Beatríz Pesquera (Berkeley: University of California Press, 1993). She observes, "Baca's illustration centers a male protagonist and a [male] child, who engage the spectator's gaze directly through frontal portraits"; the image "prevents this type of definition and engagement" in relation to the female in the drawing (55).

16. McClintock, "No Longer in a Future Heaven," 89.

17. Huaco-Nuzum, "Mi Familia/My Family," 143.

18. Ibid., 145.

19. Ibid., 147.

20. Ibid., 146.

21. McClintock, "No Longer in a Future Heaven," 89.

22. Alfredo Mirandé, "The Chicano Family: A Reanalysis of Conflicting Views," *Journal of Marriage and the Family* 39 (1977): 755.

23. Stacey, *In the Name of the Family,* 38.

24. Mirandé, "The Chicano Family," 755.

25. Deniz Kandiyoti, "Identity and Its Discontents: Women and the Nation," in *Colonial Discourse and Post-Colonial Theory: A Reader,* ed. Patrick Williams and Laura Chrisman (New York: Columbia University Press, 1994), 388.

26. Stacey, *In the Name of the Family,* 42.

27. McClintock, "No Longer in a Future Heaven," 91.

28. Also, the name of their other son — the incorrigible pachuco who dies earlier in the film — is Chucho, a nickname for Jesus.

29. David Alvirez and Frank Bean, "The Mexican American Family," in *Ethnic Families in America,* ed. Charles Mindel and Robert Hamerstein (New York: Elsevier Scientific Press, 1976), 277.

30. McClintock, "No Longer in a Future Heaven," 92.

31. Saldívar-Hull, *Feminism on the Border,* 137.

32. John Phillip Santos, *Places Left Unfinished at the Time of Creation* (New York: Viking, 1999), 26.

33. Mirandé, "The Chicano Family," 755.

34. Kandiyoti, "Identity and Its Discontents," 377.

35. Valerie Amos and Pratibha Parmar, "Challenging Imperial Feminism," *Feminist Review* 17 (Autumn 1984): 9.

36. Patricia Zavella, "The Problematic Relationship of Feminism and Chicana Studies," 27.

37. Maxine Baca Zinn, "Chicano Family Research: Conceptual Distortions and Alternative Directions," *Journal of Ethnic Studies* 7 (1979): 61.

38. See Oscar Lewis, *The Children of Sanchez* (New York: Random House, 1961), and *La Vida: A Puerto Rican Family in the Culture of Poverty, San Juan and New York* (New York: Random House, 1966).

39. See Robin D. G. Kelley, *Yo' Mama's Disfunktional!* (Boston: Beacon, 1997), 181, n. 3. Kelley sheds light on Lewis's often misunderstood arguments about working class culture, noting that "the culture they created to cope with poverty and disenfranchisement was passed down through generations and this led to passivity and undermined social organizations."

40. Heller quoted in Baca Zinn, "Chicano Family Research," 61.

41. Lewis studied a Tepoztecan village (*Life in a Mexican Village: Tepoztlán Restudied* [Urbana: University of Illinois Press, 1951]); the urban poor of Mexico City *(Five Families: Mexican Case Studies in the Culture of Poverty* [New York: Basic Books, 1959] and *The Children of Sanchez);* and Puerto Ricans in San Juan and New York *(La Vida).*

42. Morton Stith, Karen Karabasz, and Marc Taylor, "Mythology and the Mexican Family" (lecture delivered at the Biblioteca Pública, San Miguel de Allende, Guanajuato, July 2001).

43. Fernando Peñalosa, "Mexican American Family Roles," *Journal of Marriage and the Family* 30, no. 4 (1968): 682. Miguel Montiel, "The Social Science Myth of the Mexican American Family," *El Grito: A Journal of Contemporary Mexican Thought* (Summer 1970): 56.

44. Alvirez and Bean, "The Mexican American Family," 288.

45. Maxine Baca Zinn, "Familism among Chicanos: A Theoretical Review," *Humbolt Journal of Social Relations* 10 (1982–1983): 224–38.

46. Baca Zinn, "Political Familism," 18.

47. Ibid., 23.

48. Alvirez and Bean, "The Mexican American Family," 276.

49. Mirandé, "The Chicano Family," 753.

50. Baca Zinn, "Political Familism," 20–21.

51. Zavella, "The Problematic Relationship of Feminism and Chicana Studies," 27.

52. Originally written in 1973 by Ana Nieto-Gómez (see Ana Nieto-Gómez, "La Feminista," *Encuentro Femenil* 1 [1973]: 34–47); quoted in Alma M. Garcia, "The Development of Chicana Feminist Discourse," *Gender and Society* 3, no. 2 (June 1989): 225.

53. Ibid.

54. Dionne Espinoza, "'Revolutionary Sisters': Women's Solidarity and Collective Identification among Chicana Brown Berets in East Los Angeles, 1967–1970," *Aztlan* 26, no. 1 (Spring 2001): 39.

55. Ibid., 18.

56. Saldívar-Hull, *Feminism on the Border*, 132.

57. Catherine Ramirez, *The Lady Zoot-Suiter* (Durham: Duke University Press, forthcoming).

58. Ibid.

59. Richard Griswold del Castillo, *La Familia: Chicano Families in the Urban Southwest* (Notre Dame: University of Notre Dame Press, 1984), 33–39.

60. Amos and Parmar, "Challenging Imperial Feminism," 10. See especially their discussion of black women.

61. Yvette Flores-Ortiz, "The Broken Covenant: Incest in the Latino Family," *Voces: A Journal of Chicana/Latina Studies* 1, no. 2 (Summer 1997): 58.

62. Arturo J. Aldama, *Disrupting Savagism* (Durham and London: Duke University Press, 2001), 136.

63. See Keta Miranda, *Subversive Geographies* (Austin: University of Texas Press, forthcoming). See also Vicki Ruiz, who writes about comadrazgo in the context of women agricultural workers: "Commadrazgo [sic] served as one of the undergirdings for general patterns of reciprocity as women cared for one another as family and neighbors." *From Out of the Shadows* (New York and Oxford: Oxford University Press, 1998), 16.

64. Espinoza, "'Revolutionary Sisters,'" 42.

65. Ibid., 40.

Chapter Five

An earlier version of this chapter was published as "Re-Imagining Chicana Urban Identities in the Public Sphere, cool chuca style," in *Between Women and Nation: Transnational Feminisms and the State,* ed. Caren Kaplan, Norma Alarcón, and Minoo Moallem (Durham and London: Duke University Press, 1999), 72–91.

1. Catherine Ramirez, "Crimes of Fashion: The Pachuca and Chicana Style Politics," *Meridians: Feminism, Race, Transnationalism* 2, no. 2 (2002): 1–35.

2. See Nancy Fraser, *Unruly Practices,* 2d ed. (Minneapolis: University of Minnesota Press, 1991), 122.

3. Ibid., 122–24.

4. Nancy Fraser, "Rethinking the Public Sphere," *Social Text* 25, no. 26 (1994): 75.

5. Jean Franco, *Critical Passions,* ed. Mary Louise Pratt and Kathleen Newman (Durham and London: Duke University Press, 1999), 103.

6. Fraser's feminist interpretation of Habermas focuses on the gendered aspects of each of these spheres, explicitly highlighting the masculine subtext of the citizen's role in the public sphere and the feminine subtext of the child-rearing role in the familial or private lifeworld sphere. In defining citizenship, modern societies invest a higher value on the soldiering role rather than on "life-fostering child-rearing," thereby privileging the public (masculine) citizen-subject in the formation of the nation-state. Indeed, male dominance is intrinsic rather than accidental to modernity precisely because it is structural and "premised on the separation of waged labor and the state from childrearing and the household" — an institutional arrangement that for Fraser marks "the linchpin of modern women's subordination." As citizens in the public sphere and as producer in private (official) economic sphere, men are the privileged subjects of discourse and social relations, whereas women are confined to the private domestic sphere of the family and consumption. See Fraser, *Unruly Practices,* 122–29.

7. Jean Franco, "Beyond Ethnocentrism: Gender, Power, and the Third-World Intelligentsia," in *Marxism and the Interpretation of Culture,* ed. Cary Nelson and Lawrence Grossberg (Urbana and Chicago: University of Illinois Press, 1988), 507.

8. See Keta Miranda, *Subversive Geographies* (Austin: University of Texas Press, forthcoming).

9. See Ramirez, "Crimes of Fashion," 2.

10. Ibid.

11. These poems appear in Carmen Tafolla, *"Sonnets of Human Beings" and Other Selected Works* (Santa Monica, Calif.: Lalo Press, 1992).

12. Laura del Fuego, *Maravilla* (Encino, Calif.: Floricanto Press, 1989), 49.

13. Ibid., 37.

14. For other contemporary research on pachucas, cholas, and homegirls see Mary G. Harris, "Cholas, Mexican-American Girls, and Gangs," *Sex Roles* 30, nos. 3–4 (1994); Joan W. Moore, *Going Down to the Barrio: Homeboys and Homegirls in Change* (Philadelphia: Temple University Press, 1991); and Julie Bettie, "Women without Class: Chicas, Cholas, Trash, and the Presence/Absence of Class Identity," *Signs: Journal of Women in Culture and Society* 26, no. 1 (2000).

15. Miranda, *Subversive Geographies.*

16. Ramirez, "Crimes of Fashion."

17. Rosa Linda Fregoso, *The Bronze Screen: Chicana and Chicano Film Culture* (Minneapolis: University of Minnesota Press, 1993), 133–34.

18. See Rosa Linda Fregoso, "Hanging with the Homegirls in Alison Anders' *Mi Vida Loca,*" *Cineaste* 21, no. 2 (1995): 36–37.

19. Initially I wrote a favorable review that aired on National Public Radio's "Latino USA" during the summer of 1994. Favorable reviews were published in Michele Kort, "Filmmaker Alison Anders: Her Crazy Life," *Ms.,* May–June 1994; Abel Salas, "Alison Anders Discusses *Mi Vida Loca,*" *Latin Style,* August 1994; B. Ruby Rich, "Babes in Gangland," *Elle,* September 1994. See also B. Ruby Rich, "Slugging It Out for Survival," *Sight and Sound,* April 1995, 14–17.

20. Negative reviews of the film include Kevin Thomas, "The Road to '*Mi Vida Loca*' Paved with Good Intentions," *Los Angeles Times,* 22 July 1994; Pat Dowell, "Poor Creatures," *In These Times,* 8 August 1994; Rose Arrieta, "Outside Looking In," *San Francisco Bay Guardian,* 3 August 1994.

21. As a graduate student in the Department of the History of Consciousness at UC-Santa Cruz, Keta Miranda took several homegirls to screen the film at the San Francisco film festival as well as to academic conferences, where they shared their experiences with many of us. I have benefited enormously from their insights and from Keta's observations on girl gang members. The results of this ethnographic study will be published as part of Miranda's forthcoming book, *Subversive Geographies.* I would also like to thank Sylvia Escarcega-Judge, a graduate student in the Department of Anthropology at UC-Davis, whose insightful comments on a shorter published version of this research forced me to rethink some of my previous formulations. At her insistence, I reformulated this section to include some account of the agency and subjectivity of "actual" (not simply discursive) girl gang members.

22. Liela Cobo-Hanlon, "Another Side of the 'Crazy Life,'" *Los Angeles Times,* 21 July 1994; Jill Sharer, "Gang Girls on Attitude, Reality, and *Mi Vida Loca,*" *LA Weekly,* 22–28 July 1994.

23. See Miranda, *Subversive Geographies.*

Chapter Six

1. Carey McWilliams, *North from Mexico* (New York: Monthly Review Press, 1961).

2. As Mike Davis writes: "At a New York advertising convention in the early 1930s, the mission aura of 'history and romance' was rated as an even more important attraction in selling Southern California than weather or movie industry glamour." Mike Davis, *City of Quartz* (London and New York: Verso, 1990), 27.

3. McWilliams, *North from Mexico,* 42.

4. Davis, *City of Quartz,* 26.

5. Ibid., 83, 27.

6. Teresa de Lauretis, "On the Subject of Fantasy," in *Feminisms in the Cinema*, ed. Laura Pietropaolo and Ada Testaferri (Bloomington and Indianapolis: Indiana University Press, 1995), 64.

7. See Luiz Costa Lima, *The Control of the Imaginary* (Minneapolis: University of Minnesota Press, 1988), 120.

8. Ibid.

9. Ibid., 206.

10. de Lauretis, "On the Subject of Fantasy," 65.

11. Moreover, like McWilliams, Mike Davis details the ways in which the whitening of California history during the nineteenth and twentieth centuries reinforced white racial and economic supremacy just as the erasure of Mexican working-class and mixed-race identities consolidated California's nativism.

12. For more on genealogy as historical method see Michel Foucault, "Two Lectures," in *Power/Knowledge: Selected Interviews and Other Writings, 1972–1977*, ed. and trans. Colin Gordon, 78–108 (New York: Pantheon, 1980); for a feminist rereading of Foucault's genealogical method, see Jana Sawicki, *Disciplining Foucault* (New York and London: Routledge, 1991).

13. Antonio Ríos-Bustamante, "Latino Participation in the Hollywood Film Industry, 1911–1945," in *Chicanos and Film,* ed. Chon Noriega (New York and London: Garland, 1992), 22.

14. Ibid.

15. Geoffrey Bell, *The Golden Gate and the Silver Screen* (New York and London: Cornwall Books, 1984), 72.

16. Ibid., 85.

17. "Mayor Drives 6-Horse Team," *San Francisco Examiner,* 29 July 1919.

18. "Operatic Star Leaves on Concert Tour," *San Francisco Chronicle,* 10 July 1927.

19. See Joanne Hershfield, *The Invention of Dolores del Rio* (Minneapolis: University of Minnesota Press, 2000), x.

20. Ibid., 3.

21. Michelena's father is described as "member of a distinguished South American Spanish family" (see "Operatic Star Leaves on Concert Tour"); González's obituary states she was a "daughter of an old Spanish family" ("Myrtle Gonzales Dead," *Los Angeles Times,* 23 October 1918).

22. "Myrtle Gonzales Dead," 1.

23. Roughly 10 percent of the films produced during the early era of cinema survive, mostly in public and private archives. At the Library of Congress I located four of the forty-two films starring Myrtle González, but only one of the sixteen featuring Michelena.

24. See for example Clara E. Rodríguez, "Visual Retrospective: Latin Film Stars," in *Latin Looks,* ed. Clara E. Rodríguez (Boulder: Westview, 1997), 80–84; Antonio Ríos-Bustamante, "Latinos and the Hollywood Film Industry, 1920–1950," *Americas 2001* (January 1988): 6–27.

25. Ríos-Bustamante, "Latinos and the Hollywood Film Industry," 23.

26. Hershfield, *The Invention of Dolores del Rio,* 10.

27. Mexican critic quoted in Gabriel Ramírez, *Lupe Vélez: La mexicana que escupía fuego* (Mexico City: Cineteca Nacional, 1986), 53.

28. Ibid., 114. "Pocho/pocha" is a disparaging term used by Mexicans in Mexico to refer to the Mexican diaspora. Throughout the twentieth century, "pocho" served to deride Mexicans living in the United States and especially their U.S.-born children, for losing their "culture," "customs," and language. Until the Chicano Movement reclaimed "Chicano" as a political identity, the term was used interchangeably with "pocho."

29. Vicki L. Ruiz, *From Out of the Shadows* (New York: Oxford University Press, 1998), 6.

30. Ramírez, *Lupe Vélez,* 29.

31. Ibid., 28.

32. John D'Emilio and Estelle B. Freedman, *Intimate Matters: A History of Sexuality in America* (New York: Harper and Row, 1988), 241.

33. Ramírez, *Lupe Vélez,* 29.

34. D'Emilio and Freedman, *Intimate Matters,* 265.

35. Ramírez, *Lupe Vélez,* 43.

36. Ibid., 53.

37. Lane quoted in Ramírez, *Lupe Vélez,* 56. This and subsequent translations of Ramírez are mine.

38. D'Emilio and Freedman, *Intimate Matters,* 240.

39. Ruiz, *From Out of the Shadows,* 65.

40. Douglas Monroy, "'Our Children Get So Different Here': Film, Fashion, Popular Culture, and the Process of Cultural Syncretization in Mexican Los Angeles, 1900–1935," *Aztlan* 19, no. 1 (Spring 1988–1990): 87.

41. Ruiz, *From Out of the Shadows,* 59.

42. Monroy, "'Our Children Get So Different Here,'" 90.

43. Ruiz, *From Out of the Shadows,* 58.

44. Monroy, "'Our Children Get So Different Here,'" 83.

45. Ramírez, *Lupe Vélez,* 94.

46. Ibid., 62.

47. Ibid., 128.

48. See especially Ríos-Bustamante, "Latinos and the Hollywood Film Industry"; Gary D. Keller, *Hispanics and United States Film* (Tempe, Ariz.: Bilingual Press, 1994); and Luis Reyes and Peter Rubie, *Hispanics in Hollywood: An Encyclopedia of Film and Television* (New York and London: Garland, Inc., 1994).

49. See especially Reyes and Rubie, *Hispanics in Hollywood,* 20–21.

50. I thank Tatcho Mindiola for sharing his reservations about the critiques of Lupe Vélez by Chicano historiographers and also for providing me with copies of Vélez films that he had taped from television.

51. I owe my understanding of "screwball comedy" to the work of Maya Higgins, who wrote an undergraduate thesis under my supervision at UC-Davis.

52. Quoted in Hershfield, *The Invention of Dolores del Rio,* 18.

53. Published originally in *Continental* (December 1931) and quoted in Ramírez, *Lupe Vélez*, 80.

54. Emilio García Riera, *México visto por el cine extranjero* (Mexico City: Ediciones Era: Universidad de Guadalajara, Centro de Investigaciones y Enseñanzas Cinematográficas, 1987–1988), 231.

55. Ramírez, *Lupe Vélez*, 126–27.

56. Ibid., 124.

57. Ramon Garcia, "New Iconographies: Film Culture in Chicano Cultural Production," in *Decolonial Voices*, ed. Arturo J. Aldama and Naomi Quiñonez (Bloomington: Indiana University Press, 2002), 70.

58. Ibid.

59. See Yvonne Yarbro-Bejarano, "Ironic Framings: A Queer Reading of the Family (Melo)drama in Lourdes Portillo's *The Devil Never Sleeps/El diablo nunca duerme*," in *Lourdes Portillo: "The Devil Never Sleeps" and Other Films*, ed. Rosa Linda Fregoso (Austin: University of Texas Press, 2001), 110.

60. Ramírez, *Lupe Vélez*, 27.

61. Ibid., 85, 100.

62. Ibid., 93.

63. Ibid., 12.

64. Kenneth Anger, *Hollywood Babylon* (New York: Bell, 1975), 239.

65. Matthew Tinkcom, *Working like a Homosexual* (Durham and London: Duke University Press, 2002), 141. I thank Ann Cvetkovich for bringing this text to my attention.

66. Ibid., 141, 148.

67. According to the catalogue notes of a recent exhibit of Warhol's films at the Whitney, "*Lupe* was shown on three screens at its premiere." See Chrissie Isles, *Into the Light: The Projected Image in American Art, 1964–1977* (Whitney Museum of American Art, 2001).

68. Ramírez, *Lupe Vélez*, 15.

69. Labra quoted in ibid., 139.

70. Ibid., 35.

71. Ibid., 52.

72. Ibid., 82.

73. Ibid., 133.

74. Ibid., 135.

75. Kay Redfield Jamison, *An Unquiet Mind* (New York: Vintage Books, 1996), 211.

76. Kay Redfield Jamison, *Touched with Fire* (New York: Free Press Paperbacks, 1993), 2.

77. Ibid., 5, 240.

78. Ibid., 6.

Chapter Seven

1. Rosaura Sánchez, *Telling Identities* (Minneapolis: University of Minnesota Press, 1995), 287.

2. Horsman, Reginald, "Scientific Racism and the American Indian in the Mid-Nineteenth Century," *American Quarterly* 27 (May 1975): 165.

3. Quoted in José Limón, "Stereotyping and Chicano Resistance: An Historical Dimension," in *Chicanos and Film*, ed. Chon Noriega (New York: Garland, 1992), 6.

4. In chapter three I draw from Toni Morrison's notion the "Africanist presence" and discuss how the "Mexicanist presence" has been rarely acknowledged as also shaping "the imaginative and historical terrain upon which American writers [and I would add, moviemakers] journeyed."

5. Quote from Lora Romero's response to my paper "Consideration toward the Study of Racialized Sexuality on the Borderlands" (paper delivered at the annual meeting of the Modern Language Association, Washington, D.C., December 1996). I am indebted to the late Lora Romero for bringing Toni Morrison's notion of "Africanist presence" to my attention.

6. The analysis developed in this chapter is based on the actual viewing of the films I discuss herein, rather than on the reading of synopsis of films, as is usually the case in discussions of silent films on Mexicanos/Chicana/os. My focus on the significance of Mexicana/Chicana representation in the nation-building project was a research decision sparked by the writings of scholars who had identified the existence of stereotypes in films featuring Chicanos/as dating back to the beginnings of cinema. However, as I would soon discover, the only surviving evidence of early filmic representations of Mexicans and Chicanas/os is in the written synopses published in the various trade magazines of the time, including Biograph *Bulletin* and *Motion Picture World*. In general, only about 10 percent of the silent films made in the early twentieth century survive to this day. For this reason, and because written summaries of film plots (synopses) are highly mediated and subjective interpretations, it becomes difficult to make any definitive interpretations of the nature of the images of Mexicanos/Chicanas. Thus, for the purposes of my analysis, I have restricted my interpretations primarily to the films I was able to view in the various film archives throughout the country.

7. Unfortunately only a handful of the two thousand or so silent films on Mexicans survive, thereby making difficult a comprehensive assessment of cinematic discourse on Mexicana subjects.

8. "*The Red Girl:* Another Soul-Stirring Story of Life on the Frontier by the Biograph," *Bulletin* 170 (15 September 1908): 19; see also *The Moving Picture World* 3, no. 12 (15 September 1908): 221.

9. Nina Yuval-Davis and Floya Anthias, "Introduction," in *Woman-Nation State*, ed. Nina Yuval-Davis and Floya Anthias (London: Macmillan, 1989), 9.

10. Cheryl Harris, "Whiteness as Property," *Harvard Law Review* 106, no. 8 (1993): 1721.

11. Harris, "Whiteness as Property," 1785.

12. Ian Haney López, "Racial Restrictions on Law and Citizenship," in *Critical Race Theory: Essays on the Social Construction and Reproduction of "Race,"* ed. E. Nathaniel Gates (New York: Garland, 1997), 114.

13. Horsman, "Scientific Racism and the American Indian," 165.

14. Bancroft quoted in Sánchez, *Telling Identities,* 30.

15. *Southern Quarterly Review* article quoted in Horsman, "Scientific Racism and the American Indian," 166.

16. Dorothy Roberts, "Who May Give Birth to Citizens: Reproduction, Eugenics, and Immigration," in *Immigrants Out: The New Nativism and the Anti-Immigrant Impulse in the United States,* ed. Juan F. Perea (New York: New York University Press, 1997), 208.

17. As Haney López explains, it was not until after 1870 that blacks could naturalize. See Haney López, "Racial Restrictions," 44. Quote is from Harris, "Whiteness as Property," 1713.

18. Ian Haney López, "White by Law," in *Critical Race Theory: The Cutting Edge,* ed. Richard Delgado (Philadelphia: Temple University Press, 1995), 542.

19. *Motion Picture Review* 4, no. 25 (19 June 1909): 842.

20. Daniel J. Kevles, *In the Name of Eugenics* (New York: Alfred A. Knopf, 1985), 107.

21. John D'Emilio and Estelle B. Freedman, *Intimate Matters: A History of Sexuality in America* (New York: Harper and Row, 1988), 106.

22. Sander Gilman, *Difference and Pathology: Stereotypes of Sexuality, Race, and Madness* (Ithaca: Cornell University Press, 1985), 107. D'Emilio and Freedman, *Intimate Matters,* 106.

23. Raymond Paredes, "The Origin of Anti-Mexican Sentiment in the United States," *New Scholar* 6 (1977): 158.

24. Quoted in Sánchez, *Telling Identities,* 30.

25. Farnham quoted in Richard R. Peterson, "Anti-Mexican Nativism in California 1848–1853: A Study of Cultural Conflict," *Southern California Quarterly* 62, no. 4 (Winter 1980): 317–18.

26. Southerner quoted in D'Emilio and Freedman, *Intimate Matters,* 106.

27. Stephen Jay Gould, *The Mismeasure of Man* (New York: W. W. Norton, 1981), 35.

28. Nancy Leys Stepan, "Race and Gender: The Role of Analogy in Science," *ISIS* 77 (1986): 266.

29. See Gould, *The Mismeasure of Man.*

30. Horsman, "Scientific Racism and the American Indian," 39.

31. Race scientist quoted in Gould, *The Mismeasure of Man,* 39.

32. Ibid., 39–43.

33. Stepan, "Race and Gender," 263–64.

34. Agassiz quoted in Gould, *The Mismeasure of Man,* 49.

35. Stepan, "Race and Gender," 263.

36. Ibid., 275.

37. Horsman, "Scientific Racism and the American Indian," 164.

38. Michel Foucault, *The History of Sexuality Volume I: An Introduction*, trans. Robert Hurley (New York: Vintage Books, 1980), 122.

39. Ibid., 125.

40. Ibid., 123.

41. Laura Ann Stoler, *Race and the Education of Desire* (Durham: Duke University Press, 1995), 42.

42. Ibid., 8.

43. Ibid., 30–31.

44. Ibid., 84.

45. Published in the *United States Democratic Review* in 1848 and quoted in Sánchez, *Telling Identities*, 182.

46. I arrived at this conclusion on the basis of my examination of the written synopses of the following films, the actual prints of which, as I mentioned earlier, no longer exist. In some, like *A Traitor to His Country* (1914) and *Masked Dancer* (1914), Anglo men pursue Mexicans to no avail; in many other films of the period, such as *The Spirit of the Flag* (1913), *A Border Tale* (1910), *The Heart of Bonita* (1916), and *The Heart of Paula* (1916), the Mexican advances toward the white male are frustrated. Like *Mexican Sweethearts* (1909), most films feature triangular relations, and in most cases, a character flaw in the Mexicana provides the reason for her undesirability, thus fixing the impossibility of mixed-race unions in the cultural imaginary. The Mexican character is depicted as a "greaser"/cantina girl in *Masked Dancer;* a self-abnegating woman in *The Heart of Bonita* and *A Border Tale;* hot-blooded and jealous in *The Spirit of the Flag;* and criminal in *The Secret Treaty* (1913).

47. Pro-miscegenation films in which white males rescue the Mexicana from the excesses of her culture include *The Miner's Peril* (1914), *Rose of the Rancho* (1914), *The Rose of San Juan* (1913), *The California Revolution of 1846* (1911), *When California Was Won* (1911), *An American Invasion* (1912), *Margarita and the Mission Funds* (1913), *The Smuggler's Daughter* (1912), *Mike and Jake in Mexico* (1913), *The Apache Kid* (1913), *Shorty's Trip to Mexico* (1914), *The Fighting Lieutenant* (1913), *The Secret of the Dead* (1915), *The Bowl Bearer* (1915), *Along the Border* (1916), *Melita's Sacrifice* (1913), *Clouds in Sunshine Valley* (1916), *The Lady of Sorrow* (1914), *Lieut. Danny USA* (1916), *Licking the Greasers* (1915), and *Bronco Billy's Mexican Wife* (1912). Films in which a white male defeats a Mexican male in romance include *The Señorita's Conquest* (1911), *On the Border* (1913), *The Aztec Treasure* (1914), *The Mexican Rebellion* (1914), *The Trap* (1914), *The Winner* (1914), and *The Wedding Guest* (1916).

48. The following films were set in mid-nineteenth-century California: *The Miner's Peril* (1914), *Rose of the Rancho* (1914), *The Rose of San Juan* (1913), *The California Revolution of 1846* (1911), *When California Was Won* (1911), *An American Invasion* (1912), and *Margarita and the Mission Funds* (1913).

49. See Kevles, *In the Name of Eugenics*, 75.

50. Yuval-Davis and Anthias, "Introduction," 9.

51. Stoler, *Race and the Education of Desire*, 42.

52. Antonia Castañeda, "The Political Economy of Nineteenth-Century

Stereotypes of Californianas," in *Between Borders,* ed. Adelaida R. del Castillo (Encino, Calif.: Floricanto Press, 1990), 223.

53. Castañeda, "Political Economy," 218.

54. Originally published in the trade journal *Motion Picture World,* 6 December 1913. Quoted in Kathleen Karr, "The Long Square-Up: Exploitation Trends in the Silent Film," *Journal of Popular Film* 3, no. 2 (Spring 1974): 123.

55. See Kevles, *In the Name of Eugenics,* 56.

56. Deena J. González, "From La Leyenda Negra to Las Tules," in *The Mask of Zorro: Mexican Americans in Popular Media* (Los Angeles: Gene Autry Western Heritage Museum, 1994), 10.

57. D'Emilio and Freedman, *Intimate Matters,* 88. Beverly Trulio, "Anglo American Attitudes towards New Mexican Women," *Journal of the West* 12 (1973): 233.

58. Trulio, "Anglo American Attitudes," 231–32.

59. Lawyer quoted in Castañeda, "Political Economy," 218.

60. D'Emilio and Freedman, *Intimate Matters,* 86.

61. Gilman, *Difference and Pathology,* 81.

62. D'Emilio and Freedman, *Intimate Matters,* 194.

63. Ibid., 199.

64. Janet Staiger, *Bad Women* (Minneapolis: University of Minnesota Press, 1995), xiii.

65. Ibid., 67.

66. Ibid., 6, 117.

67. Ibid., 143.

68. A cursory review of film synopses from the period reveals the extent to which interdictions against female promiscuity are rendered in portrayals of hypersexualized (i.e., women with many lovers) Mexicana characters, as in *Pepita's Destiny* (1913), *The Power of Angelus* (1914), and *The Black Mantilla* (1917); taboos around unrestrained emotions like jealousy and revenge are filtered through the negative depictions of Mexicanas in films like *The Two Brothers* (1913), *Carmelita's Revenge* (1914), *A Mexican Romance* (1912), *The Jealousy of Miguel and Isabella* (1913), *The Lotus Woman* (1916), and *His Mexican Bride* (1909). There are no extant prints of any of these films in the various archives.

69. Allan Brandt, *No Magic Bullet: A Social History of Venereal Disease in the United States since 1880* (New York: Oxford University Press, 1987), 14.

70. Quoted in Kevles, *In the Name of Eugenics,* 107.

71. Ibid.

Chapter Eight

1. My recollection of my grandmother's memories of the Amusu's opening day has been reconstructed through descriptions taken from L. G. Collins, "Amusu Theater Being Erected on Mesquite Street at Cost of $20,000," *Corpus Christi Caller-Times,* 8 August 1914.

2. For detail on the history of labor and race relations in Texas see David Montejano, *Anglos and Mexicans in the Making of Texas, 1836–1986* (Austin: University of Texas Press, 1987).

3. Charles Musser, *History of American Cinema: The Emergence of Cinema to 1907* (New York: Charles Scribner's and Sons, 1990b), 425.

4. According to Musser, in 1908 only four of these machines were operating in the country. See Charles Musser, "The Nickelodeon Era Begins: Establishing the Framework for Hollywood's Mode of Representation," in *Early Cinema: Space, Frame Narrative,* ed. Thomas Elsaesser (London: British Film Institute, 1990a), 265.

5. Advertisement quoted in Bill Walraven, "Step Right Up to Corpus Christi's Vaudeville Theaters, *Corpus Christi Caller-Times,* 10 October 1980.

6. Information taken from an unpublished article written by Frank Wagner, "Early Moviehouses in Corpus Christi."

7. Tío Charlie Garza, interview with author, Corpus Christi, Tex., 23 August 1993.

8. For details on the Spanish dancer Carmencita, see Terry Ramsaye, *A Million and One Nights: A History of the Motion Picture* (New York: Simon and Schuster, 1926), 115–17.

9. The exhibitor's name was John P. Harris. See Benjamin A. Hampton, *A History of the Movies* (New York: Covici, 1931), 41–56.

10. According to Frank Wagner, only Harry Elliot, the owner of the Lyric Theater, had windstorm insurance. He was able to repair the Amusu and borrow money to rebuild the Aldine on Chaparral.

11. Hampton, *A History of the Movies,* 41.

12. Information taken from Wagner's "Early Moviehouses in Corpus Christi."

13. Hampton, *A History of the Movies,* 73.

14. "Seaside Opening," *Corpus Christi Democrat,* January 1912.

15. Hampton, *A History of the Movies,* 41.

16. See Montejano, *Anglos,* 113–16.

17. Newspaper editorials quoted in José Limón, "Stereotyping and Chicano Resistance: An Historical Dimension," in *Chicanos and Film,* edited by Chon Noriega (New York: Garland, 1992), 10–11.

18. For further details, see Felix Sánchez, "Projectionist Smooth Operator," *Corpus Christi Caller-Times,* 7 December 1978, 1.

19. Film historian Charles Musser has documented that by 1910, fire marshals and insurance underwriters were requiring that projection booths be lined with asbestos in order to avoid fires. See Musser, *History of American Cinema,* 442.

20. Ibid.

21. Ibid.

22. Emilio García Riera, *México visto por el cine extranjero: Vol. 1, 1894–1940* (Mexico City: Ediciones Era, 1987–1990).

23. See Arnoldo de León, *They Called Them Greasers* (Austin: University of Texas Press, 1983), 16.

24. Mary Louise Pratt, *Imperial Eyes: Travel, Writing, and Transculturation* (London and New York: Routledge, 1992), 6.

25. Cornelius Smith Jr., *A Southwestern Vocabulary: The Words They Used* (Glendale, Calif.: Arthur H. Clark Company, 1984), 104.

26. de León, *They Called Them Greasers,* 17.

27. Elizabeth Grosz, *Volatile Bodies* (Bloomington: Indiana University Press, 1994), 201.

28. Mary Douglas, *Purity and Danger: An Analysis of Concepts of Pollution and Taboo* (New York and Washington: Praeger, 1966), 2.

29. Ibid., 35. Douglas continues: "[This approach] implies two conditions: a set of ordered relations and a contravention of that order. Dirt, then, is never a unique, isolated event. Where there is dirt there is a system. Dirt is the by product of a systemic ordering and classification of matter, in so far as ordering involves rejecting inappropriate elements. This idea of dirt takes us straight into the system of symbolism and promises to link-up with more obviously symbolic systems of purity."

Epilogue

1. John Phillip Santos, *Places Left Unfinished at the Time of Creation* (New York: Viking, 1999), 80.

2. "The Gold Rush Spirit Lives on in California," *San Francisco Chronicle,* 25 January 1998, D6.

3. Ann Laura Stoler, *Race and the Education of Desire* (Durham: Duke University Press, 1995), 7.

Bibliography

Agamben, Giorgio. "Form-of-Life." In *Means without End*. Translated by Vincenzo Binetti and Cesare Casarino, 3–14. Minneapolis: University of Minnesota Press, 2000.

Alarcón, Norma. "Anzaldúa's Frontera: Inscribing Genetics." In *Displacement, Diaspora, and Geographies of Identity*, edited by Smadar Lavie and Ted Swedenburg, 41–53. Durham: Duke University Press, 1995.

Aldama, Arturo J. *Disrupting Savagism*. Durham and London: Duke University Press, 2001.

Alonzo, Ana María. *Thread of Blood: Colonialism, Revolution, and Gender on Mexico's Northern Frontier*. Tucson: University of Arizona, 1995.

Alvirez, David, and Frank Bean. "The Mexican American Family." In *Ethnic Families in America*, edited by Charles Mindel and Robert Hamerstein, 271–92. New York. Elsevier Scientific Press, 1976.

Amos, Valerie, and Pratibha Parmar. "Challenging Imperial Feminism." *Feminist Review*, 17 (Fall 1984): 3–19.

Anger, Kenneth. *Hollywood Babylon*. New York: Bell, 1975.

Arguelles, Lourdes, and Anne M. Rivero. "Gender/Sexual Orientation Violence and Transnational Migration: Conversations with Some Latinas We Think We Know." *Urban Anthropology and Studies of Cultural Systems and World Economic Development* 22, nos. 3–4 (1993): 259–71.

Arias, Patricia. "La migración femenina en dos modelos de desarrollo: 1940–1970 y 1980–1992." In *Relaciones de genero y transformación agraria: Estudios sobre el campo mexicano*, edited by Soledad González Montes, 223–53. Mexico City: El Colegio de México, 1995.

Baca Zinn, Maxine. "Political Familism: Toward Sex Role Equality in Chicano Families." *Aztlan* 6, no. 1 (Spring 1975): 13–26.

———. "Chicano Family Research: Conceptual Distortions and Alternative Directions." *Journal of Ethnic Studies* 7 (1979): 59–71.

———. "Familism among Chicanos: A Theoretical Review." *Humbolt Journal of Social Relations* 10 (1982–1983): 224–38.

Bahar, Saba. "Women's Rights Are Human Rights." In *Global Feminism since 1945,* edited by Bonnie G. Smith, 265–89. London and New York: Routledge, 2000.

Bales, Kevin. *Disposable People.* Berkeley: University of California Press, 1999.

Bauman, Zygmunt. *Globalization: The Human Consequence.* New York: Columbia University Press, 1998.

Bejarano, Cynthia. "Las Super Madres de Latino América: Transforming Motherhood and Houseskirts by Challenging Violence in Juárez, Mexico, Argentina, and El Salvador," *Frontiers* 23, no. 1 (2002): 126–50.

Bell, Geoffrey. *The Golden Gate and the Silver Screen.* New York and London: Cornwall Books, 1984.

Benítez, Rohry, et al. *El silencio que la voz de todas quiebra.* Chihuahua, Mexico: Ediciones del Azar, 1999.

Benjamin, Walter. "Theses on the Philosophy of History." In *Illuminations,* edited by Hannah Arendt. Translated by Harry Zohn, 253–64. New York: Schocken, 1969.

———. "The Work of Art in the Age of Mechanical Reproduction." In *Illuminations,* edited by Hannah Arendt. Translated by Harry Zohn, 217–52. New York: Schocken, 1969.

Bernardi, Daniel. "The Voices of Whiteness: D. W. Griffith's Biograph Films (1908–1913)." In *The Birth of Whiteness: Race and the Emergence of U.S. Cinema,* edited by Daniel Bernardi, 103–28. New Brunswick: Rutgers University Press, 1996.

Bettie, Julie. "Women without Class: Chicas, Cholas, Trash, and the Presence/Absence of Class Identity." *Signs: Journal of Women in Culture and Society* 26, no. 1 (2000): 1–35.

Bhabha, Homi K. *The Location of Culture.* London and New York: Routledge , 1994.

Bonilla-Santiago, Gloria. "Latina Battered Women: Barriers to Service Delivery and Cultural Considerations." In *Helping Battered Women: New Perspectives and Remedies,* edited by Albert R. Roberts, 229–34. New York: Oxford University Press, 1996.

Bowden, Charles. "While You Were Sleeping: In Juárez, Mexico, Photographers Expose the Violent Realities of Free Trade." *Harper's,* December 1996, 44–52.

———. *Juárez: The Laboratory of Our Future.* New York: Aperture, 1998.

———. "I Wanna Dance with the Strawberry Girl." *Talk,* September 1999, 113–18.

Brandt, Allan M. *No Magic Bullet: A Social History of Venereal Disease in the United States since 1880.* New York: Oxford University Press, 1987.

Brown-Guillory, Elizabeth. "Introduction." In *Women of Color: Mother-*

Daughter Relationships in Twentieth-Century Literature, edited by Elizabeth Brown-Guillory, 1–16. Austin: University of Texas Press, 1996.

Burawoy, Michael. "Grounding Globalization." In *Global Ethnography: Forces, Connections, and Imaginations in a Postmodern World,* edited by Michael Burawoy et al., 337–50. Berkeley: University of California Press, 2001.

Burton, Julianne. "Oedipus Tex/Oedipus Mex: History, Mystery, and the Paternal Gaze in John Sayles's *Lone Star.*" In *Multiculturalism, Transnationalism, and Film,* edited by Ella Shohat and Robert Stam. New Brunswick: Rutgers University Press, forthcoming.

Castañeda, Antonia. "The Political Economy of Nineteenth Century Stereotypes of Californianas." In *Between Borders,* edited by Adelaida R. del Castillo, 213–36. Encino, Calif.: Floricanto Press, 1990.

Chabram-Dernersesian, Angie. "And, Yes . . . The Earth Did Part: On the Splitting of Chicana Subjectivity." In *Building with Our Hands,* edited by Adela de la Torre and Beatríz Pesquera, 34–56. Berkeley: University of California Press, 1993.

Chomsky, Noam. "Preface: Notes on NAFTA: The Masters of Mankind." In *Juárez: The Laboratory of Our Future,* edited by Charles Bowden, 13–20. New York: Aperture, 1998.

Cisneros, Sandra. *"Woman Hollering Creek" and Other Stories.* New York: Vintage, 1991.

Comisión Nacional de Derechos Humanos de México. "The Case of Assassinated Women in Cuidad Juárez and the Lack of Collaboration of the Offices of the Attorney General of Chihuahua." Mexico City: Comisión Nacional de Derechos Humanos de México, 1998.

Coontz, Stephanie. *The Way We Really Are.* New York: Basic Books, 1997.

Crawley, Heaven. "Engendering the State in Refugee Women's Claims for Asylum." In *States of Conflict,* edited by Susie Jacobs, Ruth Jacobson, and Jennifer Marchbank, 87–104. New York: Zed Books, 2000.

Crenshaw, Kimberlé Williams. "Mapping the Margins: Intersectionality, Identity Politics, and Violence against Women of Color." In *Critical Race Theory: The Key Writings That Formed the Movement,* edited by Kimberlé Williams Crenshaw, Neil Gotanda, Gary Peller, and Kendall Thomas, 357–83. New York: The New Press, 1995.

Davis, Mike. *City of Quartz.* London and New York: Verso, 1990.

de la O Martínez, María. "Maquiladora, mujer, y cambios productivos: Estudio de caso en la industria maquiladora de Cuidad Juárez." In *Mujeres, migración, y maquila en la frontera norte,* edited by Soledad González Montes et al., 241–70. Mexico City: El Colegio de México, Programa Interdisciplinario de Estudios de la Mujer, 1995.

de Lauretis, Teresa. "On the Subject of Fantasy." In *Feminisms in the Cinema,* edited by Laura Pietropaolo and Ada Testaferri, 63–85. Bloomington and Indianapolis: Indiana University Press, 1995.

de León, Arnoldo. *They Called Them Greasers.* Austin: University of Texas Press, 1983.

del Fuego, Laura. *Maravilla*. Encino, Calif.: Floricanto Press, 1989.

D'Emilio, John, and Estelle B. Freedman. *Intimate Matters: A History of Sexuality in America*. New York: Harper and Row, 1988.

Douglas, Mary. *Purity and Danger: An Analysis of Concepts of Pollution and Taboo*. New York and Washington: Praeger, 1966.

Espinoza, Dionne. "'Revolutionary Sisters': Women's Solidarity and Collective Identification among Chicana Brown Berets in East Los Angeles, 1967–1970," *Aztlan* 26, no. 1 (Spring 2001): 17–58.

Ferguson, Roderick. "The Nightmares of the Heteronormative." *Cultural Values* 4, no. 4 (October 2000): 419–44.

Fernández-Kelly, María Patricia. *For We Are Sold, I and My People: Women and Industry in Mexico's Frontier*. Albany: State University of New York Press, 1983.

Fischer, Lucy. *Cinematernity: Film Motherhood, Genre*. Princeton: Princeton University Press, 1996.

Flores, Lisa A., and Michelle A. Holling. "Las Familias and las Latinas: Mediated Representations of Gender Roles." In *Mediated Women: Representations in Popular Culture*, edited by Marian Meyers, 339–53. Cresskill, N.J.: Hampton Press, 2000.

Flores-Ortiz, Yvette. "La Mujer y la Violencia: A Culturally Based Model for the Understanding and Treatment of Domestic Violence in Chicana/Latina Communities." In *Chicana Critical Issues*, edited by Mujeres Activas en Letras y Cambio Social, 169–82. Berkeley: Third Woman Press, 1993.

———. "The Broken Covenant: Incest in the Latino Family." *Voces: A Journal of Chicana/Latina Studies* 1, no. 2 (1997): 48–70.

Foucault, Michel. *The History of Sexuality Volume I: An Introduction*. Translated by Robert Hurley. New York: Vintage Books, 1980.

———. "Two Lectures." In *Power/Knowledge: Selected Interviews and Other Writings, 1972–1977*, edited and translated by Colin Gordon, 78–108. New York: Pantheon, 1980.

Franco, Jean. "Beyond Ethnocentrism: Gender, Power, and the Third World Intelligentsia." In *Marxism and the Interpretation of Culture*, edited by Cary Nelson and Lawrence Grossberg, 503–15. Urbana and Chicago: University of Illinois Press, 1988.

———. *Critical Passions*, edited by Mary Louise Pratt and Kathleen Newman. Durham and London: Duke University Press, 1999.

———. *The Decline and Fall of the Lettered State*. Cambridge and London: Harvard University Press, 2002.

Fraser, Nancy. *Unruly Practices*. 2d ed. Minneapolis: University of Minnesota Press, 1991.

———. "Rethinking the Public Sphere." *Social Text* 25, no. 26 (1994): 56–90.

Fregoso, Rosa Linda. *The Bronze Screen: Chicana and Chicano Film Culture*. Minneapolis: University of Minnesota Press, 1993.

———. "Hanging with the Homegirls in Alison Anders' *Mi Vida Loca*." *Cineaste* 21, no. 2 (1995): 36–37.

———. "Voices without Echo: The Global Gendered Apartheid," *Emergences* 10, no. 1 (May 2000): 137–56.

———, ed. *Lourdes Portillo: "The Devil Never Sleeps" and Other Films*. Austin: University of Texas Press, 2001.

Garcia, Alma M. "The Development of Chicana Feminist Discourse." *Gender and Society* 3, no. 2 (1989): 217–38.

Garcia, Ramon. "New Iconographies: Film Culture in Chicano Cultural Production." In *Decolonial Voices,* edited by Arturo J. Aldama and Naomi Quiñonez, 64–77. Bloomington: Indiana University Press, 2002.

García Riera, Emilio. *México visto por el cine extranjero: Vol. 1, 1894–1940*. Mexico City: Ediciones Era: Universidad de Guadalajara, Centro de Investigaciones y Enseñanzas Cinematográficas, 1987–1990.

Garza, Charlie. Interview with author. Corpus Christi, Tex., 23 August 1993.

Gil, Rosa Maria, and Carmen Inoa Vásquez. *The Maria Paradox: How Latinas Can Merge Old World Traditions with New World Self-Esteem*. New York: G. P. Putnam's Sons, 1996.

Gilman, Sander L. *Difference and Pathology: Stereotypes of Sexuality, Race, and Madness*. Ithaca: Cornell University Press, 1985.

González, Deena J. "From La Leyenda Negra to Las Tules." In *The Mask of Zorro: Mexican Americans in Popular Media*. Los Angeles: Gene Autry Western Heritage Museum, 1994.

Gould, Stephen Jay. *The Mismeasure of Man*. New York: W. W. Norton, 1981.

Gray, Herman. "Anxiety, Desire, and Conflict in the American Racial Imagination." In *Media Scandals,* edited by James Lull and Stephen Hiverman, 85–98. Malden, Mass.: Blackwell, 1997.

Grewal, Inderpal. "On the New Global Feminism and the Family of Nations." In *Talking Visions,* edited by Ella Shohat, 501–30. Cambridge and London: MIT Press, 1998.

Griswold del Castillo, Richard. *La Familia: Chicano Families in the Urban Southwest*. Notre Dame: University of Notre Dame Press, 1984.

Grosz, Elizabeth. *Volatile Bodies*. Bloomington: Indiana University Press, 1994.

Hampton, Benjamin A. *A History of the Movies*. New York: Covici, 1931.

Haney López, Ian. "Racial Restrictions on Law and Citizenship." In *Critical Race Theory: Essays on the Social Construction and Reproduction of "Race,"* edited by E. Nathaniel Gates, 109–25. New York: Garland, 1997.

———. "White by Law." In *Critical Race Theory: The Cutting Edge,* edited by Richard Delgado, 542–50. Philadelphia: Temple University Press, 1995.

Harris, Cheryl L. "Whiteness as Property." *Harvard Law Review* 106, no. 8 (1993): 1710–91.

Harris, Mary G. "Cholas, Mexican-American Girls, and Gangs." *Sex Roles* 30, nos. 3–4 (1994): 1770–91.

Harvey, David. *Spaces of Hope*. Berkeley: University of California Press, 2000.

Heller, Celia. *Mexican American Youth: Forgotten Youth at the Crossroads*. New York: Random House, 1966.

Hershfield, Joanne. *The Invention of Dolores del Rio*. Minneapolis: University of Minnesota Press, 2000.

Hom, Sharon K. "Female Infanticide in China." In *Global Critical Race Feminism,* edited by Adrien Katherine Wing, 251–59. New York: New York University Press, 2000.

Horsman, Reginald. "Scientific Racism and the American Indian in the Mid-Nineteenth Century." *American Quarterly* 27 (1975): 153–67.

Huaco-Nuzum, Carmen. "Mi Familia/My Family." *Aztlan* 23, no. 1 (Spring 1998): 141–53.

Human Rights Watch, Women's Rights Project. *The Human Rights Global Watch Report on Women's Human Rights*. New York: Human Rights Watch, 1995.

Hurtado, Aida. "The Politics of Sexuality in the Gender Subordination of Chicanas." In *Living Chicana Theory,* edited by Carla Trujillo, 383–428. Berkeley: Third Woman Press, 1998.

Iglesias-Prieto, Norma. *Entre yerba, polvo, y plomo: Lo fronterizo visto por el cine mexicano*. Tijuana, Mexico: El Colegio de la Frontera-norte, 1991.

Isles, Chrissie. *Into the Light: The Projected Image in American Art, 1964–1977*. New York: Whitney Museum of American Art, 2001.

Jacobs, Susie, Ruth Jacobson, and Jennifer Marchbank. "Introduction: States of Conflict." In *States of Conflict,* edited by Susie Jacobs, Ruth Jacobson, and Jennifer Marchbank, 1–24. New York: Zed Books, 2000.

Jamison, Kay Redfield. *Touched with Fire*. New York: Free Press, 1993.

———. *An Unquiet Mind*. New York: Vintage Books, 1996.

Kandiyoti, Deniz. "Identity and Its Discontents: Women and the Nation." In *Colonial Discourse and Post-Colonial Theory: A Reader,* edited by Patrick Williams and Laura Chrisman, 376–91. New York: Columbia University Press, 1994.

Kang, Laura Hyun Yi. "Si(gh)ting Asian/American Women as Transnational Labor." *Positions: Positions: East Asia Cultures Critique* 5, no. 2 (Fall 1997): 403–37.

Kaplan, E. Ann. "Dialogue: Ann Kaplan Replies to Linda Williams's 'Something Else besides a Mother: Stella Dallas and the Maternal Melodrama.'" *Cinema Journal* 24, no. 2 (Fall 1984): 40–73.

———. "Feminist Film Criticism: Current Issues and Problems." *Studies in Literary Imagination* 19, no. 1 (1992a): 7–20.

———. *Motherhood and Representation*. London and New York: Routledge, 1992b.

Karr, Kathleen. "The Long Square-Up: Exploitation Trends in the Silent Film." *Journal of Popular Film* 3, no. 2 (Spring 1974): 107–28.

Keller, Gary D. *Hispanics and United States Film*. Tempe, Ariz.: Bilingual Press, 1994.

Kelly, Liz. "Wars against Women: Sexual Violence, Sexual Politics and the Militarized State." In *States of Conflict,* edited by Susie Jacobs, Ruth Jacobson, and Jennifer Marchbank, 45–65. New York: Zed Books, 2000.

Kelly, Robin D. G. *Yo' Mama's Disfunktional!* Boston: Beacon, 1997.

Kevles, Daniel J. *In the Name of Eugenics.* New York: Alfred A. Knopf, 1985.

Kort, Michelle. "Filmmaker Alison Anders: Her Crazy Life." *Latin Style,* May–June 1994.

Lewis, Oscar. *Life in a Mexican Village: Tepoztlán Restudied.* Urbana: University of Illinois Press, 1951.

———. *Five Families: Mexican Case Studies in the Culture of Poverty.* New York: Basic Books, 1959.

———. *The Children of Sanchez.* New York: Random House, 1961.

———. *La Vida: A Puerto Rican Family in the Culture of Poverty, San Juan and New York.* New York: Random House, 1966.

Lima, Luiz Costa. *The Control of the Imaginary.* Minneapolis: University of Minnesota Press, 1988.

Limón, José. "Stereotyping and Chicano Resistance: An Historical Dimension." In *Chicanos and Film,* edited by Chon Noriega, 3–20. New York: Garland, 1992.

———. *American Encounters: Greater Mexico, the United States, and the Erotics of Culture.* Boston: Beacon, 1998.

Lomnitz, Larissa A., and Marisol Pére-Lizaur. "Dynastic Growth and Survival Strategies: The Solidarity of Mexican Grand-Families." In *Kinship, Ideology, and Practice in Latin America,* edited by Raymond T. Smith, 183–95. Chapel Hill and London: University of North Carolina Press, 1984.

Lowe, Lisa. *Immigrant Acts.* Durham and London: Duke University Press, 1996.

———. "Toward a Critical Modernity." *Anglistica* 4, no. 1 (2000): 69–89.

Macaulay, Fiona. "Tackling Violence against Women in Brazil: Converting International Principles into Effective Local Policy." In *States of Conflict,* edited by Susie Jacobs, Ruth Jacobson, and Jennifer Marchbank, 144–62. New York: Zed Books, 2000.

Mayne, Judith. *Cinema and Spectatorship.* London and New York: Routledge, 1983.

McClintock, Anne. "No Longer in a Future Heaven: Gender, Race, and Nationalism." In *Dangerous Liaisons: Gender, Nation, and Postcolonial Perspectives,* edited by Anne McClintock, Aamir Mufti, and Ella Shohat, 89–112. Minneapolis: University of Minnesota, 1997.

McWilliams, Carey. *North from Mexico.* New York: Monthly Review Press, 1961.

Miranda, Keta. *Subversive Geographies.* Austin: University of Texas Press, forthcoming.

Mirandé, Alfredo. "The Chicano Family: A Reanalysis of Conflicting Views." *Journal of Marriage and the Family* 39 (1977): 747–56.

Monárrez, Julia Estela. "La cultura del feminicidio en Ciudad Juárez, 1993–1999." *Frontera Norte* 12, no. 23 (January–June 2000): 87–117.

Monroy, Douglas. "'Our Children Get So Different Here': Film, Fashion,

Popular Culture, and the Process of Cultural Syncretization in Mexican Los Angeles, 1900–1935." *Aztlan* 19, no. 1 (Spring 1988–1990): 79–108.

Montejano, David. *Anglos and Mexicans in the Making of Texas, 1836–1986.* Austin: University of Texas Press, 1987.

Montiel, Miguel. "The Social Science Myth of the Mexican American Family." *El Grito: A Journal of Contemporary Mexican Thought* (Summer 1970): 56–63.

Moore, Joan W. *Going Down to the Barrio: Homeboys and Homegirls in Change.* Philadelphia: Temple University Press, 1991.

Moraga, Cherríe. *Loving in the War Years: Lo Que Nunca Pasó por Sus Labios.* Boston: South End Press, 1983.

Morrison, Toni. *Playing in the Dark: Whiteness and the Literary Imagination.* Cambridge: Harvard University Press, 1992.

Musser, Charles. "The Nickelodeon Era Begins: Establishing the Framework for Hollywood's Mode of Representation." In *Early Cinema: Space, Frame Narrative,* edited by Thomas Elsaesser, 25–273. London: British Film Institute, 1990a.

———. *History of the American Cinema: The Emergence of Cinema to 1907.* New York: Charles Scribner's Sons, 1990b.

Nathan, Debbie. "Death Comes to the Maquilas: A Border Story." *The Nation,* 13–20 January 1997, 18–22.

———. "Work, Sex, and Danger in Cuidad Juárez." *NACLA* 33, no. 3 (November–December 1999): 24–30.

Neft, Naomi, and Ann D. Levine. *Where Women Stand: An International Report of the Status of Women in 140 Countries.* New York: Random House, 1997.

Nesiah, Vasuki. "Toward a Feminist Intersectionality: A Critique of U.S. Feminist Legal Scholarship." In *Global Critical Race Feminism,* edited by Adrien Katherine Wing, 42–52. New York: New York University Press, 2000.

Obiora, Leslye Amede. "Bridges and Barricades: Rethinking Polemics and Intransigence in the Campaign against Female Circumcision." In *Global Critical Race Feminism,* edited by Adrien Katherine Wing, 260–74. New York: New York University Press, 2000.

Oliver, Kelly. *Subjectivity without Subjects.* Lanham, Md.: Rowan and Littlefield, 1998.

Oré-Aguilar, Gaby. "Sexual Harassment and Human Rights in Latin America." In *Global Critical Race Feminism,* edited by Adrien Katherine Wing, 362–74. New York: New York University Press, 2000.

Oropeza, Lorena. "His Story and Beyond: César Chávez, Vietnam, and the Chicana/o Movement." Paper presented at the annual meeting of the American Studies Association, Washington, D.C., November 1997.

Paredes, Raymond. "The Origin of Anti-Mexican Sentiment in the United States." *New Scholar* 6 (1977): 158–60.

Peñalosa, Fernando. "Mexican American Family Roles." *Journal of Marriage and the Family* 30, no. 4 (1968): 680–88.

Pérez, Emma. *The Decolonial Imaginary: Writing Chicanas into History.* Bloomington and Indianapolis: Indiana University Press, 1999.

Peterson, Richard R. "Anti-Mexican Nativism in California, 1848–1853: A Study of Cultural Conflict." *Southern California Quarterly* 4, no. 80 (1962): 309–27.

Pratt, Mary Louise. *Imperial Eyes: Travel, Writing, and Transculturation.* London and New York: Routledge, 1992.

Ramirez, Catherine. "Crimes of Fashion: The Pachuca and Chicana Style Politics." *Meridians: Feminism, Race, Transnationalism* 2, no. 2 (2002): 1–35.

———. *The Lady Zoot-Suiter.* Durham: Duke University Press, forthcoming.

Ramírez, Gabriel. *Lupe Vélez: La mexicana que escupía fuego.* Mexico City: Cineteca Nacional, 1986.

Ramsaye, Terry. *A Million and One Nights: A History of the Motion Picture.* New York: Simon and Schuster, 1926.

Reyes, Luis, and Peter Rubie. *Hispanics in Hollywood: An Encyclopedia of Film and Television.* New York: Garland, 1994.

Rich, Adrienne. *Of Woman Born: Motherhood as Experience and Institution.* New York: Norton, 1976.

Rich, B. Ruby. "Babes in Gangland." *Elle,* September 1994.

———. "Slugging It Out for Survival." *Sight and Sound,* April 1995, 14–17.

Ríos-Bustamante, Antonio. "Latinos and the Hollywood Film Industry, 1920–1950." *Americas 2001* (January 1988): 6–27.

———. "Latino Participation in the Hollywood Film Industry, 1911–1945." In *Chicanos and Film,* edited by Chon Noriega, 21–32. New York and London: Garland, 1992.

Roberts, Dorothy. "Who May Give Birth to Citizens: Reproduction, Eugenics, and Immigration." In *Immigrants Out: The New Nativism and the Anti-Immigrant Impulse in the United States,* edited by Juan F. Perea, 205–17. New York: New York University Press, 1997.

Rodríguez, Clara E. "Visual Retrospective: Latin Film Stars." In *Latin Looks,* edited by Clara E. Rodríguez, 80–84. Boulder: Westview, 1997.

Romany, Celina. "Themes for a Conversation on Race and Gender in International Human Rights Law." In *Global Critical Race Feminism,* edited by Adrien Katherine Wing, 53–66. New York: New York University Press, 2000.

Ruiz, Vicki L. *From Out of the Shadows.* New York: Oxford University Press, 1998.

Russell, Dianna, and Jill Radford. *Feminicide: The Politics of Woman Killing.* New York: Twayne, 1999.

Salas, Abel. "Alison Anders Discusses *Mi Vida Loca.*" *Latin Style,* August 1994, 42.

Saldívar-Hull, Sonia. *Feminism on the Border: Chicana Gender Politics and Literature.* Berkeley: University of California, 2000.

Salzinger, Leslie. "From High Heels to Swathed Bodies: Gendered Meanings under Protection in Mexico's Export Processing Industry." *Feminist Studies* 23, no. 3 (Fall 1997): 549–74.

Sánchez, Rosaura. *Telling Identities*. Minneapolis: University of Minnesota Press, 1995.

Santos, John Phillips. *Places Left Unfinished at the Time of Creation*. New York: Viking, 1999.

Sassen, Saskia. *Losing Control? Sovereignty in an Age of Globalization*. New York: Columbia University Press, 1996.

——. *Globalization and Its Discontents*. New York: The New Press, 1998.

Sawicki, Jana. *Disciplining Foucault*. New York and London: Routledge, 1991.

Shah, Nayan. *Contagious Divides: Epidemics and Race in San Francisco's Chinatown*. Berkeley: University of California Press, 2001.

Shohat, Ella. "Gender and Culture of Empire: Toward a Feminist Ethnography of the Cinema." *Quarterly Review of Film and Video* 13, nos. 1–3 (1991–1992): 45–79.

——. "Multicultural Feminism in a Transnational Age." In *Talking Visions*, edited by Ella Shohat. Cambridge and London: MIT Press, 1998.

Smith, Cornelius C., Jr. *A Southwestern Vocabulary: The Words They Used*. Glendale, Calif.: Arthur H. Clark Company, 1984.

Smith, Michael Peter. *Transnational Urbanism*. Malden, Mass.: Blackwell, 2001.

Smith, Valerie. "Telling Family Secrets: Narrative and Ideology in *Suzanne Suzanne* by Camille Billops and James V. Hatch." In *Multiple Voices in Feminist Film Criticism*, edited by Linda Dittman, Diane Carson, and Janice R. Walsh, 380–90. Minneapolis: University of Minnesota Press, 1994.

Stacey, Jackie. *Star Gazing: Hollywood Cinema and Female Spectatorship*. New York: Routledge, 1994.

——. *In the Name of the Family*. Boston: Beacon, 1996.

——. "Family Values Forever." *The Nation*, 9 July 2001, 26–30.

Staiger, Janet. *Bad Women*. Minneapolis: University of Minnesota Press, 1995.

Steifert, Ruth. "War and Rape: A Preliminary Analysis." In *Mass Rape: The War against Women in Bosnia-Herzegovina*, edited by Alexandra Stiglmeyer, 54–72. Lincoln: University of Nebraska Press, 1994.

Stepan, Nancy Leys. "Race and Gender: The Role of Analogy in Science." *ISIS* 77 (1986): 261–77.

Stepan, Nancy Leys, and Sander L. Gilman. "Appropriating the Idioms of Science: The Rejection of Scientific Racism." In *The Bounds of Race: Perspectives on Hegemony and Resistance*, edited by Dominick LaCapra, 72–103. Ithaca: Cornell University Press, 1991.

Stith, Morton, Karen Karabasz, and Marc Taylor. "Mythology and the Mexican Family." Lecture presented at the Biblioteca Pública, San Miguel de Allende, Guanajuato, July 2001.

Stoler, Ann Laura. *Race and the Education of Desire*. Durham: Duke University Press, 1995.

Tafolla, Carmen. *"Sonnets of Human Beings" and Other Selected Works.* Santa Monica, Calif.: Lalo Press, 1992.

Taussig, Michael. *Shamanism, Colonialism, and the Wild Man.* Chicago and London: University of Chicago Press, 1987.

———. *Defacement.* Stanford: Stanford University Press, 1999.

Thouard, Sylvie. "Performances of *The Devil Never Sleeps/El diablo nunca duerme.*" In *Lourdes Portillo: "The Devil Never Sleeps" and Other Films,* edited by Rosa Linda Fregoso. Austin, 119–43: University of Texas Press, 2001.

Tinkcom, Matthew. *Working like a Homosexual.* Durham and London: Duke University Press, 2002.

Trujillo, Rafael. *Olvídate del Alamo.* Mexico City: La Prensa, 1965.

Trulio, Beverly. "Anglo American Attitudes towards New Mexican Women." *Journal of the West* 12 (1973): 229–39.

United Nations. *Domestic Violence against Women in Latin America and the Caribbean.* Series on Women and Development. Santiago, Chile: Social Development Division, United Nations, 1990.

———. *Domestic Violence against Women in Latin America and the Caribbean.* Series on Women and Development. Santiago, Chile: Social Development Division, United Nations, 1992.

Velasco Ortiz, Laura. "Migración femenina y estrategias de sobrevivencia de la unidad doméstica: Un caso de estudio de mujeres mixtecas en Tijuana." In *Mujeres, migración, y maquila en la frontera,* edited by Soledad González Montes et al., 37–63. Mexico City: Colegio de México, Programa Interdisciplinario de Estudios de La Mujer, 1994.

Wagner, Frank. N.d. "Early Moviehouses in Corpus Christi."

West, Joan, and Dennis West. "Borders and Boundaries: An Interview with John Sayles." *Cineaste* 22, no. 3 (1996): 14–17.

Willis, Holly. "Uncommon History: An Interview with Barbara Hammer." *Film Quarterly* 47, no. 4 (1994): 7–13.

Wing, Adrien Katherine. "A Critical Race Feminist Conceptualization of Violence." In *Global Critical Race Feminism,* edited by Adrien Katherine Wing, 332–46. New York: New York University Press, 2000.

Wright, Melissa. "Maquiladora Mestizas and a Feminist Border Politics: Revisiting Anzaldúa." *Hypatia* 13, no. 3 (Summer 1998): 114–31.

Yarbro-Bejarano, Yvonne. "Ironic Framings: A Queer Reading of the Family (Melo)Drama in Lourdes Portillo's *The Devil Never Sleeps/El diablo nunca duerme.*" In *Lourdes Portillo: "The Devil Never Sleeps" and Other Films,* edited by Rosa Linda Fregoso, 102–18. Austin: University of Texas Press, 2001.

Yuval-Davis, Nina, and Floya Anthias. "Introduction." In *Woman-Nation State,* edited by Nina Yuval-Davis and Floya Anthias, 1–15. London: Macmillan, 1989.

Zavella, Patricia. "The Problematic Relationship of Feminism and Chicana Studies." *Women's Studies* 17 (1989): 25–36.

Index

Compositor:	BookMatters, Berkeley
Indexer:	Marcia Carlson
Text:	10/13 Galliard
Display:	Galliard
Printer and Binder:	Sheridan Books, Inc.